PRIMARY SCIENCE
FOR TRAINEE TEACHERS

PRIMARY SCIENCE
FOR TRAINEE TEACHERS

JUDITH RODEN and
JAMES ARCHER

 |

Los Angeles | London | New Delhi
Singapore | Washington DC

Learning Matters
An imprint of SAGE Publications Ltd
1 Oliver's Yard
55 City Road
London EC1Y 1SP

SAGE Publications Inc.
2455 Teller Road
Thousand Oaks, California 91320

SAGE Publications India Pvt Ltd
B 1/I 1 Mohan Cooperative Industrial Area
Mathura Road
New Delhi 110 044

SAGE Publications Asia-Pacific Pte Ltd
3 Church Street
#10-04 Samsung Hub
Singapore 049483

Editor: Amy Thornton
Development Editor: Jennifer Clark
Production Controller: Chris Marke
Project Management: Deer Park Productions
Marketing Manager: Lorna Patkai
Cover design: Wendy Scott
Typeset by: C&M Digitals (P) Ltd, Chennai, India
Printed by Henry Ling Limited at The Dorset Press,
Dorchester, DT1 1HD

Library of Congress Control Number: 2014942707

British Library Cataloguing in Publication data

A catalogue record for this book is available from
the British Library.

MIX
Paper from
responsible sources
FSC
www.fsc.org FSC™ C013985

ISBN 978-1-4462-9656-1 (pbk)
ISBN 978-1-4462-9655-4

At SAGE we take sustainability seriously. Most of our products are printed in the UK using FSC papers and boards.
When we print overseas we ensure sustainable papers are used as measured by the Egmont grading system.
We undertake an annual audit to monitor our sustainability.

Contents

Acknowledgements

We would like to thank the headteachers and staff of:

- Newington Community Primary School, Ramsgate

- Hythe Bay Church of England Primary School and Children's Centre

- Sturry Church of England Primary School, Canterbury

- St. John's Church of England Primary School, Canterbury

Thanks go to colleagues Kerry Jordan-Daus, William Stow, the Primary Science Team at Canterbury Christ Church University past and present especially Tim Smith and Sarah Gourlay.

We would also like to thank the students from our past and present primary science courses at Canterbury Christ Church University, and especially our PGCE-Enhanced Studies groups from recent years and the 2012 and 2013 Teach First Primary and Early Years participants.

Thanks also to David Ponsonby for permission to use notes on classification of plant and animal kingdoms, in Chapter 5, based on standard nomenclature used by the Royal Botanic Gardens, Kew.

Finally, with special thanks to Amy Archer and Paddy Grinter for their support and encouragement, especially in the writing of this book.

About the authors and series editor

Judith Roden is a Principal Lecturer at Canterbury Christ Church University where she is involved in teaching primary science. Much of her work is spent in school supporting Teach First participants, School Direct students and other students in PGCE and undergraduate Teacher Education Programmes. Currently she is the national lead tutor for Teach First Primary Science. She has written and edited a number of popular primary science textbooks over the past ten years. She has also held chartered Science Teacher Status for a number of years and in 2014 received a Teaching Fellowship Award from her university.

James Archer has wide experience in supporting trainee primary teachers in science. Currently he is a Lecturer in Primary Science Education at Bradford College. Previously he was a Senior Lecturer in Primary Science Education at Canterbury Christ Church University. He has a passion for child-centred science enquiry. Prior to working at Canterbury James taught in both the primary and secondary phases in England and South Africa. In these settings he held various responsibilities for leading and co-ordination of science. He has also been an advisor in primary science supporting a cluster of schools.

Alice Hansen is the Director of Children Count Ltd, an education consultancy company that provides continuing professional development for teachers in primary mathematics education and primary schools in curriculum development in England and abroad. Prior to her current role, she was a primary school teacher and senior lecturer in primary education before becoming a programme leader of a teacher-training programme. Alice is an active researcher and her research interests include technology-enhanced learning. Her current research focuses on developing effective tasks for children to develop their conceptual understanding of fractions.

Introduction

A high quality science education provides the foundations for understanding the world through the specific disciplines of biology, chemistry and physics. Science has changed our lives and is vital to the world's future prosperity, and all pupils should be taught essential aspects of knowledge and methods, processes and uses of science. Through building up a body of key foundational knowledge and concepts, pupils should be encouraged to recognise the power of rational explanation and develop a sense of excitement and curiosity about national phenomena. They should be encouraged to understand how science can be used to explain what is occurring, predict how things will behave, and analyse causes. (DfE, 2013, p.3)

This statement of purpose invites scrutiny and comment and raises questions about how best to implement the 2014 science National Curriculum at Key Stages 1 and 2.

About this book

This book is intended to support all Early Years and primary trainees on all courses of initial teacher training in England and has been tailored to the 2014 science National Curriculum. Newly qualified and more experienced primary teachers may also find this book useful as they begin to make sense of the new science National Curriculum. The Teaching Standards require all teachers to have a secure understanding of the subjects that they are required to teach and an awareness of the strategies that can foster effective learning in science. You may feel that you already have a secure knowledge of the science that underpins the science National Curriculum, but this in itself is insufficient in terms of helping children to learn science at an appropriate level and to encourage them to be scientists. You need to provide an excellent role model to enthuse and inspire the next generation of young scientists.

Scientific literacy

Language and literacy run deeply in the human experience. Within science it has been suggested there are numerous literacies (Webb, 2007). Developing a child's competence and confidence in their ability to converse in the language of science, a language that can be familiar and alien at the same time, is one of the most important tasks of the primary teacher. To do this a level of sophistication in scientific dialect is required. This book aims to support the beginning teacher's quest for conceptual knowledge development through the use of examples and practical guidance in order to enhance the student teacher's scientific literacy.

More importantly, developing a children's scientific literacy involves supporting their emergent enquiry skills in a way that enables them to engage in the scientific process. Just as language acquisition starts with the basic building blocks of listening and turn-taking, developing a child's scientific literacy is firmly rooted in improving the foundational skills of observing and exploring. Through the development of a scientific literacy in this sense children are afforded the opportunity to improve skills such as questioning, critical thinking and evaluating that benefit the wider curriculum.

The importance of science

It is important that the UK has enough well-qualified scientists to meet the demand, but there is much evidence to suggest that there is a shortfall in the numbers of young people coming through into science-related occupations. This explains why science continues to hold core subject status with the National Curriculum. The ASPIRE Project reported concern that women, and working-class and some minority ethnic groups are under-represented in the study of science, especially in the physical sciences and engineering (Archer et al., 2013). Nevertheless, scientists in the UK remain among the best in the world. Schools and universities prepare the most talented and able scientists extremely well, but there is a big gap in achievement between the most able and the least able pupils in terms of success in science subjects. Compared to other countries in the world, many young people in the UK who have potential in science fail to opt for science subjects that would lead them to careers in science. Overall, this situation is very worrying.

Children not only need to perform well in science in primary schools but also need to enjoy science and to recognise that science is important in their lives. Ofsted (2013, p.4) reported that the best science teachers set out first to 'maintain curiosity' in their pupils and that this not only fosters enthusiasm for science, but also helps pupils fulfil their potential. Children must find their science education stimulating and memorable so they continue to study science for as long as possible. Indeed, there is evidence to suggest that many children do enjoy science at primary level (Archer et al., 2013), especially practical work (Ofsted, 2013), particularly when it is well taught and when they have ownership over some of their work. However, despite enjoying science, they do not see themselves as scientists and do not consider taking up a scientific job when they leave education. The ASPIRE Project (Archer et al., 2013) found that only approximately 15 per cent of young people aspire to become scientists. Surprisingly, perhaps, they concluded that at least among the 10–14 year olds in the study, negative views of school science are not the problem. Their findings showed that most young people report liking school science from Year 6 to Year 9 and that 42 per cent of Year 9 students were interested in studying more science in the future. Students also reported positive views of scientists and said that their parents thought that it was important for them to learn science. However, despite these widely-held positive views, the majority of 10–14 year olds do not aspire to become scientists.

The problem seems to relate to children not fully understanding what scientists do, except at a very superficial level. Archer et al. (2013) found that most students and families are not aware where science can lead to and that 'the brainy image of scientists and science careers' puts many pupils off. Children's perceptions of science and scientists have been the focus of research for many years across the world. Although there may be some evidence to suggest that children's perceptions may now go beyond the stereotypical view of the scientist, due to recent changes in the ways that scientists are presented in the media and to Science, Technology, Engineering and Mathematics (STEM) initiatives, clearly there is still a problem, particularly with girls continuing to see science as male dominated.

The challenge for you is to raise your children's awareness of the importance of science in their lives, whether they are male or female, no matter what their socio-economic background. You need to help children not only to enjoy science and to be curious, but also to see the relevance of science in their lives. We hope that this book will help you to achieve this in your teaching.

Further reading

Harlen, H. (ed) (2012) *Principles and big ideas of science education*. Hatfield: Association for Science Education (ASE). Available at: www.ase.org.uk (accessed 11/6/14).

References

Archer, L., Osborne, J., Dewitt, J., Dillon, J., Wong, B. and Willis, B. (2013) *ASPIRES Young people and career aspirations 10–14*. London: King's College London

Department for Education (2013) *Science programmes of study: Key stages 1 and 2* September 2013 London: DfE.

Ofsted (2013) *Maintaining curiosity: A survey into science education in schools.* Manchester: Ofsted.

Webb, p. (ed) (2007) *Scientific literacy: A new synthesis*. Port Elizabeth, South South Africa: Bay Books.

1 Working scientifically

Learning outcomes

By reading this chapter you will develop:

- an awareness of the importance of working scientifically;
- an understanding of the key scientific processes that underpin working scientifically;
- a knowledge of the progression in the process skills that underpin working scientifically;
- an understanding of effective pedagogic strategies for the teaching of working scientifically.

Teachers' Standards

2. Promote good progress and outcomes by pupils

- be aware of pupils' capabilities and plan teaching to build on these
- demonstrate knowledge and understanding of how pupils learn and how this impacts on teaching.

3. Demonstrate good science subject and curriculum knowledge

- have a secure knowledge of science and foster and maintain pupils' interest in science
- demonstrate a critical understanding of the developments in the subject and curriculum area.

Introduction
What is science?

The biggest challenge for you as a teacher in the Early Years or primary phase of education is to understand what exactly science is in the primary school and to have a clear view as to how it should be taught for optimum learning. Science in the primary school is a unique interpretation of what it means to engage in science activity. Roden and Ward (2008, p.6) suggest that there are numerous facets that go to make up the construct of primary science. They encourage us to see science both as a body of knowledge and as a way of working. The new primary curriculum (DfE, 2013) sets out aims to develop knowledge and conceptual understanding as well as children's ability to work in a scientific manner.

Davies and Howe (2003) suggest that science should be both a hands-on and a minds-on activity. At the heart of outstanding primary practice in enquiry is allowing children to construct and investigate their own questions. The Cambridge Primary Review highlights the importance of providing learners with a real sense of autonomy (Alexander, 2010). One child reported in the review that 'we learn things best when we can find out things for ourselves' (Alexander, 2010, p.148). In order to facilitate this it is important, therefore, to be mindful of what counts in terms of 'working scientifically' and how this can be integrated into everyday practice in primary science.

Key scientific concepts

- The process skills in science

- Working scientifically

- Progression in working scientifically

- Types of investigations

Research focus

A recent report undertaken by Ofsted (2013) in 91 primary and 89 secondary good and outstanding schools found the following.

- In the best schools visited, teachers ensured that pupils understood the 'big ideas' of science. They made sure that pupils mastered the investigative and practical skills that underpin the development of scientific knowledge and could discover for themselves the relevance and usefulness of those ideas.

- Science achievement in the schools visited was highest when individual pupils were fully involved in planning, carrying out and evaluating investigations that they had, in some part, suggested themselves.

The report made the following recommendations.

School leaders, including governing bodies, should:

- provide sufficient weekly curriculum time so that individual pupils develop good scientific enquiry skills as well as the knowledge they need.

Science subject leaders should:

- in primary schools, monitor pupils' progress in science regularly to ensure they are supported effectively to reach their potential.

Science teachers should:

- use assessment effectively to plan lessons that build on individual pupils' prior knowledge and provide feedback that genuinely helps pupils to improve their work in science.

Reflection

Given the increased emphasis in the new programme of study on creating opportunities for enquiry and working scientifically, how do these findings and recommendations relate to your experience of primary science? To what extent is there an opportunity for children to work scientifically in the primary schools known to you? What are the implications of the recommendations on your practice and on the weekly timetable of a class?

The process skills in science

As primary science educators our aim is to develop the children's knowledge, understanding and skills. In science the particular skills that help us in working scientifically are known as the process skills. Although there is not as such an agreed definitive list of process skills, these can often be found in curriculum documents. The DfE (2013) programme of study for science lists particular process skills and is very explicit in suggesting that they should be seen as being on equal terms and weighting with that of conceptual knowledge and understanding. The programme of study continually emphasises that knowledge and process skills should always be taught together. Ofsted (2011) highlights, however, that there is a tendency by primary practitioners to focus almost exclusively on conceptual development, often missing opportunities for process skill development. The following section will explore what the process skills are and provide practical examples of how these can be nurtured and developed in the primary phase.

Observation and questioning

Observation is using our senses to explore in a way that assists the raising of questions. It is important that children are taught to identify questions that can and cannot be investigated. Observation and questioning are fundamental process skills from which all other process skills can be developed. Fictional texts such as *Why?* by Lindsay Camp and Tony Ross highlight the inquisitive nature of young children in an amusing and playful way. Questions such as 'Are we nearly there yet?' have become synonymous with our view of young children. Entering a Foundation Stage classroom there appears to be a culture of questioning as children engage in their many activities.

Curriculum links

The Early Years Foundation Stage (EYFS) framework (Early Education, 2012) provides the expectation that all children should be engaged in and respond to questions and questioning and so supports a culture characterised by practitioners responding to children's inquisitive nature. However, while there may well be provision for this kind of approach within many Early Years settings, interestingly, it has been noted that these abilities often do not develop beyond the Foundation Stage and that, indeed, in many cases they regress over a child's career in primary education (Ofsted, 2008; Ofsted, 2011; Ofsted, 2013).

To develop children's questioning ability in science takes time. Questions are often created in response to an individual engaging in exploring and observing a particular phenomenon. Barnes (2012, p.239) suggests that children should be submerged in powerful learning experiences at the start of any new learning. It is essential that children are allowed to engage in exploration at the start of the investigation process. Trying to facilitate the process of children raising productive and relevant questions outside of an observational experience often proves futile. When children have not been given the opportunity to observe a phenomenon they often create questions that seem irrelevant to the teacher. The teacher becomes frustrated by the children's inability to raise questions that can be investigated and so provides the children with questions to investigate. It is often after observing a phenomenon that children are spurred into considering what they have observed and have genuine questions that they wish to explore. Enquiry work that seeks to engage learners and support their discovery must begin with an observational experience.

Case study: Candles

Matt, a third year BA (Hons) student participant, was working with a group of Year 4 children to develop their ability to raise questions about light. He provided them with a single lit tea light on a heat-proof mat. He asked the children to write down as many observations as they could about the candle and its light.

Figure 1.1   Tea light

Some of the observations raised were that:

- the candle made a circle of light on the mat;
- the further away from the candle the fainter the light got;
- as the flame moved the light also moved.

After the children had gathered their observations together Matt spoke with the children about the different type of question words that could be used to raise a scientific question. He encouraged the children to look at the science display where they could see a range of question words including 'why', 'when' 'what' and 'how'. Together as a class Matt and the children worked to create a model question. They asked:

'How can you increase the distance of the light travelled?'

Following this, children in pairs were encouraged to develop as many questions as they could using their observations and the question word. Once complete, the children were asked to use the sorting grid in Figure 1.2. One column was entitled 'Questions I *can* investigate now' and the other 'Questions I *can't* investigate now'.

Figure 1.2   Sorting grid

If the children were unsure as to which column their question belonged they were asked questions like 'Explain/describe the investigation that you could do to answer your question.' and 'What equipment do you think you would need?' If the children were unsure they were encouraged to place the question in the 'can't' column. The children were encouraged to share their 'can' questions with another pair. After this they shared their 'can't' questions in their fours. They were encouraged to try to change their 'can't' questions into 'can' questions.

An example of this was seen when one group changed:

'Why does the light get fainter the further away you get from the candle?'

to:

'What happens to the amount of light there is the further away you get?'

Although through observation the children were able to come to a simple conclusion about the concentration of light the further you get away from a light source, there is still merit in their seeking to carry out this investigation. By finding an answer to their question using accurate measures the children would be able to provide the required evidence to support their findings.

'Can' questions were also improved during this time with:

'Does the distance of light increase if we add one more candle?'

This implies a simple investigation with only two stages of investigation to:

'What happens to the distance of the light when the number of candles increases?'

This suggests a more complex investigation that should provide richer data that will enable children to come to a more reliable conclusion.

Activity

Take a natural object. Observe it using all of your senses. Draw an enlarged version of a section of the object onto a large piece of paper and label it. Look at your observations. Using your question words turn your observations into questions. Sort your questions into two columns:

- questions I *can* investigate now;

- questions I *can't* investigate now.

Once sorted, seek to turn the 'can't' questions into 'can' questions. Select a 'can' question to investigate and carry out the investigation. You could record the entire process in a floor book and use this as a resource to model to children alternative ways to record the enquiry process.

Figure 1.3   Example of a floor book

Predicting and hypothesising

Predicting is the act of saying what you consider is likely to happen before the outcome is known. However, it is important to realise that predicting is not simply guessing. A prediction is based upon previous knowledge and understanding of the idea under study, i.e. based on a particular hypothesis or a set of findings. Hypothesising is the ability to suggest why an observed phenomenon occurs by applying knowledge, skills and experience. Put simply a hypothesis is a proposed reason for an observed occurrence that is discovered during the enquiry process. A prediction draws on the hypothesis to help suggest what may happen for a new scenario prior to the investigative element of the enquiry process. In the primary classroom this can be further distilled down to 'I think … because', 'I think' being the prediction and an explanation after 'because' becoming a hypothesis.

Within the primary phase these two skills are used as mandatory elements in each enquiry. However, the curriculum introduces prediction at lower Key Stage 2. Why do you think this is? To be able to predict meaningfully a child needs to have had a wide experience in science and previous experience of the concept under study. The child needs to hold relevant knowledge and understanding that can be applied to a new situation. Children of a young age often find prediction difficult. Predictions made by young children are often simply guesses and are frequently not founded on prior scientific knowledge or experience. Asking children at this early stage to make predictions in relation to topics that they have no prior experience or knowledge of can have damaging effects. Children can easily become despondent as their predictions are either incorrect or, worse, deemed as irrelevant by the class teacher. This experience can be extremely off-putting. The emphasis on developing observational and questioning skills in Key Stage 1 should provide the foundation for children to be able to make predictions and hypotheses later on in their primary science career.

Often in the heat of an exciting enquiry older children can miss opportunities to formally record their hypotheses. Using digital recording aids such as electronic thought bubbles and talk buttons can prove an invaluable tool in assisting children in this area. Having the physical resource prompts children to make hypotheses throughout the enquiry experience.

Figure 1.4   Thought bubble

Figure 1.5   Talk buttons

Gathering evidence: recording and presenting

The primary phase offers huge potential for creativity in science. When gathering data, children should be encouraged to use a range of recording strategies that are meaningful to them. Traditional and formal methods that set rigid expectations on outcomes and outputs do not necessarily support understanding. Common practice requires children to write at length prior, during and post the recording stage. This raises two issues. Firstly, when assessing and marking this work the teacher feels obliged to feedback on writing and language conventions as well as the science focus. This equal focus in feedback on science and English can be confusing to children. The child's understanding of science becomes one that perceives science to be inextricably linked to language conventions. In some areas of science the link to language is less obvious and the greater link to number and mathematics is more apparent, such as in aspects of physics. Continually feeding back on language conventions therefore seems to be slightly unhelpful. In addition it has long been reported that children find it hard to read and understand the work recorded in their own books.

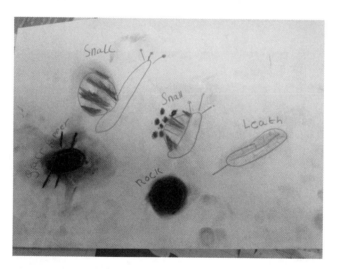

Figure 1.6   Drawings used to record work

In Figure 1.6 you will see that the child has used drawings as a method of recording. There is a greater chance that younger children particularly will be able to recall what they have found through pictures and images than through formal written methods. It is important, however, to realise that the opportunity for assessment with this method should not stop merely with marking the children's drawings. A discussion should be had with the children about the drawings and what they show. This discussion will provide a rich environment in which useful assessment can take place.

Presenting data also provides a range of creative opportunities. Challenging the conventions of graph and chart making is really important. When starting to learn about presenting information children should be able to consider a variety of ways. Arts-based responses such as songs, raps or living graphs (see Figure 1.7), with each child taking a value and presenting it using their bodies, are great examples of this. Other approaches such as using materials or simply placing a scale on their recordings are also beneficial.

Figure 1.7 A living graph – a record of height in centimetres

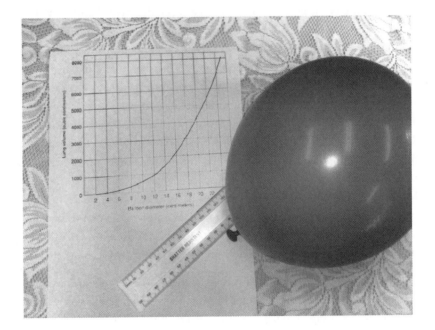

Figure 1.8 A creative approach to recording work

Creative approaches often lend themselves to collaborative work among teachers and children (for example see figure 1.8). Using approaches such as these are not only playful and fun but they also provide a platform for children to build the understanding, knowledge and skills for formal presenting methods.

Activity

Reflect on the ways you have asked children to record their work in science or the way you have seen children record during the science lessons you have observed. To what extent were the methods suggested above evident?

Interpreting findings

Collecting data is relatively easy. Looking at, analysing and understanding what the data is saying is a higher level skill. When interpreting findings children need to organise and/or reorganise data in a way that supports them in exploring and identifying patterns in their data. This leads children to draw conclusions. Giving children already collected data can help enhance their ability to analyse data and draw conclusions. Children need to have an opportunity to focus on this skill alone without having to worry about the other process skills.

Drawing conclusions

The ability to draw conclusions from data is an important skill. Often left to the end of a lesson, this skill is an integral process that should be seen as active throughout an enquiry. Concluding is the act of saying what has been discovered and why this may be, drawing on the evidence gathered. Most children find concluding difficult and often provide a brief descriptive summary of what they have done. Children need this process modelled for them. There are opportunities for shared reading and writing activities here for children analysing conclusions written by others, drawing out the key elements and looking to improve the annotated examples. Getting children to stop what they are doing and to tell each other what they have discovered in plenaries and mini-plenaries should also help develop children's ability to draw conclusions. Using the word phenomenon here can be useful. Playing the Muppets' 'phenomenon' song and getting the children to join in with the song is a good way to introduce this term. After this fun introduction the children should be asked to share what phenomenon they have discovered. As each individual uses the word phenomenon the whole class could sing the song. This is important as it focuses the children on writing conclusions that centre on discovery rather than conclusions that repeat and recount the process.

To develop concluding as an active skill it may be useful to use tools such as dictaphones and computer programmes or applications to provide a tool for regular concluding. Children could be encouraged to begin with to make digital conclusions at regular set intervals until this becomes a natural process for the children to undertake themselves.

Evaluating: identifying barriers and ways forward

Evaluation is an important process skill. At the end of an investigation children need to engage in the process of reviewing what has gone on in order that they can improve future work. Children need to be able to question the validity and reliability of their findings. As time progresses the children need to consider whether their findings are congruent with the wider body of knowledge of science. At this stage the children need to consider why this may be. It could be due to the discovery of new knowledge or, alternatively, it could be that there were issues with the methodology of the investigation. If this is the case children need to identify the potential barriers and limitations that were involved in the investigation. For this to be successful children need to be supported through this process by means of scaffolds such as questions.

Table 1.1   Progression mapping in process skills for Key Stages 1 and 2

Process skill	Key Stage 1	Lower Key Stage 2	Upper Key Stage 2
Questioning	Asking simple questions	Asking relevant questions	Planning different types of scientific enquiries to answer questions
Observation	Observing closely	Making systematic and careful observations	Making systematic and careful observations
Prediction		Using conclusions to make predictions for new values	Using tests to make predictions
Selecting equipment	Using simple equipment Performing simple tests	Setting up simple practical enquiries	Using equipment that assists observing and recording with increased precision, accuracy, and complexity (additional)
Selecting the one mode of enquiry		Using different types of scientific enquiries to answer questions, for example comparative investigations and fair tests	Planning different types of scientific enquiries including recognising and controlling variables where necessary Using tests to set up further comparative and fair tests
Recording	Gathering and recording data	Where appropriate taking accurate measurements using standard units with a range of equipment Gathering and recording in a variety of ways to help in answering questions Recording using simple scientific language, drawings, labelled diagrams, keys, bar charts and tables	Taking measurements, using a range of scientific equipment, increasing in accuracy and precision, taking repeat readings when appropriate Recording data and results of increased complexity using scientific diagrams and labels, classification keys, tables, scatter graphs, bar and line graphs

(Continued)

Table 1.1   (Continued)

Process skill	Key Stage 1	Lower Key Stage 2	Upper Key Stage 2
Classifying	Identifying and classifying	Classifying in a variety of ways to help in answering questions	
Presenting		Presenting data in a variety of ways to help in answering questions Reporting findings	Reporting and presenting findings including conclusions, causal relationships
Concluding	Using observations and ideas to suggest answers to questions	Drawing simple conclusions Using straightforward evidence to support findings	Identifying scientific evidence that has been used to support or refute arguments
Evaluating: Identifying barriers and ways forward		Identifying barriers, suggesting improvements and raising further questions Identifying differences and similarities or changes related to ideas and processes	Evaluating the trust/reliability of findings

Progression in working scientifically

It is important for the primary practitioner to be aware of the progression in the skills that assist children in working scientifically. The curriculum document maps the progression in these skills over three phases. Table 1.1 maps the progression in the new programme of study at Key Stages 1 and 2. Scrutiny of the Early Years Foundation Stage documentation, including DfE (2012), shows that the process skills are embedded in Foundation Stage practice.

When planning for progression and curriculum mapping teachers need to take into account process skill development. Teachers need to decide on how these skills are built up and developed in children. Far too often children are expected to use all of these processes immediately as they enter the primary phase and constantly in all science sessions. This is confusing to children and does not allow them to see how these skills are developed. Additionally, children need to be given the opportunity to refine and develop individual process skills. For the majority of science sessions teachers should seek to develop a single process skill that is relevant to the children.

Case study: Planning for working scientifically

Fiona, a part-time PGCE student, was on a course placement in a Year 2 class. She wanted to develop the children's ability to identify and classify. In addition she wanted to develop the children's ability to identify the animal group types.

→

As a starter activity Fiona took the children outside to the playground. The children were asked to 'pair up' with children who had similar features to theirs: the same colour eyes, height, hair length, gender and so on. She then introduced the term 'classification' and explained that this was similar to grouping and sorting.

Back indoors Fiona provided the children, in groups of four, with a range of plastic animals including a human figure and asked them to sort them into as many different group types as possible. Fiona held a plenary and asked the groups to share what they had discovered. Through this process Fiona was able to identify a common misconception. The children often left the human figure out of the groups as they did not perceive the human to be an animal and therefore did not include the human in their groupings.

Using her assessment information Fiona decided that the children needed to have the misconceptions addressed and needed supporting in being able to group the plastic figures in a more scientific manner. Fiona was aware that the 'Top Trump' cards games were popular with her class so she created a framework for the different animal groups using a Top Trump format and made large copies that she then laminated. Each group was given a set of cards and the same plastic animals as before but now had a framework to support their classification. After much debate among the children they came to the joint conclusion that a human must be an animal as it met all of the features of a mammal and all other mammals were animals.

Types of investigation and enquiries

A scientific investigation has clear characteristics. In an investigation children should have a real sense of ownership. Children should have choice and should be making autonomous decisions either as an individual or by working in groups. Ideally in investigative work children should have the opportunity to raise their own questions and investigate these fully and have time to do so (Ofsted, 2013). Additionally, investigations should allow for the use and development of the aforementioned process. Not all process skills will be able to be developed in all investigations.

It is important to acknowledge that there are different types of investigations that occur within the primary phase. One of the unfortunate effects of the previous programme of study and its level descriptors was that there was only ever one type of investigation listed. The phrase 'in their own investigative work, they decide on an approach [for example, using a fair test] to answer a question' (DfES, 2004, p.55), led to a fixation, in many schools, on the fair test mode of investigation leaving other forms neglected. This was worsened by a perception that a fair test is always required no matter what was being investigated. Sadly this has had an impact on children's perception as to what counts as a scientific investigation.

Research focus

Watson, Goldsworthy and Wood-Robinson (1998, pp4–5) highlighted that in the primary phase, there are at least six different kinds of investigation taking place. These are:

1. classifying and identifying: the classification and identification of plant types;

2. fair testing: identifying, selecting and changing one variable while all others remain the same, seeking to use equal measures and methods on each occasion;

3. pattern seeking: these are also known as survey investigations, or '...er and ...er investigations', where a correlation between two factors is being explored, for example 'does the longer the leg mean the further the jump?';

4. investigating models: topics such as electricity are particularly tricky as children are not able to observe the phenomenon itself but merely its effects; models are used to help replicate the science to assist understanding, such as passing a cord joined to form a loop through hands as children stand in a circle to replicate the flow of an electrical current;

5. exploring: playing with and observing a phenomenon such as buoyancy through playing with objects in the water tray;

6. making things: this is often considered as a separate subject within the primary phase; however, primary pedagogues would be wise to consider the possibility of making links between design and technology teaching and science teaching.

When planning for investigations teachers need to be mindful of the various forms of investigation. Children need to be exposed to each of these and be aware of the differences. Once this is achieved more able children should be able to identify and select which type of investigation they should use, regardless of key stage.

Teaching strategies

It has been suggested that previous versions of the primary curriculum were overloaded. When this was combined with the disjointed way that science was 'taught', this often led children to believe that science was too difficult and lacked any sense of relevance (Duggan and Gott, 2002). Craft et al. (2001) suggested that children need to have their creative potential developed. In science a child's creative potential is largely linked to the process skills. The main barrier to this may be tests that appear to reward recall and learning by rote (Duggan and Gott, 2002). Rather than being able to

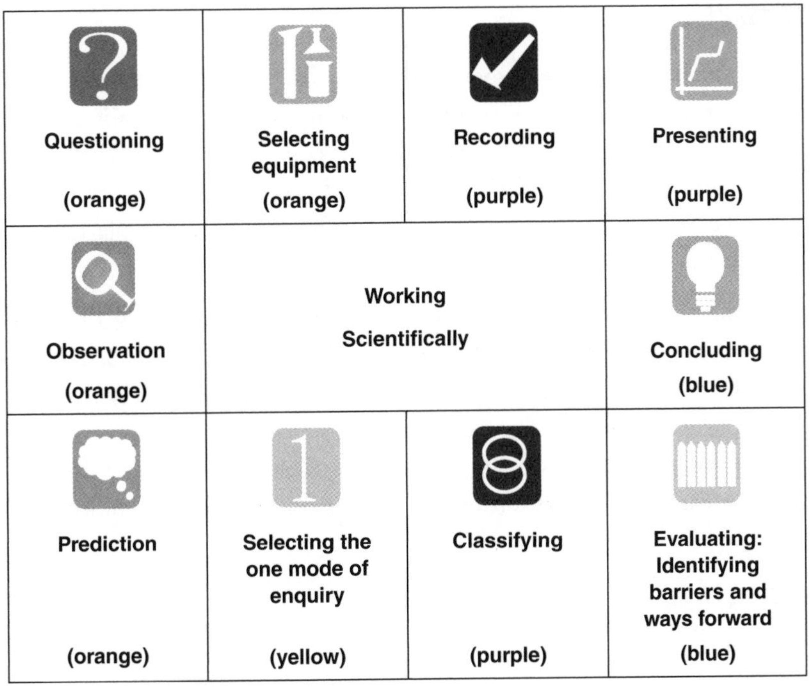

Questioning (orange)	**Selecting equipment** (orange)	**Recording** (purple)	**Presenting** (purple)
Observation (orange)	**Working Scientifically**		**Concluding** (blue)
Prediction (orange)	**Selecting the one mode of enquiry** (yellow)	**Classifying** (purple)	**Evaluating: Identifying barriers and ways forward** (blue)

Figure 1.9 Working Scientifically – process skills symbols

recall facts, it is more important that children are able to find information and weigh up evidence, come to a conclusion and decide what is relevant (Roden, 2005). Ofsted (2011) highlights, however, that teacher confidence and understanding of the processes and how they develop is significantly low. One strategy to tackle this is through using the 'Working Scientifically' materials produced by Archer (2009).

The symbols have been used to group the stages in which the processes are undertaken. The groups are:

- oranges and yellows for planning;
- purples for obtaining and presenting;
- blues for considering and evaluating.

When planning lessons that seek to develop these skills it would be advantageous to consider the groupings of these areas.

Focused teaching

Within the Working Scientifically materials there are ten symbols that relate to different scientific processes. Teachers are encouraged to identify the processes and thereby the symbols that relate to the area they are seeking to develop. Either electronically or by using physical cards, the symbol is placed next to the learning objectives to assist learners in appreciating which process skill they are developing within the session.

Working walls

The enquiry process takes time. Experience shows that there is little space for science displays in the primary classroom. In addition traditional working walls can be troublesome and can take considerable amounts of time to construct. This approach uses Magic Whiteboards® with Velcro® spots in the centre and another Velcro® spot on the back of a Working Scientifically symbol. With the symbol in place the children can record their work, be it observations, questions, etc.

Once the session is over the Magic Whiteboards® can be transferred literally to any surface in the room. The work becomes a permanent feature in a class and can be added to outside of the formal session time. When the following sessions take place work can be taken down and further symbols and work can be added. There is a greater fluidity to working that comes through using this approach. This approach therefore assists children to better understand the enquiry process of formal science.

Sequencing

To assist the children in the planning of the investigation, cards of the symbols can be provided. This visual sequencing assists the children to talk through the planned enquiry process with others.

Figure 1.10   Example of using symbols to plan an investigation

In the example in Figure 1.10 the child has considered what will be needed to observe in order to raise investigative questions. This strategy supports all pupils, including those with specific special educational needs and disabilities (SEND) related to processing. Often children see scientific enquiry as a linear process. More sophisticated learners need to appreciate that the enquiry process is considerably more messy than this. A simple way to assist this understanding would be by providing the children with more than one of the card symbols.

Flexible frameworks

Children have been provided for far too long with overly prescriptive frameworks in science that give them specific ways of working. A common example of this is predrawn and labelled photocopied tables. Using the Working Scientifically symbols children can be provided with flexible frameworks. Children can be given frameworks with sections that contain specific process skill symbols. Alternatively the children can be given frameworks with the entire set of symbols in all sections and they can simply circle the symbol to which they believe the section relates. Using the symbols children can construct their own frameworks for writing; this sees the children being able to work with an even greater sense of autonomy.

Figure 1.11   Examples of vocabulary pin wheels – showing vocabulary for specific phases of an investigation

Vocabulary wheels

Increasingly, and rightly so, there is a focus on children using correct scientific vocabulary. In addition best practice should be seeking ways and means of extending children's vocabulary.

Within the working scientifically approach children are provided with phase appropriate vocabulary pin wheels. This tool can be used, regardless of method of recording, to assist children's precise and extended use of scientific vocabulary.

Summary

This chapter has explored what is meant by working scientifically. It has been suggested that this is an area of science that is extremely important and should be seen as equal to the development of conceptual understanding. The key scientific processes have been discussed on an individual basis and strategies for developing each of these in the primary phase have been explored. This chapter has sought to identify which of the processes occur in each phase in the new programme of study and how these develop and progress. Finally this chapter has sought to introduce the 'Working Scientifically' approach and its associated resources. There is significant room now for primary science practitioners to work on their own strategies to develop this important area of primary science education.

Self-assessment questions

1. What is science?
2. What are the process skills?
3. What are the different types of investigation that are seen in the primary phase?

Further reading

Johnston, J. (2014) *Emergent science: Teaching science from birth to 8.* Abingdon: Routledge.

Roden, J. (2005) *Reflective reader: Primary science.* London: Learning Matters SAGE.

Roden, J. (2008) Raising questions, in Ward, H., Roden, J., Hewlett, C. and Foreman, J. *Teaching science in the primary classroom,* 2nd edition. London: SAGE.

References

Alexander, R. (ed.) (2010) *Children, their world, their education: Final report and recommendations of the Cambridge Primary Review.* London: Routledge.

Archer, J. (2009) An introduction to One Science. Unpublished.

Barnes, J. (2012) An introduction to cross-curricular learning, in Driscoll, P., Lambirth, A. and Roden, J. (eds) *The Primary Curriculum: A Creative Approach.* London: SAGE.

Craft, A., Jeffery, B. and Leibling, M. (2001) *Creativity in education.* London: Continuum.

Davies, D. and Howe, A. (2003) *Teaching science, design and technology in the early years.* London: David Fulton.

Department for Education (2012) *Statutory framework for the Early Years Foundation Stage.* Runcorn: DfE.

Department for Education (2013) *Science programmes of study: Key Stages 1 and 2.* London: DfE.

Department for Education and Science (2004) *Science: The National Curriculum for England, Key Stages 1–4,* revised 2004. London: DfES.

Duggan, S. ad Gott, R. (2002) What sort of science education do we really need? *International Journal of Science Education,* 24(7): 661–79.

Early Education (2012) *Framework development matters in the Early Years Foundation Stage.* London: Early Education.

Ofsted (2008) *Success in science.* London: Ofsted.

Ofsted (2011) *Successful science.* London: DfE.

Ofsted (2013) *Maintaining curiosity: a survey into science education in schools.* Manchester: Ofsted.

Roden, J. (2005) *Reflective reader: primary science.* London Learning Matters SAGE.

Roden, J. and Ward, H. (2008) What is science? in Ward, H., Roden, J., Hewlett, C. and Foreman, J. *Teaching science in the primary classroom,* 2nd edition. London: SAGE.

Watson, R., Goldsworthy, A. and Wood-Robinson, V. (1998) *ASE–King's College Science Investigations in Schools (AKSIS) project, second interim report to the QCA.* London: Kings College.

2 Plants

Learning outcomes

By reading this chapter you will develop:

- an awareness of the importance of plants in everyday life;
- an understanding of the key scientific concepts that underpin the teaching of plants;
- a knowledge of progression in the teaching and learning of plants;
- an understanding of effective pedagogic strategies for teaching plants including starting with the outdoor environment.

Teachers' Standards

1. **Set high expectations which inspire, motivate and challenge pupils**

- set goals that stretch and challenge pupils of all backgrounds, abilities and dispositions.

2. **Promote good progress and outcomes by pupils**

- be aware of pupils' capabilities and their prior knowledge, and plan teaching to build on these
- demonstrate knowledge and understanding of how pupils learn and how this impacts on teaching.

3. **Demonstrate good subject knowledge and curriculum knowledge**

- have a secure knowledge of science and curriculum areas, foster and maintain pupils' interest in science, and address misunderstandings.

4. **Plan and teach well-structured lessons**

- promote a love of learning and intellectual curiosity.

Introduction

Plants are amazing living things, but frequently the reaction of learners of all ages is that they are boring. This may well be symptomatic of how it was and often continues to be taught. Teachers may feel very secure in their understanding of biological topics including plants, but research in the past suggests that many adults may hold misconceptions about biological processes (Driver et al., 1994). Possibly because of this, teaching is frequently limited to a few, well-known activities such as growing cress, labelling the parts of a stereotypical drawing of a plant and investigating what a plant needs to grow. These are often repeated at different stages throughout the primary phases without thought for progression in learning. Such activities might be legitimate in teaching basic, but limited, information about plants, but on the whole, such an approach suggests lack of insight and imagination in delivery.

There are two notable reasons why it is important for young children to learn about plants. Firstly, children need to understand the world around them including, for example, where their food comes from. Secondly, there is currently a significant shortage of young people entering the world of plant science. There is a great need to produce more plant scientists in the future for economic and social reasons. It is imperative that primary children are introduced to plant science in a way that encourages their curiosity, helping them to be fascinated by the world of plants as incredible living things and worthy of later study. This last point should not be underestimated as it is well known that children's attitudes towards school subjects affect their choice of further study (Simon and Osborne, 2010).

Research focus

Research carried out on behalf of the British Nutrition Foundation (BNF) involved the questioning of 27,500 children aged 5–16 in May 2013. Among other findings were that:

- almost one-third of primary pupils think cheese is made from plants;

- nearly one in ten secondary pupils think that tomatoes grow underground;

- there is much confusion among younger pupils about where staples like bread and pasta come from – about one-third of 5–8 year olds think they are made from meat;

- almost one-fifth of 5–8 year olds do not realise that potatoes grow under-ground with 10 per cent thinking they grow on bushes or trees.

Activity

Reflect on the link between plants and the cross-curricular topic of healthy eating. What is your view on the findings of this research? Do your children hold these ideas? If so, what could you do to challenge these ideas?

The outdoor environment in the Early Years

Like some older children, younger children will probably find it difficult to understand that a tree is a plant. They may recognise a 'tree' in general terms, but are unlikely to be able to distinguish one tree from another unless they are given the opportunity to observe, at first hand, the different characteristics of different trees, both broadleaved (deciduous) and evergreen. Starting early in the EYFS it is important for children to look at, for example, leaves from different trees in autumn so that they come to understand the wide variety of this type of plant. Unless children compare and contrast trees and other plants at first hand, they are unlikely to appreciate the wide variety of particular plants and will continue to hold very narrow ideas of what plants are.

Case study: Looking closely at trees with Year R children

Lisa, a first year Teach First participant, was working with her Reception children to develop their understanding of the world. This provided an excellent opportunity to make use of the local environment. During a regularly scheduled 'change walk', when children visited the local environment at different times of the year using the same route each time, Lisa encouraged her children to look at the various trees on the route, on this occasion in autumn. Lisa provided her class with choice. Some children decided that they would like to collect leaves that had fallen from the trees; some showed interest in the fruits that had fallen from the trees, for example conkers, sweet chestnuts and a variety of winged seeds which were collected and taken back into the classroom; others decided to make bark rubbings of different trees using wax crayons and thin white paper. Armed with cameras, some children took photographs of different trees on their route and were reminded to take turns over using the camera.

Once back in the classroom, Lisa asked the children to put their collections on the table for closer observation. Using a simple magnifying glass, the children looked more closely at their finds. Working together, Tara and Josh realised that not all leaves looked the same. Tara noticed that some of the leaves 'looked like hands' and that others had a number of leaves on one stem. Similarly, other children discovered that the bark rubbings from different trees were different and that not all the fruits from trees were the same.

Lisa decided that she would take her children out to look at the trees again to see if they could find out, by matching, from which trees each of the different leaves had come. During the whole experience, Lisa and her adult helpers were able to watch what the children were doing, noting anything that interested them and listening to what individual children said as they went on their focused walk together. Later the evidence was matched to each child's profile as evidence against relevant Early Learning Goals.

Later in the day, Lisa talked to the class about what they had done and found out. They looked at the photographs that the children had taken. The work that the children had completed formed the basis of a wall display and the objects were placed on a table. Over the next few days, children brought in additional items from the outside environment to add to the display. Lisa made a point of asking children to sort the objects into groups, for example leaves, fruits, etc., and to make simple comparisons between things in the same group and to ask their own questions to extend their learning even further.

When interest in the objects' table began to wane, Lisa provided children with simple equipment to plant the seeds that had been collected, for example horse chestnuts, sweet chestnuts, acorns and sycamore seeds. Later, as growth occurred, Lisa planned for her children to draw a sequence of pictures of the emerging plants and later to pull up the plants to look closely to see what had happened to the developing seeds underneath the soil.

Curriculum links

Practitioners in the EYFS are encouraged to give children opportunities for exploration of the natural environment providing simple equipment such as microscopes to aid close observation. Such activities help them to look for patterns in nature and to see similarities and differences (DfE, 2012).

The 'nature table' has been a popular feature of Early Years classrooms for decades, particularly during autumn.

This provision can create interest and extend children's understanding of plants and the seasons. Seasonal change can seem magical to very young children. In spring the changes to the apparently 'dead' trees can be awesome. Change walks provide an enjoyable opportunity to observe change over time and should not be restricted to the EYFS. If the same route is taken in every season, even the very youngest children observe how the observable features of trees change over time and can note the steady changing of the colours of leaves on the trees over the seasons. From winter buds to leaf fall and the development of new buds the opportunities for observation across a range of trees are significant in developing awareness of the natural world.

School gardens or wild areas can be used to undertake simple investigations of growth over time. Even very young children can record the rate of growth through adopting and taking photographs of a plant as it grows. This goes beyond advice to Early Years practitioners for children to take care of flower beds (NADA, 2012, p.40)

Key scientific concepts

- Plants as living things

- Variation in plants

- Parts of a plant and their function

- Growth, germination and survival

- Pollination, seed formation and seed dispersal

Plants as living things

Plants are living organisms. They grow, feed, respire, move, reproduce, are sensitive to stimuli and excrete. Most plants are green. Unlike animals, plants are able to make their own food. Green plants are called primary producers. Green plants make their own food through a process called photosynthesis. During photosynthesis, solar energy is converted into chemical energy.

Activity

Look at the surface of some leaves under a hand lens or simple microscope. You should notice many small round structures. These are called chloroplasts.

Chloroplasts contain chlorophyll. Chlorophyll absorbs sunlight. Sunlight is a form of energy. During photosynthesis, a chemical reaction, energy from sunlight is converted into chemical energy in the form of sugars.

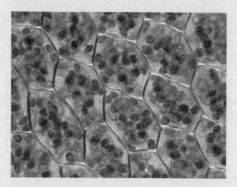

Figure 2.1 Chloroplasts in a plant cell

Look again at the leaf. What other features do you notice? Make a quick observational drawing. Find out what function chloroplasts and the other observable features perform in the survival of a plant.

Photosynthesis

Photosynthesis occurs in the presence of chlorophyll, carbon dioxide and water. Most photosynthesis takes place in leaves. Chlorophyll, in chloroplasts in leaves, absorbs light energy. Water is transported from the roots of a plant to the leaves. Carbon dioxide is absorbed from the air by leaves. Photosynthesis involves a number of processes that work together.

Table 2.1 Chemical reaction involved in the production of energy in the presence of light

Carbon dioxide	+	Water	In the presence of light and chlorophyll	Sugar	+	Oxygen
$6CO_2$		$6H_2O$		$C_6H_{12}O_6$		$6O_2$

Photosynthesis involves the gas carbon dioxide (CO_2). Carbon dioxide diffuses from the air into leaves through structures called stomata. Mechanisms called guard cells control diffusion of carbon dioxide and the amount of water absorbed by the leaf, by osmosis, for photosynthesis.

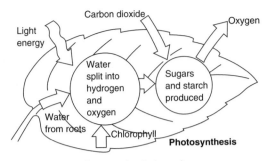

Figure 2.2 Diagram of a leaf showing photosynthesis in action

Leaf fall in autumn

Photosynthesis mainly occurs in leaves and depends on the amount of light available. As days in the northern hemisphere grow shorter, the amount of light available for photosynthesis decreases. The shortening of days through autumn into winter causes other effects in trees: from late summer, leaves begin to fall. Observing everyday changes in the outdoor environment, children find the change of colour of leaves from green to reds, yellows and oranges fascinating. Children often ask why this happens and are interested that this process does not happen to all trees. Trees that keep their leaves all year round are called evergreen. Trees that lose their leaves in autumn are called broadleaved or deciduous. Leaf fall is a natural process. Old leaves die and new leaves are produced. In the UK and in some other parts of the world this happens at particular times of the year. New leaves form in the spring and trees lose their leaves in the autumn. In other, less temperate parts of the world where there is little seasonal change in conditions, leaf fall and renewal is a continuous process all through the year, so the process is less noticeable over time and less dramatic than in the UK. During the spring and summer in the UK and northern Europe and in North America, leaves exhibit many different shades of green.

The reason for leaf fall is linked to day length: as day length becomes shorter, trees produce less chlorophyll. This exposes other chemicals stored in the leaves such as carotene which has a yellow colour. In the summer, carotene is masked by the green chlorophyll. As temperatures drop in the autumn, chlorophyll breaks down and shows the other pigmented chemicals that are not affected by the drop in temperature. Many leaves turn from green to yellow and others from green to orange and red.

When trees lose their leaves, each leaf leaves a scar on the twig.

New buds begin to grow immediately above the leaf scars.

A leaf colour survey can provide an interesting simple investigation for children collecting and comparing the colour of leaves from different trees or the same tree over time as they fall in the autumn. This not only increases their awareness of trees as living things but also extends their observational skills which are important when children are 'working scientifically'. Following close observation and identification of winter twigs, upper Key Stage 2 children can make a key for younger children to use to identify the tree from which the twigs came.

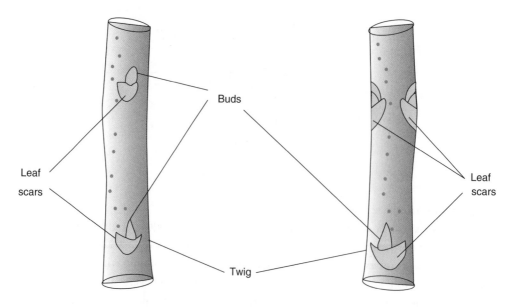

Figure 2.3   Leaf scars and buds located on a twig

Figure 2.4   Leaf scars on a twig

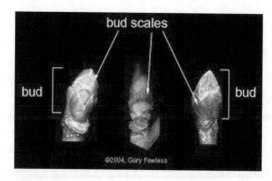

Figure 2.5   Buds and bud scales

Case study: Key Stage 1 children looking at plants

Sanjay, a postgraduate Certificate in Education (PGCE) (full-time) student was planning for his class to look at plants in the new year. In particular he wanted his Key Stage 1 class to identify and name a variety of common wild and garden plants, including deciduous and evergreen trees. He decided that because it was winter, he would help children to identify some common broadleaved (deciduous) trees by looking at their winter buds. He visited the Woodland Trust website at www.woodlandtrust.org.uk and consulted books and other secondary sources to support his planning and further develop his own subject knowledge about trees.

He thought that it was a good opportunity to help children to develop their ability to use keys by asking them to identify the trees using simple keys like the ones produced by the Natural History Museum at www.nhm.ac.uk/resources-rx/files/urban-tree-survey-key-69444.pdf or the Forestry Commission at www.forestry.gov.uk/treenametrail and to identify winter twigs using the Woodland Trust website at www.naturedetectives.org.uk/NR/rdonlyres/344CA3AC-3973-465F-9E30-828247B9770D/0/twigs.pdf.

Within the same term he was planning for his children to describe the basic structure of flowering plants, including trees. He also gave them the opportunity to continue to monitor the growth of the sprouts and potatoes they had planted during the previous autumn.

Sanjay decided that he would make each child a simple diary to record the growth of the plants over time. He also planned that on a mild day he would give his class a challenge: to find a plant in the 'wild area' of the school grounds with the longest roots. Before that, he knew that he would have to teach his class the parts of a plant so that he could reinforce the names of the main parts of a green plant, i.e. leaves, flowers (blossom), petals, fruit, roots, bulb, seed, trunk, branches, stem. He made a note to himself to remember to repeat this activity again, in the same area of the school grounds, to note seasonal change later in the year.

Sanjay decided the best way for the children to learn the main parts of a green plant was to ask the children to make a close observational drawing of the plant. He decided that weeds like the dandelion, and flowers grown from bulbs such as the daffodil, snowdrops and tulips, were good plants for study. He considered health and safety issues related to the study of plants and consulted the Association for Science Education (ASE) Be Safe! He bore in mind the fact that although they look very similar to onions or shallots, many bulbs are poisonous and need to be treated with great care in the classroom. The children had planted some bulbs during the first term. Sanjay decided that he would ask some children to dig up a small number of the bulbs to see what was happening to them. Once again they made close observational drawings and named the parts of the plant for reinforcement of these ideas before they returned the developing plants to their original position in the ground.

Curriculum links

In Key Stage 1 Year 1 pupils should be taught to identify and name a variety of common wild and garden plants, including deciduous and evergreen trees, and also to identify and describe the basic structure of a variety of common flowering plants, including trees.

Activity: Floor book

Floor books are fantastic! They are promoted by Ofsted (2013) as a great way for assessing and recording a learning journey. Floor books can be as simple as two pieces of paper stuck together. However, Early Years practitioners often construct more elaborate examples with books taking the shape of objects linked to the topic under study and with children's work, 3D elements and photographs incorporated within them.

Select a natural object such as a leaf. Create a page in a prepared floor book for observations of the object. Prepare another page for questions that arise from your observations. Prepare final pages that demonstrate the scientific process that you employed to answer one of the questions. The tool will prove to be useful as a model for children to develop their own floor books on a range of topics.

Reflect on the ways that you might use floor books in your teaching.

Variation in the plant kingdom

Variation is an important scientific concept. It is concerned with the diversity of living things. Although children are more likely to be familiar with flowering plants such as daffodils, daisy, dandelion, sweet peas or common trees and shrubs, there are other plants that are non-flowering. There are five main groups of non-flowering plants:

- algae (including seaweeds);

- mosses;

- liverworts;

- ferns;

- lichens.

The study of plants obviously lends itself to work in the outside environment. Children may well not be aware of the appearance of examples of the above groups. Potential homework challenges for older primary children could include individual research of a small number of examples of plants from one group, for example collecting information about and downloading or collecting pictures or photographs of examples from each group. Pooling and presenting findings later as a display gives children the opportunity to communicate what they have found out to the rest of the class and also provides an authentic link with literacy skills. Children may have other ideas of how to present this information as a record of their work. Later, follow-up activities could include going to their local environment, a local garden centre or a woodland environment armed with their new knowledge. Work might be extended to include the use of keys or plants from outside these groups such as cacti, air plants or Venus fly traps which are always popular. The knowledge and understanding gained during this period would provide a springboard for later study of habitats.

Parts of a plant and their function

All parts of a plant have different jobs to do. They work together to ensure survival and reproduction of the whole plant.

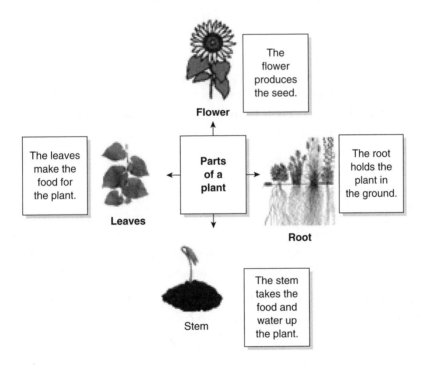

Figure 2.6 Parts of a plant

What a plant needs to grow

Many children think that plants need soil to grow. This is a reasonable but false assumption. Close observation of many outdoor habitats reveals that many plants grow without soil, including some common plants that grow on walls and others, like those that invade and establish themselves in areas of land next to the sea and cacti, that can grow in sand or between rocks.

Plant growth is affected by the availability of light and water and by temperature. This can be explored in the classroom by children carrying out simple investigations such as finding out the effects of excluding light or water from growing plants.

Research focus: Children's ideas about plants

Large-scale research was carried out in the 1980s and 1990s into the ideas that primary children hold about a range of scientific ideas including plants. Much of this is now dated, but it is still worth considering as long as it is recognised that the context of primary education is now very different in the second decade of the twenty-first century. Harlen and Qualter (2009) concluded that younger children often recognise that plants need soil, water and light. They posited that older primary children might well go further, but their explanations were unlikely to refer to processes but rather to need (Harlen and Qualter, 2009).

Plants breathe. Although they do not have lungs like humans and other mammals, they 'breathe' in carbon dioxide during photosynthesis and breathe out oxygen. Children may find this idea difficult. Photosynthesis takes place during the day. Oxygen is a waste product of photosynthesis. Just like animals, plants need to break down carbohydrates to produce energy.

$$\text{Sugar + oxygen} \rightarrow \text{carbon dioxide}$$

$$C_6H_{12}O_6 + 6H_2O \rightarrow 6CO_2 + \text{water} + \text{energy}$$

Oxygen is involved in this process called respiration. Respiration is the process of breaking down carbohydrates (sugars) to release energy to be used in other parts of the plant. The energy that is released during respiration is used by the plant in various ways to help the plant to function as a living organism.

Although plants release oxygen into the air during the day they do not give out all the oxygen that has been produced during respiration. At night, plants still need to

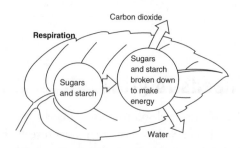

Figure 2.7 Diagram of a leaf showing respiration in action

respire. When it is dark at night, in the absence of light, plants need to absorb oxygen from the air and give off carbon dioxide.

The important thing to remember is that photosynthesis takes place in the light, but respiration occurs all the time. The amazing thing to note here is that if trees and other plants did not release oxygen into the atmosphere in this way, animals would not be able to live on Earth. All life on Earth depends on the basic life processes in plants.

Roots

Roots are important parts of a plant. Roots anchor plants and stop them from being uprooted or washed away. Roots are involved in transporting water around the plant. Plants contain lots of very thin tubes which carry liquids up, down and around the plant. Tubes called xylem carry water and mineral salts up the stem to the leaves. Tubes called phloem carry dissolved food like sugars and amino acids that are made in the leaves by photosynthesis to every part of the plant. Phloem also carries hormones to other parts of the plant. Hormones control growth.

Water is essential to the life of a plant. Green plants need water for photosynthesis and to stop the plant wilting. Plants lose water most of the time. Water evaporates from leaves. Leaves have a large surface area. This process is called transpiration. More evaporation from the leaves takes place during the day than at night. Stomata on leaves are open during the day and are closed at night. Plants need to be able to control the amount of water entering the plant and the amount of water leaving so stomata may also close during very hot weather when conditions are very dry. Plants will wilt if they do not get enough water. Water is pulled up the xylem in the stem from the roots. Clearly, plants are highly organised complex living things being dependent on some amazingly complex structures, mechanisms and processes: well worth more than a cursory study at an appropriate level. The key to this is to maintain the curiosity of children as they discover the amazing diversity and complex lives of plants, the success of which are essential for other life on Earth.

Activity

There are a number of productive starting points for raising questions about plants and plant processes that can be investigated at the primary level. Stimuli for raising questions can include close observation of leaves or other parts of the plant. Here, for example, is the opportunity for pupils to notice that some evergreen leaves such as the holly are usually very shiny and more rigid than broadleaved leaves such as the oak, ash or beech, which are usually thinner and more fragile. After raising questions from the stimulus, pupils could raise questions about how water can be retained in a leaf – how can transpiration be stopped? Alternatively, children could monitor what happens

(Continued)

(Continued)

to a range of different leaves over time, making observational drawings or taking photographs of this change over time. Children could monitor the change in weight of a particular mass of leaves over time using simple but sensitive weighing scales.

If you are teaching upper Key Stage 2 children, you could think about providing your children with the opportunity to investigate any comparative relationships, for example whether there is a relationship between the size of leaf and the height of a tree, or between the girth and height of a tree. Investigating such comparative relationships provides opportunities for a wealth of authentic survey investigations that pupils will find interesting and, if you give them the opportunity to problem solve, for example finding out how to measure the height of a tall tree, ones that will extend their skills across curriculum areas. The potential for investigation is enormous. Identify other comparative relationships for yourself.

The life cycle of flowering plants

Reproduction in plants can happen sexually or asexually.

Asexual reproduction in plants

Many flowering plants reproduce asexually. Instead of being pollinated by insects, they reproduce through a process called vegetative propagation. Some flowers develop from bulbs, corms or tubers. Bulbs, corms and tubers are similar in that they all store food that is essential for the future growth of new plants. The term 'bulb' has come to mean any plant that has an underground food storage capacity (International Bulb Society, 2013).

Flowers like tulips and daffodils grow from bulbs. Flowers like crocuses grow from corms. A corm is a short underground stem. New corms form on the side of old ones. When these break off they form a new plant. Irises grow asexually from underground stems called rhizomes. The stored food in the rhizome feeds the new plant as it develops. Other plants such as strawberries have side branches called runners. Runners grow over the soil and form buds. Each bud grows into a new strawberry plant. A potato is grown asexually from a tuber. A tuber is a swollen underground root. New shoots grow from 'buds', sometimes called eyes. All these are examples of asexual reproduction in plants.

Sexual reproduction in plants

Flowering plants carry out sexual reproduction. Sexual reproduction takes place in the flowers. Flowers have sex cells. The male sex cells are called pollen grains and the female sex cells are called egg cells. A seed forms when a pollen grain fertilises an egg cell. Pollen grains from one plant usually fertilise another. This is advantageous to the plant as, like in animals, a mix of genetic material results in more variation.

Flowers all have the same basic structure.

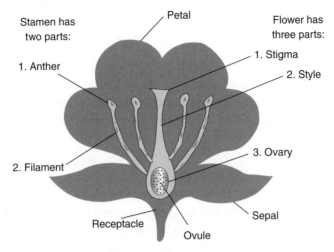

Figure 2.8 Diagram of a flower showing essential parts

Sepals protect the developing flower in the bud.

Petals are often coloured and scented to attract insects. Petals often have a **nectary** at the base. The nectary makes a sugary substance called nectar.

Stamens are male sex organs. Each stamen is made up of two parts, the **anther** where pollen is made and the **filament** which holds the anther. The stamens are usually easy to see.

Carpels are female sex organs. Each carpel is made up of a **stigma,** a **style** and an **ovary.** The **ovule** is inside the ovary. The ovule is the female egg cell. Carpels are usually found in the middle of the flower.

Activity

Using a hand lens, look carefully at some common flowers such as the tulip, apple, pear or sweet pea. While all flowers have the same basic parts, they are often shaped differently and have different numbers of petals, stamens and carpels.

Can you identify all the parts labelled in the above drawing?

Some flowers, such as those produced by some grasses, cereals and some trees, are not coloured or scented. They are sometimes difficult to see which may lead to the conclusion that they are not flowers at all. Grasses and cereals do not have sepals or petals, but they do have large anthers that make lots of light pollen and hang down outside the flower. Feathery stigmas catch the pollen grains in the air. In high summer pollen levels in the air are often very concentrated because of the amount of pollen taken from the anthers of grasses as the wind blows. This high level of pollen is the cause of much discomfort for hay fever sufferers.

Pollination

Pollen grains are made inside anthers. When they are ripe, anthers split open to release the pollen. Pollen grains have to transfer from the anthers of one flower to the carpels of another. This is called pollination. Pollen can be transferred from one plant to another in two main ways: it can be carried by insects or blown by the wind.

Insect pollination

Flowers attract insects by their colourful scented flowers that often contain nectar. When the insect lands on a flower its body rubs against the flower's anthers and stigma. Pollen is sticky, so it sticks to the bodies of insects. When the insect visits other flowers, some of the pollen it is carrying is transferred onto the stigma of other flowers. This is called cross-pollination. Sometimes the pollen from one flower lands on the stigma of another flower of the same species. This is called **self-pollination.**

Fertilisation

When a pollen grain lands on the female stigma pollination is complete. During fertilisation a pollen nucleus must join with an egg nucleus to make a seed. This means that the pollen nucleus must travel down though the ovary to reach the egg cell. Once it has landed on the stigma it begins to form a pollen tube.

Each pollen grain starts to grow a pollen tube down through the style to the ovary. As it grows, the pollen tube takes the pollen nucleus with it. When it reaches the egg cell nucleus, the pollen nucleus fuses with the egg cell nucleus. This is called fertilisation. The fertilised egg grows into the embryo. The ovule forms the seed with the embryo inside it and the ovary forms the fruit with the seeds inside it.

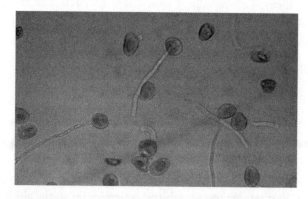

Figure 2.9   Pollen tubes from birch at 75 mins (SAPS Science and Plants for Schools, Student Sheet 4 – Pollen Tube growth)

Fruits and seeds

Seed production

The Seed: an amazing little package of life

Plants invest their futures in seeds. Each seed contains an embryo with its inherited set of genes, and a food store to start the plant off until it can support itself by making its own food. Seeds have to be tough to withstand harsh conditions, and attacks by animals. Their survival can be astonishing. A seed dug up from the arctic Tundra germinated after being frozen for 10,000 years. Seeds of desert plants regularly last for decades waiting for the rain that signals time for germination.

(Braund, 2001, p.27)

Following fertilisation the petals of the flower fall off. The fertilised egg grows into an embryo which will eventually grow into a new plant. Each ovule grows into a seed. The seed is a food store for the next generation of the plant. The idea of what counts as a seed can be very confusing. Confusion stems from the inconsistent use of terms in everyday language and the fact that different terms are used for different seeds. There is a general misconception held by many children that seeds come from packets and that, for example, beans are not seeds but pulses, and nuts are not seeds. Some seeds such as peaches or plums are surrounded by a hard 'stone' covered by a soft, edible fruit. Other seeds like pears, blueberries and apples have small seeds in the centre of the fruit. Others like the raspberry have many seeds each covered by its own small fruit. Only the strawberry has its seeds on the outside of the fruit. Other fruits like peppers, aubergines and cucumbers are often not thought of as fruits at all, but nevertheless contain seeds within them.

Seed dispersal: fruits and seeds

For the best chance of survival, seeds need to be scattered over as wide an area as possible. If seeds from the same plant were dispersed over a very limited space, they would be crowded and would have to compete for light and space and water. Plants have evolved a number of different ways of dispersing their seeds. Some seeds like those of the dandelion and thistle are attached to very fine 'parachutes' that catch the wind. Others like the ash, elm and sycamore produce winged seeds. These slow the rate of descent to the ground and allow for the seeds to be carried further by the wind. Poppy seeds are shaken out when the wind moves the fruits. They are dispersed like salt from a salt box.

Some seeds eaten by animals are dispersed miles away from the plant from which they are produced. Some fruits containing seeds such as rosehip or hawthorn are brightly coloured to attract birds and other animals. When the fruits are eaten by the animals, the seeds, being indigestible, are passed out of the body in faeces during excretion. Squirrels store nuts such as hazelnuts and acorns in the ground. Far more are stored than can be eaten so some germinate and have a good start in life.

Some seeds, such as those of the broom self-disperse.

Figure 2.10 Broom seeds explode out of the pod when the seeds are ripe

When the seeds are ripe the seed case dries and shrinks spreading the seeds away from the original plant in an explosion. For more information see: http://apps.rhs.org.uk/schoolgardening/uploads/documents/seed_dispersal_548.pdf

Activity

Collect some winged seeds from different trees. Look at them closely. In particular look at the relative weight and size of the various parts of the winged seed. Take some measurements. Drop the seed from a height. How long do they take to fall? Use a fan to investigate how far the seed can travel at different speeds of the fan.

Take some measurements of the various parts of the winged seed then make a winged seed out of craft material. Can you make a representative model then investigate what happens when you change some of the features? What could you change and what could you measure?

Germination

When seeds land in places where conditions are good for their growth, when the time is right they will germinate. Germination occurs when the embryo begins to grow.

For more information see: www.kidsgrowingstrong.org/bean_seed_grows

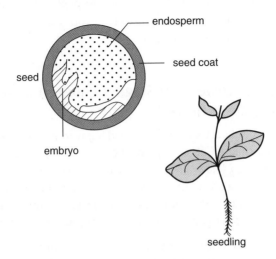

Figure 2.11 The inside of a seed

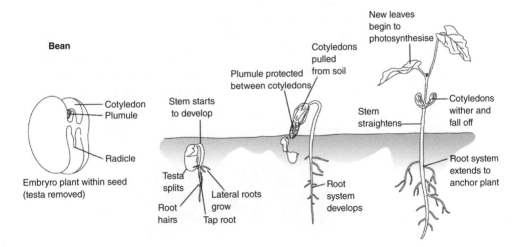

Figure 2.12 Beans beginning to grow

Conditions for germination

Seeds germinate when the conditions are right. Before a seed can germinate it needs water to enable the seed to swell up and to make the food stored in the seed ready to feed the embryo. Oxygen is needed for respiration and the temperature needs to be right. Many seeds do not begin to grow until spring or summer for this reason.

Growth in plants

Plants respond to light, gravity and water. Parts of the plant grow towards them or away from them. These growth responses are called tropisms. Plants grow towards the light. This response is called positive phototropism. Under the effects of gravity, no matter which way up a seed is planted, the shoot always grows upwards and the roots grow downwards. The response to gravity is called geotropism. Shoots are negatively geotropic and roots are positively geotropic.

Case study: Lower Key Stage 2 children looking at reproduction in flowering plants

Daniel, a School Direct student, was working with his lower Key Stage 2 class teaching his children about reproduction in flowering plants. He decided to assess what they knew already about this process by providing them with a box of craft resources. He asked them, in pairs, to construct a flower and watched with interest as flowers were produced. He then asked some of the pairs to explain their flower and the parts they had put on their flower.

He then gave them a real flower, with obvious parts, for example a sweet pea or a tulip, and asked them to pull the pieces of the flower apart. He also gave them a diagram of the names of the parts of a flower and asked them to research, using a tablet computer, the function of each part of the flower and carry out more specific research about pollination and seed formation. To consolidate their learning, Daniel decided that it would be nice to record some of the class's work as a role-play. He asked his class, in groups of about six, to make up a role-play to show the stages in the process. He gave them time to work out their role-play and allowed them to make props to support their work.

He was conscious that parts of many plants are used as foodstuff and that it is important to reinforce the main parts of a plant, i.e. root, stem, flower, etc.

Figure 2.13   Children sorting pictures of parts of plants into groups

He was also aware that there is often much confusion about fruits and seeds, etc. The problem stems from the difference in the usage of terms in everyday life and in the scientific world. Confusion can be rife: for example, is a nut a seed, or are peppers and cucumbers vegetables or fruit?

To help clarify terms and develop a better understanding, he planned to give his class an opportunity to sort plants into groups.

Daniel also planned to give his pupils the opportunity to explore what seeds and bulbs need to grow. He knew that there was a common misconception held by many about the role of soil in the growth of a seed. He knew that seeds and bulbs need water to grow, but most do not need light: seeds and bulbs have a store of food inside them. He knew that corms, bulbs and seeds all contain a store of food for the early developing seed and that they need water to grow. He planned to challenge his children's misconceptions about the need for soil by encouraging them to put seeds like broad beans into tubes and watching what happened as they germinated and grew over time without the need for soil.

Curriculum links

Work on plants provides the opportunity for pupils to work scientifically by observing and recording the growth of a variety of plants over time from seeds or bulbs. They could observe similar plants at different stages of growth and set up comparative tests to show that plants need light and water to stay healthy. (DfE, 2013)

In lower Key Stage 2 pupils should be given the opportunity to identify and describe the functions of different parts of flowering plants (roots, stem/trunk, leaves and flowers) and to explore the requirements of plants for life and growth (air, light, water, nutrients from soil and room to grow) and how they vary from plant to plant. (DfE, 2013).

A very common illustrative activity, popular in many schools uses either cut white carnations or stems of celery placed for a time in coloured water to help children to understand, at a simple level, the way water is transported in plants. They should also explore the part that flowers play in the life cycle of flowering plants, including pollination, seed formation and seed dispersal.

Activity

Collect together some pictures of different fruits, stems, roots and leaves. Sort the examples of fruits, stems, flowers and roots in groups.

Compare your sorting with the information provided. Did you find any problematic? Which and why?

Self-assessment questions

1. What will your approach be to teaching about plants both in the inside and outside environments? Can you explain why you will adopt this approach?
2. What are the main points of learning about plants that are important for your age group of children?
3. How will this translate into practice in your classroom?

Look back at the subject knowledge that underpins the teaching of this topic.

1. Make a quick sketch of the parts of a plant.
2. Explain what the roots are for.
3. Explain why flowering plants have flowers.
4. Explain the role of the stem.
5. Explain why a plant has seeds or fruits.
6. Explain how fertilisation occurs in flowering plants.
7. What do corms, seeds and bulbs all have in common?
8. Explain the conditions needed for germination.

Further reading and websites

Braund, M. (2001) *Primary plants: A handbook for teaching plant science in the primary school*. Birmingham: The Questions Publishing Company Ltd.

Growing seeds in a bag: www.saps.org.uk/primary/teaching-resources/639-growing-seeds-in-a-plastic-bag

How fast does a root grow? www.saps.org.uk/primary/teaching-resources/217-how-fast-does-a-root-grow-

Plants and fertiliser: www.saps.org.uk/primary/teaching-resources/216-adding-mineral-salt-do-radishes-grow-better

Rapid cycling brassicas: www.saps.org.uk/primary/teaching-resources/226-growing-rapid-cycling-brassicas

Root growing through a maze: www.saps.org.uk/primary/teaching-resources/611-making-a-root-move-through-a-maze

SAPS – Science and Plants for Schools: www.saps.org.uk

What do plants need to grow? – booklet: www.saps.org.uk/primary/teaching-resources/236-living-processes-and-what-plants-need-to-grow

Woodland Trust: www.woodlandtrust.org.uk

References

Braund, M. (2001) *Primary plants: A handbook for teaching plant science in the primary school*. Birmingham: The Questions Publishing Company Ltd.

Department for Education (2012) *Statutory framework for the Early Years Foundation Stage 2012*. Runcorn: DfE. Available at: www.education.gov.uk/publications/standard/AllPublications/Page1/DFE-00023-2012 (accessed 11/6/14).

Department for Education (2013) *Science programmes of study: Key stages 1 and 2.* National Curriculum in England, September 2013. London: Crown copyright 2013.

Department for Education (2013) *The National Curriculum for England*, framework document. London: DfE. Available at: www.education.gov.uk/nationalcurriculum (accessed 11/6/14).

Driver, R., Squires, A., Rushworth, P. and Wood-Robinson, V. (1994) *Making sense of secondary science: Research into children's ideas.* London: Routledge.

Harlen, W. and Qualter, A. (2009) *The teaching of science in primary schools*, 5th edition. London: Routledge.

International Bulb Society (IBS) Available at: bulbsociety.org (accessed 11/6/14).

Ofsted (2013) *Maintaining curiosity: A survey into science education in schools.* Manchester: Ofsted.

Simon, S. and Osborne, J. (2010) Students' attitudes to science, in Osborne, J and Dillon, J (eds) *Good practice in science teaching: What research has to say*, 2nd edition. Maidenhead: Open University Press.

3 Animals, including humans: the parts of the body, the senses, teeth, nutrition and the digestive system

Learning outcomes

By reading this chapter you will develop:

- an understanding of key scientific concepts that underpin the teaching of animals including humans, specifically the parts of the body, the senses, nutrition, teeth and the digestive system;
- effective pedagogic strategies for teaching about the parts of the body, the senses, teeth, nutrition and the digestive system in humans;
- your understanding of how misconceptions can be used as starting points for learning in science.

Teachers' Standards

3. Demonstrate good science subject and curriculum knowledge

- have a secure knowledge of science, foster and maintain pupils' interest in science, and address misunderstandings.

4. Plan and teach well-structured lessons

- promote a love of learning and children's intellectual curiosity
- reflect systematically on the effectiveness of lessons and approaches to teaching.

Introduction

Children in the EYFS and primary stages of education are just as interested in themselves and how their body works as older children and adults. Indeed, they may be more so! This makes teaching this aspect of science potentially very rewarding and interesting for everyone. This is, however, dependent on how the topic is taught. More traditional teaching of this topic has tended to focus on facts to be learned and worksheets to be labelled and completed. Here, for many, the interest in and the awe and wonder of the processes and mechanisms of the working of the human body have often been lost in the learning of names and transmission of information where that approach has been used instead of developing 'joined-up' understanding of the interrelated and complex processes involved in everyday living. What is needed is a much more practical approach that incorporates simple but potentially memorable experiences that stimulate thought and discussion. Indeed, it could be argued that many children might not be able to relate to the stereotypical diagrammatic representations frequently used in the teaching of this topic and that textbooks and other information are generally aimed at the adult rather than the child. In this chapter, alternative strategies will be explored. These will be suitable for the development of your own science subject knowledge, but will also enable you, with careful planning, to tailor the ideas to specific groups of children.

Progression in learning and for understanding is very important. Although the topics of nutrition, teeth and digestion are often taught separately, it may well be more effective to teach them together as integral parts of the complex workings of the body. Additionally, science, and these topics in particular, have huge potential for making cross-curricular links, in this case, healthy eating and healthy living. Furthermore, children need to understand how they can live healthy lives. They need the adults around them to present complex ideas in a way that they can understand, and be shown how to 'manage' their bodies to keep them well and happy.

Key scientific concepts

- How our bodies work: (life processes)

- The senses

- Nutrition and hygiene

- Teeth

- Digestion

How our bodies work

Animals are amazing. The extent of the diversity of animal groups is amazing. Different kinds of animals have evolved different ways of ensuring survival. The bodies of mammals, including humans, have numerous complex systems to support life, growth and reproduction. The human animal has many things in common with other mammals, but also has significant differences. Children need to visit and revisit different aspects of the human body in action as they get older and need to be presented with learning experiences that develop a holistic understanding of the complex workings of the human body where every different part has a role in the survival of the whole body.

Parts of the body: external and internal parts of the body

Action rhymes, poems and songs have a useful role in helping children to learn scientific ideas and to develop their knowledge and understanding. Very young children will be familiar with the action song 'Heads, shoulders, knees and toes'. This action rhyme not only reinforces the names of external parts of the body, but also helps them to link the word for each part to its position on the human body. You might want to explore whether your children can name all the external parts of the body before you start to formally teach them the parts. Give them pictures of the various external parts of the body and ask them to locate these on a life-size outline of a child's body. Use their answers and drawings to assess what they know. Use this information to tailor the next steps in their learning to what they already know.

If you are teaching older children, explore their ideas about how the digestive system works before you start teaching the topic. Ask them to discuss, in pairs or small groups, what they already know and what questions they have about the digestive process and to record their understanding in any way they like. Ask them to draw the location of the part of the digestive system. Rather than give them a template to represent the human body, ask them to make an outline drawing of a child's body and then to add their ideas of where they think each part is located.

Nutrition and hygiene

Allied to a study of the senses and teeth and digestion is nutrition, including hygiene.

Curriculum links

Pupils at Key Stage 1 need to know about the right amounts of different types of food to eat to remain healthy. However, at this stage they would not need to be introduced to the names of major food groups. The emphasis throughout education should be on encouraging children to understand and, if possible, adopt a balanced diet.

Some available resources in the past have labelled foodstuffs as good or bad which has sometimes had an unfortunate effect on the preferred eating habits of some children. The term 'diet' is often associated with controlling the amount of food and therefore calories eaten when diet really means what we eat.

The Food Standards Agency (2007) recommends that all healthy individuals should consume a diet that contains:

- plenty of starchy foods such as rice, bread, pasta and potatoes (choosing wholegrain varieties when possible);

- plenty of fruit and vegetables: at least five portions of a variety of fruit and vegetables a day;

- some protein-rich foods such as meat, fish, eggs, beans and non-dairy sources of protein, such as nuts and pulses;

- some milk and dairy, choosing reduced fat versions or eating smaller amounts of full fat versions or eating them less often;

- just a little saturated fat, salt and sugar.

Healthy eating advice

The Eatwell plate is a pictorial representation of the proportion that different food groups should contribute to the diet. This representation of food intake relates to individuals over the age of five (FSA, 2007).

Use the Eatwell plate to help you get the balance right. It shows how much of what you eat should come from each food group.

Fruit and vegetables

Bread, rice, potatoes, pasta and other starchy foods

Meat, fish, eggs, beans and other non-dairy sources of protein

Foods and drinks high in fat and/or suger

Milk and dairy foods

Figure 3.1 The Eatwell plate

In order to be healthy a diet needs to include items from each of the different groups. It would not be healthy if a diet consisted only of fruit or lots of cakes and sweets. Today, many people regularly eat processed food and ready prepared meals. Food packaging is required to indicate the proportions of different types of food on the labels. There is often concern about the amounts of hidden sugar and salt contained in popular snacks such as crisps, cakes and breakfast cereals.

Obviously, hygiene is linked to healthy eating. Young children need to be taught not only the importance of washing their hands before eating, but also how to do this. Some will need close supervision while they are washing hands themselves. It has to be remembered that drying hands after washing is also important.

Activity

Reflect on your own diet. Make a note of everything you eat for a day. Using information from food packets, etc., try to work out how much of each different type of food you consumed in the day. Take a particular note of how much salt and sugar you have ingested. How does this amount relate to recommended adult guidelines?

The senses

One of the characteristics of all living things is that they respond to stimuli. While we would not expect children in the EYFS or Key Stage 1 to name the seven characteristics of living things, children at Key Stage 1, when learning about the parts of the body, are expected to say which part of the body is associated with each sense. Humans have five senses that respond to a variety of stimuli in our environment. These are called receptors or sense organs. Human animals have five sense organs: eyes, ears, nose, skin and tongue.

Table 3.1 The five senses

Sense organ	What the sense organ responds to	Sense
Eyes	Light rays	Sight
Ears	Sound vibrations and movements	Hearing (and also balance)
Nose	Chemicals in the air	Smell
Tongue	Chemicals in food and drink	Taste
Skin	Pressure, pain, heat and cold.	Touch

Topics that involve the senses are popular in the Early Years and Key Stage 1. Although many children have been asked to label drawings of the eye and ear in the past, this is really not appropriate. Instead, it is much more valuable and productive to give children the opportunity to observe and to 'work scientifically' using all their senses (when this is safe).

Case study: Use of senses

Thomas, a second year undergraduate trainee, was working with his Key Stage 1 class. Over the term he wanted to improve their observation skills through providing a series of simple investigations using all their senses. He planned to offer them some activities set in a familiar context.

Sight

Starting with sight tests he planned to talk to his children about their sight. He made some different sized letters and stuck them to a large piece of card using Velcro®. Using these resources as a stimulus, he decided that he would encourage them to think about what questions they could raise about sight and how they could find out about their sight, for example how far they could see the letters clearly. He knew that he would have to try to encourage them to provide their own ideas for finding out the answers to their investigative questions, therefore scaffolding their learning. He also planned for them to make their own cardboard framed 'glasses' over which they could stick coloured transparent acetate sheets to explore what different coloured objects looked like through different coloured 'lenses'.

Taste

Knowing that his class were enthusiastic investigators, he planned to challenge them to explore their sense of taste. He provided them with blindfolds and small quantities of familiar foods such as crisps, sweets or fruit for them to identify. He wanted them to identify the foodstuff through the sense of taste only so he planned that they should hold their noses while they took turns to taste the food. He thought about the need to check his children for allergies to certain foodstuffs. He planned to use his teaching assistant to give the food to each blindfolded group of children in turn. He planned to ask her to encourage the children, in small groups, to describe the taste of the food rather than just merely trying to identify each example. One further activity he wanted to include was to colour familiar soft drinks such as lemonade and orangeade so they were not recognisable by sight. He then planned that children would try to identify the drink using taste only.

Smell

Using small, clean plastic food pots covered with clean cotton fabric and held in place with an elastic band, Thomas planned to ask his children to initially describe and then to try to identify the smell in the pot, for example herbs and spices. He knew that this would be quite difficult for many children as they might not be familiar with the herb or spice, or might not know the name of the herb or spice even if they were familiar with it. With this in mind he provided named pots of the same herbs and spices to enable them to compare and match the smell in the pot to the herb or spice. To extend this further, he also

➡

gave them some diluted essential oils put into mini-vaporisers. Reminding them to take care, he would ask them to spray a small amount of the liquid into the air in front of them and to try to identify, by matching, the essential oil.

Figure 3.2 Essential oils

Hearing

Thomas was keen to encourage his children to raise their own questions about hearing. Although he was slightly anxious about this open-ended approach, he thought that it would be good to ask them what they would like to find out about hearing. He hoped that among their responses would be some investigative questions or at least some questions that could be turned into investigative questions. He researched the sorts of questions that children might be able to investigate and decided that productive ones might relate to how far away a sound could be heard or whether there was a relationship between the size of an animal's ears and the loudness of the heard sound. He decided that to prompt questions about size of ears he would download some pictures of animals with different sized ears as a stimulus discussion point. He planned to ask small groups of children to choose their own question to investigate, allowing them to think about what resources they would need and to choose how they might record their data.

Touch

Always a popular activity, feely bags or boxes could provide his class, Thomas thought, with an opportunity to describe objects. He planned to include some objects that would be familiar and some that would not. He knew that some children would just identify the object without describing it, but that he would have to ask his class to use their sense of touch to help them to describe the object, therefore linking their work in science effectively to literacy.

Research focus: What do children think?

Research suggests (see, for example, Osborne et al., 1992) that older children frequently are unaware of some of the internal parts of the body, despite being able to name the parts. This suggests that children need not only to name parts of the body, but also to locate parts of the body, both internal and external, from a young age. Although pictures and models might have a role in helping children to learn and understand, nothing beats the experience of relating parts of the body to a child life-size diagram to enhance understanding.

However, this research, though highly valued, is now over twenty years old. More recent research with a smaller number of children suggests that some children today have little understanding of what is inside their bodies.

Figure 3.3   Inside my body – Yr 5 child

Figure 3.4   Inside my body – Yr 1 child

Case study: Action rhymes, poems and songs

Amelia, a third year undergraduate student, was working with her Year 3 class. She was interested in developing her children's understanding of how the human body works and decided she would make use of their previous knowledge. She encouraged her class to remember the 'Heads, shoulders knees and toes' action rhyme from their earlier years in school. She then encouraged them to 'add in' other parts of the body not included in the original rhyme so extending their understanding of common characteristics of humans as animals. For example:

Brain, lungs, liver, diaphragm, diaphragm

Brain, lungs, liver, diaphragm, diaphragm

And gullet and stomach and skin and intestine

Brain, lungs, liver, diaphragm, diaphragm

She then asked them to make up their own poems or action rhymes for a younger audience, based on their new learning.

Amelia was keen to encourage cross-age working, so she planned to pair up her own class with Year 1 children and built in an assessment activity so that two older children and two younger children worked together. She planned that before they worked with the younger children, her class would produce some life-size coloured pictures of different external parts of the body for the younger children to place on the outline as an assessment activity. After naming the parts, the older children would talk to the younger children about the five senses to find out if they could say which part of the body is associated with each sense. At the end of the session, the older children would be asked to assess the knowledge of the younger children and to report their assessment to the younger pupils' teacher.

Following the cross-age activity, Amelia planned to include a similar activity for her own children, giving them coloured pictures of the internal parts of the body to place on a life-size outline of their own bodies. She planned to use this as an initial activity to find out what they knew at the start of her planned teaching and then again at the end to assess what they had learned.

Curriculum links

Here there is a fantastic opportunity to make cross-curricular links. In English in lower Key Stage 2, pupils should be taught to prepare poems and play scripts to read aloud and to perform, showing understanding through intonation, tone, volume and action. In science they should develop scientific vocabulary and confidence in using scientific words in a range of contexts, engaging with a range of audiences.

Humans as mammals

Humans are just one type of the group of animals called mammals. A common misconception is that humans are not animals, so all children need to recognise that despite having some differences, humans have similar external features to other mammals such as dogs or cats or familiar farm or zoo mammals. To extend this idea further, younger children in Key Stage 1 could be encouraged to look at other mammals, or pictures of them, and to identify the location of the simple parts of the body with which they are already familiar. They may even be able to amend the original action rhyme to apply the idea to another mammal of their choice.

Digestion

In humans and other mammals digestion takes place in the gut. The gut starts at the mouth and ends at the anus and is approximately nine metres in length. Digestion involves food which is the energy source for the body. Unlike plants, animals are unable to make their own food and therefore have to digest the food that they eat to release the nutrients and energy needed by the body to live. Digestion is a slow process. Some foods take longer to digest than others. Food is processed in the gut and has to go through a number of different stages. Also, the total time taken for food to be processed within the digestive system varies from person to person.

Digestion: the mouth and teeth

In mammals, the mouth and the teeth play an important role in the digestive process. It could be argued that the process of digestion begins even before food is put into the

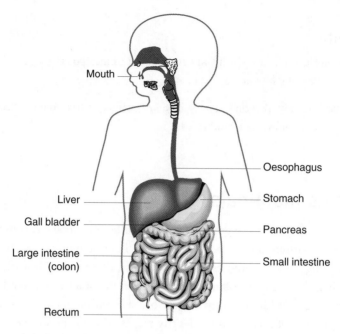

Figure 3.5 Parts of the body involved in the digestive system

mouth. Children will be familiar with the fact that their mouth, in everyday terms, begins to 'water' when they see, smell or even sometimes think about food that they like. Making the link between this and the start of the digestive process is important. What is also important is that children begin to realise that salivation, possibly more noticeable in dogs than humans, relates to a healthy digestive system. Salivation is the process and saliva is the liquid which breaks down food through chemical reactions of which we are virtually unaware when we eat. There is a widely held misconception that chemical reactions take place very rapidly and involve much heat being produced. This is not the case. Many chemical reactions take place slowly over time (please see Chapter 7 for more links to this idea in other areas of the science National Curriculum).

Activity

Try this simple activity which focuses on the idea of salivation as the first step in the digestive process with your class:

- Provide each child in groups of three with a jelly baby (sweet) or a 'polo' mint or similar (take care to check for allergies beforehand).

- One child should break the sweet into as many pieces as possible (suggest nine), one should break their sweet into three pieces and the last should keep the sweet whole.

- At a given signal, each child should suck the sweet, without swallowing, until the sweet has dissolved in the saliva.

- The time at which each sweet dissolves should be noted.

- Subsequent discussion should focus on what factors might have affected the time that each sweet took to dissolve.

Obviously this is a very simple illustrative activity and it is quite easy to see that in theory the smaller the pieces, the faster they should dissolve. The whole sweet should take longer than the three pieces which should take longer than the sweet broken into nine pieces. The reason for this is that the greater surface area of the nine pieces allows the saliva to react with the sweet more quickly. However, like many other simple investigations, it is really difficult to control other factors. In this case, the rate of production and the amount of saliva produced by different individuals may not be the same. Other factors may also affect the rate at which each sweet dissolves. However, this provides a great opportunity for discussion among the children.

Case study: Teeth

Lucinda, a second year undergraduate student, was teaching her lower Key Stage 2 placement class about teeth. She started off by finding out what her class knew or thought they knew about their teeth and how to care for them. She recorded this on a large coloured drawing of a mouth. The upper teeth recorded what the children knew and the lower teeth recorded what questions they had about teeth. She gave each child a small clean mirror and asked them to look at their teeth and to feel their own teeth with their tongue. Next she asked them, in pairs, to talk about any differences they noticed between the different shaped teeth in their mouths. Some of the children were able to tell each other that some teeth were 'a bit square', that others were 'pointed' and that some were 'bigger and were a bit flat'. She then introduced the names of the different types of teeth to those children who did not yet have the vocabulary to describe the teeth accurately. Lucinda talked to them about their experiences of losing teeth and about the 'tooth fairy', and did a quick survey of any children who had lost teeth that week.

Following this she brought some fruit into the classroom as a stimulus for thinking about which teeth are used for different purposes when eating. The children were then given some fruit to eat. She prepared the fruit and gave each child a small piece to eat. The children were reminded how important it is to chew all the food they eat very well and were asked to notice which teeth they used at different times as they chewed their food into small pieces ready for the next stage of digestion. They were given a range of foods including bread, apples and cheese and asked to repeat the process. They

$\longrightarrow$

were encouraged just to use one type of tooth at a time with each type of food. Next they had a general discussion about which teeth were best for biting, chewing, etc. and all the while she was assessing the children to see if they were using the newly introduced vocabulary correctly. They also considered the kind of food that babies and very old people eat.

Cleaning teeth regularly and thoroughly is an important thing for any child to do from a hygiene and health perspective. Cleaning teeth in school can help reinforce good practice in teeth cleaning and can particularly help those whose parents do not supervise cleaning at home.

Lucinda also wanted to assess to what extent individuals in the class could plan and carry out an investigation. She gave them a question as a starting point. Which toothpaste makes the most froth? (Roden et al., 2007 p.45). She asked them how they might find out which toothpaste was the most effective cleaner and then scaffolded the learning as they planned their own simple investigation.

The journey of food through the body – starting in the mouth: the role of teeth

In mammals, teeth have an important role in digestion. Teeth break down food into smaller pieces to enable the enzymes in saliva to start to break down the food through the chemical reaction mentioned earlier. Children of primary age do not need to know the precise reactions involved – this comes at a later stage – but understanding the process at a simple level will enable them to build on their understanding when they revisit the topic.

Teeth
Adult humans normally have 32 teeth. There are different types of teeth each with different jobs.

- Incisors are chisel shaped and are for biting and cutting.

- Canines are pointed for piercing and tearing.

- Premolars are for grinding and chewing.

- Molars are for chewing.

Children will normally have 20 teeth, ten in the top jaw and ten in the bottom jaw – four incisors, two canines and four molars in each jaw.

Children will be familiar with the fact that part of growing up involves gaining then losing 'baby' or 'milk' teeth and that new ones grow. This aspect of the topic links well to the topic of growth. Losing teeth is a big event in the lives of young humans. Here there is a great opportunity to link science to health education and to reinforce messages about tooth hygiene, including cleaning teeth and healthy eating. Eventually

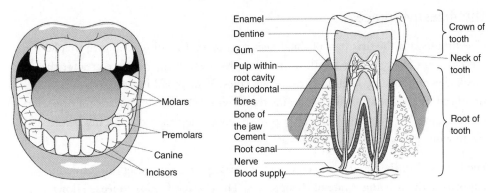

Figure 3.6 The different teeth and their position in a human's body

they will, as a normal adult, have eight incisors, four canines, eight premolars and twelve molars, but these appear over a relatively long period of time.

Milk teeth start to emerge from the gums of human babies when they are about five to ten months old and children usually have a full set by the time they are about two and a half years old. The first teeth to appear are the incisors followed by the canines and finally the molars.

Children need to recognise not only that humans belong to a group of animals called mammals but also that they share many similarities with other mammals, for example in relation to teeth and other parts of the digestive tract or gut, as it is usually known.

Activity: Other mammals and their teeth

Find out if other mammals also have two sets of teeth as they grow from birth to adult.

Find out what types of teeth carnivores, herbivores and omnivores have. Undertake a survey. Is there a relationship between the food that an animal eats and the number and size of their teeth? Use reference books and safe internet sources to find out.

- Which animals will you choose?

- How could you record your information?

Can you use your findings to predict what food animals not included in the survey might eat?

How might this approach be used in children's learning?

The digestive process

Chewing food is the first part of the digestive process. Chewing food into smaller pieces makes food easier to swallow, but also provides a bigger surface area for the break-down of food by chemicals called enzymes. When food is eaten, saliva is produced by the mouth. Saliva contains the enzymes that are important for digestion. Children need to know that it is important to chew their food thoroughly before swallowing so that food is digested easily.

Food chewed in the mouth, when swallowed, passes into the gullet. Swallowing happens without being aware of this process. The chewed food is squeezed down from the mouth into the gullet. The gullet, also called the oesophagus, is like a long tube linking the mouth to the stomach. The gullet transports food to the stomach. The stomach is like a muscular bag that can hold up to 2 litres of food. The stomach makes digestive juices that help further digest food. Digestive juices are important in breaking down food into a form that can then be absorbed in other parts of the gut. Hydrochloric acid is one chemical made in the stomach, so stomach juices are acidic. Children will probably be familiar with the taste of stomach juices when they have had a stomach upset involving sickness. The stomach is a strong muscle which churns the food and mixes it with the digestive juices. After about two hours, the mixture becomes a runny liquid which is slowly passed into the small intestine through a mechanism in the stomach which controls the flow.

It should not be assumed that children will be able to visualise what the stomach looks like, nor what a volume of two litres looks like! Manufactured models might be useful here, but if one is not available, children can simply explore the idea of the stomach being a bag by filling a plastic bag with a measured amount of water. Having a simple practical experience of this kind can really help them to remember ideas in the longer term.

From the stomach, food is slowly squeezed along a very long tube called the small intestine, which is about six metres long. Digested food is able to pass into the blood stream in the small intestine. This can happen, slowly over time, because the long tube-like small intestine has, in total, a very large surface area where the digested food can be absorbed into the blood stream for use in other parts of the body. Of course, primary age children do not need to understand the process in great detail because they will revisit this topic again later. Absorption happens through the walls of the small intestine. However, not all eaten food can be digested in this way. Some parts of food, for example hard seeds like those found in tomatoes or bran from cereals, are indigestible. The undigested food is less useful to the body and passes eventually into the large intestine. The less useful food is transported through the large intestine to the rectum before being passed out of the body through the anus. Solid waste is called faeces, which are stored in the rectum and are eventually passed from the body.

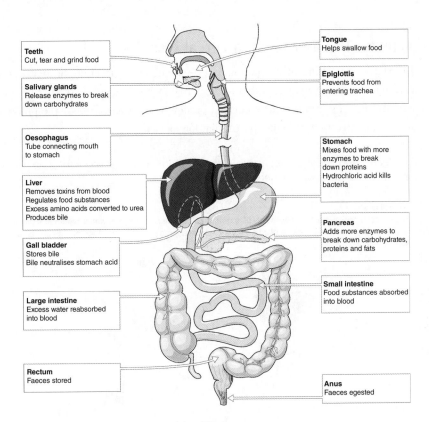

The following labels appear in the figure:

Teeth
Cut, tear and grind food

Salivary glands
Release enzymes to break down carbohydrates

Oesophagus
Tube connecting mouth to stomach

Liver
Removes toxins from blood
Regulates food substances
Excess amino acids converted to urea
Produces bile

Gall bladder
Stores bile
Bile neutralises stomach acid

Large intestine
Excess water reabsorbed into blood

Rectum
Faeces stored

Tongue
Helps swallow food

Epiglottis
Prevents food from entering trachea

Stomach
Mixes food with more enzymes to break down proteins
Hydrochloric acid kills bacteria

Pancreas
Adds more enzymes to break down carbohydrates, proteins and fats

Small intestine
Food substances absorbed into blood

Anus
Faeces egested

Figure 3.7 The human digestive system (simplified)

The whole digestive process in humans normally takes between one and two days.

Activity

How do other mammals such as sheep and cows digest their food? Find out about their digestive system. How are they the same and how are they different from the human animal?

- Find out how long it takes for digestion to take place in other familiar mammals such as cows, sheep or other familiar farm or zoo animals.

- Find out how worms, snails and birds digest their food.

- Choose some other animals that interest you and compare their digestive systems with your own.

- What are the main differences between the animals that you have researched in terms of their digestive systems?

Could the information you have researched be useful in informing planning for your children's learning?

Activity: The journey of a cereal biscuit

Illustrative modelling investigations can be useful in the teaching of digestion as children cannot investigate this process at first hand. Below is a teacher-directed activity that children can carry out and become really excited about the processes involved in digestion. Why not try this out for yourself!

For **Health and Safety** reasons the authors recommend that you substitute water for saliva and dilute white vinegar for stomach acid.

You will need:
Two cereal biscuits, a small bowl, bottle of 'saliva', a pair of scissors, large dowel or hammer, a plastic knife, a bottle of 'stomach acid', a plastic bag, a leg from a large pair of tights, 1 leg of a small pair of tights and a tray.

Pour in some of the 'saliva' to gently wet and start to break down the cereal biscuit.

To replicate the job of the upper and lower incisors use the scissors to roughly cut the cereal biscuit in the bowl.

Place the cereal biscuit in the bowl

Use the knife to replicate the chopping action of the canines.

Next use the dowel or hammer to simulate the grinding action of the molars,

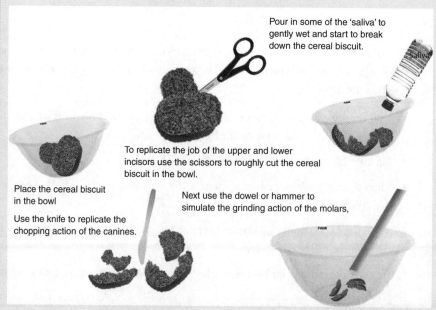

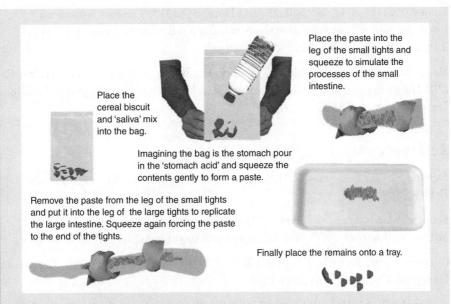

Place the cereal biscuit and 'saliva' mix into the bag.

Imagining the bag is the stomach pour in the 'stomach acid' and squeeze the contents gently to form a paste.

Place the paste into the leg of the small tights and squeeze to simulate the processes of the small intestine.

Remove the paste from the leg of the small tights and put it into the leg of the large tights to replicate the large intestine. Squeeze again forcing the paste to the end of the tights.

Finally place the remains onto a tray.

Figure 3.8 An investigation into the digestive system – the journey of a cereal biscuit

Reflection

- What were the benefits of this activity on your understanding of the processes involved in digestion and what further questions do you have about this topic?

- What might be the benefits of children undertaking this activity for themselves as part of a topic on humans as animals?

Self-assessment questions

1. Name the main parts of the body associated with the digestive system. What function does each part perform?
2. Name the different kinds of teeth found in the human body. Explain the difference in the shape and function of each in preparing food for digestion.
3. In this chapter we have begun to explore potential cross-curricular links to support the teaching of humans and other animals. What other possible links can you identify? How might these be developed?

Further reading

Department for Education (2012) *Statutory framework for the Early Years Foundation Stage 2012*. Runcorn: DfE. Available at: www.education.gov.uk/publications/standard/AllPublications/Page1/DFE-00023–2012 (accessed 11/6/14).

Haigh, A. (2010) *The art of creative teaching: Primary science – big ideas, simple rules.* Chapter 8. Edinburgh: Pearson.

Loxley, P., Dawes, L., Nicholls, L. and Dore, B. (2014) *Teaching primary science: Promoting enjoyment and developing understanding*, 2nd edition. Chapter 15, pages 248–252 and 254–257. Abingdon: Routledge.

Sharp, J., Peacock, G., Smith, R., Johnsey, R., Simon, S., Cross, A. and Harris, D. (2012) *Primary science: Teaching theory and practice*, 6th edition. Chapter 4. London: Learning Matters SAGE.

References

Department for Education (2013) *Science programmes of study: Key stages 1 and 2*. London: DfE.

Food Standards Agency (FSA) (2007) *Nutrient and food based guidelines for UK institutions*. October 2007. Available at: www.food.gov.uk (accessed11/6/14).

Osborne J., Wadsworth, P. and Black P. (1992) *Primary SPACE project: Life processes*. Liverpool: Liverpool University Press.

Roden, J., Ward, H. and Ritchie, H. (2007) *Extending knowledge in practice: Primary science*. Exeter: Learning Matters.

4 Animals including humans: growth, reproduction and the circulatory system

Learning outcomes

By reading this chapter you will develop:

- your understanding of key scientific concepts that underpin the teaching of animals including humans: specifically growth and movement, the basic needs for survival and the circulatory system;
- effective pedagogic strategies for teaching about these concepts;
- an understanding of the misconceptions that children might hold in this area of science.

Teachers' Standards

3. **Demonstrate good science subject and curriculum knowledge**

- have a secure knowledge of science, foster and maintain pupil's interest in science and address misunderstandings.

4. **Plan and teach well-structured lessons**

- promote a love of learning and children's intellectual curiosity.

Introduction

Humans belong to a larger group of animals with backbones called mammals. Mammals are warm blooded. They give birth to and suckle their young. The structures and systems that make up the bodies of animals, including humans, are sophisticated. Humans and other mammals have many structures and systems in common with other animals with backbones but, incredibly, similar systems are even found in other less complex animals without backbones. The workings of any living thing, albeit animal or plant, are complex. Each different system contributes to the working of the whole. Each part has a different job to do. This is remarkable!

Although different structures or systems can be identified and learned about independently from each other, in truth, every healthy body depends on the sound workings of all the various parts that make up the whole. In some ways it is illogical to try to isolate each structure or process because of their interdependence, but in reality, breaking down the study of animals including humans into smaller manageable chunks is essential. However, it is important for children to see the links between the various areas of science that are often taught independently. It is part of the teacher's role to 'see the bigger picture' and to help children make the links between the complex interplay between aspects of the traditionally, but artificially separate physical and biological sciences. Children generally love carrying out practical work but this topic does not really lend itself to this. However, while practical work is an important aspect of effective learning in science, there are other methods that can be used to create interest and curiosity, not least through discussion, asking questions and the use of models, analogies, simulations and role-play. All these can add variety, but are also important in providing cross-curricular links, particularly with English through speaking and listening and drama, and with personal social and health education (PSHE), including well-being.

Key scientific concepts

- How bodies work: movement, support and transportation
- Growth and the basic needs of animals including humans
- Reproduction
- The circulatory system

Movement, support and transportation

The basic unit of life is the cell. All living things contain cells. Cells are the building blocks of life. Cells of plants and animals have different structures and not all cells within one living thing are identical. The amoeba is a very simple unicellular animal that consists of just one cell. Amoebas live in ponds and other still water habitats. All the functions of the animal, i.e. to feed, reproduce, etc., happen within the one cell. Other simple animals such as spirogyra are multicellular and have a more complex structure than the amoeba. In more complex living things, different cells perform different functions within different parts of the plant or animal.

Different groups of animals have evolved different structures for the support of their bodies. The outer cells of different invertebrates have evolved differently to enable them to adapt to their particular environment. Vertebrates, i.e. the group of animals with backbones which includes mammals, birds, fish, amphibians and reptiles, on the other hand, all have internal skeletons that give them structure. The vertebrate group of animals called mammals, which includes humans, have specialised cells that perform highly complex functions within the animal, such as bone cells, white blood cells, red blood cells, nerve cells, egg cells and sperm cells. While having basic similarities, each of these different cells would look different if viewed under a microscope. They are different because they have different jobs to do within the animal.

Tissues and organs

A group of similar cells working together is called a tissue. Every cell in a particular tissue looks identical and performs the same function, for example muscle tissue is made up of identical muscle cells. Organs consist of groups of tissues working together, for example the heart is made up of muscle tissue that pumps blood around the body. Other organs in the human body include:

- the brain: controls the other organs;

- the lungs: bring oxygen into the body and remove carbon dioxide from the body;

- the diaphragm: helps air to move in and out of the body;

- the stomach: breaks down food into smaller chemical units;

- the intestines: takes water from food into the blood stream;

- the kidneys: regulate the amount of water lost from the body and get rid of waste products especially urea;

- the bladder: stores urine, a waste fluid;

- the uterus: is involved in the development of a foetus.

Groups of organs working together make a system, for example the heart and blood vessels make up the blood or cardiovascular system. Blood is carried around the body by the blood system. Other systems include:

- the nervous system: consisting of the brain, spinal cord and nerves;

- the digestive system: consisting of the gullet, stomach and intestines;

- the excretory system: consisting of the kidneys, ureters and bladder.

Growth

Case study: Growth

Morgan, a PGCE student, was working with his Key Stage 1 class. He wanted them to understand that animals, including humans, have offspring which grow into adults. In previous years he knew that they had learned about and could recognise the young of baby mammals such as dogs, cats, sheep, pigs, horses and cows, and knew the names of the young of these mammals. They knew that, for example, lambs grow up to be sheep.

Morgan asked all the children in the class to bring in some photographs of themselves, including some of when they were just born and others as they became older. He invited the mother of one of the children in the class who had recently had a new baby to come into school to talk about the baby and its needs. The mother not only talked about and actually fed the baby but also bathed the baby in front of the class. Morgan encouraged his class to ask the mother questions about the baby, for example what the baby ate and how long

→

it slept. They were all very interested to hear the answers to their own questions. Although he knew that some children would have experienced a new baby in their home, quite a number had not. For these children, the experience was particularly interesting and important. This also linked nicely for role-play during child-initiated time which also should be part of the Year 1 experience, not just restricted to Reception.

Morgan linked this experience with discussion about the needs of animals including humans for survival, i.e. the need for water, food and air. He also asked them to think about how the diet of the baby differed from their own and he helped them to understand that many baby mammals, including pets such as cats and dogs, have great similarities: they all start off life feeding on milk and then, as they get older, they increasingly eat food more like that of their parents. While discussing food with his class he reminded them of the need for them to eat the right amounts of different types of food and that cleanliness is a very important factor in staying healthy. They also thought about the need for exercise. He included some important questions for them to discuss during circle time, therefore linking the topic with PSHE, for example what might happen if they ate all the wrong sorts of foods all the time and what might happen if they did not get enough exercise.

Morgan also asked each child to bring into school some photographs of the people they lived with so they could look at the similarities and differences of people at different stages of their lives.

The human life cycle

There are six stages of the human life cycle: foetus, baby, childhood, adolescence, adulthood and old age. Each stage has particular characteristics and the changes that happen over time are so gradual that they are almost unnoticeable.

Curriculum links

Upper Key Stage 2 children need to understand these stages of growth as well as the changes experienced in puberty. Younger pupils are not expected to understand how reproduction occurs (DfE, 2013, p.11); this area of science can link well with PSHE and issues can be dealt with sensitively rather than merely teaching the physical aspects of growth.

Healthy growth from one stage to another in humans depends on gaining enough energy from food that is eaten. Food provides the body with energy and is the fuel that keeps the body working and healthy. Unlike plants, animals cannot make their own food. The energy released from eating food helps to keep muscles and other organs working. New cells are made and old or damaged cells are replaced as the animal grows. New cells are made from the chemicals in food. Chemical reactions take place in the cells in an animal's body.

Curriculum links

Lower Key Stage 2 children need to understand that animals, including humans, need the right types and amount of nutrition and also that they cannot make their own food; they get nutrition from what they eat.

The importance of nutrition is an area of science that needs to be visited and revisited regularly and cross-curricular links are important here, especially because of the worrying levels of obesity among children of school age (Howells, 2012).

Reproduction

Simple animals like amoeba reproduce asexually. Single cells divide into two and both are genetically the same. Hydra, simple freshwater animals made up of many cells, also reproduce asexually by growing buds on the parent's body. When they separate each bud becomes a new animal. Other animals reproduce sexually where two parents are involved. Each parent has sex organs which contain sex cells. Sperm are the sex cells of male animals and are made in the sex organs called testes. Eggs are female sex cells and are made in the ovaries. During sexual reproduction, a sperm and an egg join together. This is called fertilisation. A fertilised egg is called a zygote. The fertilised egg divides many times to form an embryo. The embryo develops into a separate individual with genes (hereditary units) from both parents. Sexual reproduction provides greater variation in a species than asexual reproduction.

In animals such as mammals, birds and reptiles fertilisation takes place inside the body. This is called internal fertilisation. In most amphibians and fish fertilisation takes place outside the body. This is called external fertilisation.

Movement and support

Animals move about and need support for their bodies. Their supporting framework is called a skeleton. The skeleton supports the body and gives it shape. Skeletons protect the softer parts of the body and, working with muscles, they move the body about.

Some animals such as jellyfish and worms have liquid skeletons and appear not to have a skeleton. Other animals like arthropods such as crabs, spiders and insects have hard exoskeletons. This means that they have their skeleton on the outside. Exoskeletons provide good support and protection for the softer parts inside. Exoskeletons do not grow as the animal grows so, from time to time during the life of such animals, they shed their exoskeleton and a new one grows. This is called moulting.

Skeletons inside the body of vertebrates, i.e. birds, fish, mammals, amphibians and reptiles, are called endoskeletons. Endoskeletons are made from hard bone and cartilage. Bone and cartilage are living tissues and therefore the skeleton grows as the other parts of the animal grows. Amazingly, living cells are able to repair broken bones. All vertebrate skeletons have the same basic parts:

- a skull;

- a jointed backbone;

- a rib cage that protects the thorax;

- limbs (arms and legs) and limb girdles (shoulders and hips).

The human skeleton

The adult human skeleton is made up of 205 bones and has four main functions:

- support – holding the body upright and providing a framework for tissues and organs;

- protection – the heart and lungs are protected by the rib cage and the skull protects the brain;

- movement – bones and muscles work together;

- production of blood cells – red and white blood cells, essential for life, are made inside the bone marrow.

Upper Key Stage 2 pupils need to revisit the importance of nutrition and should be introduced to the main parts of the body associated with the skeleton and muscles, finding out how different parts of the body have special functions (DFE, 2013).

Activity: Other mammals, their skeletons and how they move

- Find out if other mammals also have the same basic skeletal structure as humans.

- Collect pictures and x-ray pictures of other animals.

How might you use these in your teaching?

Activity: X-rays of vertebrates

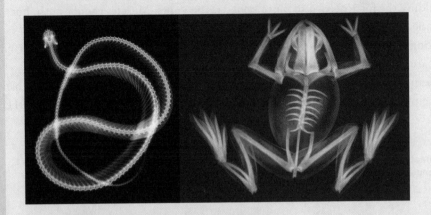

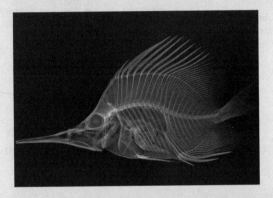

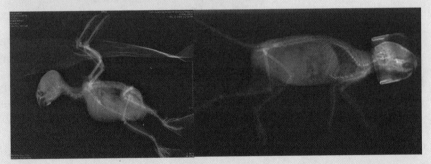

Figure 4.1 X-rays of vertebrates

- What similarities and differences do you notice between these animals?

- Can you identify to which group of vertebrates these five x-ray photographs belong?

- Do you have any further observations about these pictures?

Muscles

Humans have over 350 muscles in the body. Muscles make the body move by providing the force needed to move bones at the joints. Muscles cannot push, but provide forces to pull or squeeze things. They work together by contracting and relaxing in turn. When muscles are relaxed they are long and thin. When they contract they are short and fat. This is easy for children to understand as they can feel it happening in their own arms. Making models out of stiff cardboard and elastic bands can reinforce this idea. Can you work out how the muscles in the leg work together?

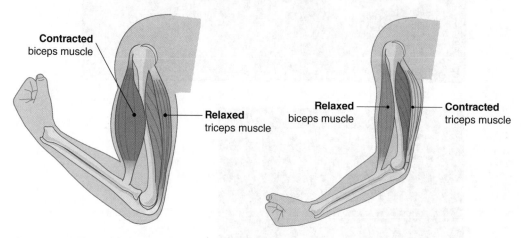

Figure 4.2 Muscles in the arm showing biceps muscles contracting when the triceps muscles relax and vice versa

There are three main types of muscle.

- Voluntary muscles – attached to bones by tendons. They move joints. Animals can control voluntary muscles themselves. Voluntary muscles are strong, but soon tire.

- Involuntary muscles – contract and relax automatically and continuously to make parts of the body work, for example they move food through the digestive system and blood along blood vessels.

- Cardiac muscles – very strong muscles that are found only in the heart and work automatically and continuously. They contract more quickly or more slowly to make the heart beat faster or slower.

Activity

The workings of the human body, how the skeleton is moved by muscles and how the internal organs work are a fascinating area for study. There is far more to know than can be included in a book like this. However, there are many resources available to help you to provide worthwhile learning experiences for your children. Rather than set out to 'teach' this topic didactically, i.e. you as the teacher providing information for your children to learn, try instead to identify resources from which your children can find the answers to the questions that they want to ask. This can be a much more enjoyable and effective way of teaching and learning.

Find out more about the human skeleton and how the body moves using muscles. Explore the skeletons of other vertebrates and look at x-rays of vertebrates and invertebrates. Children often hold the misconception that reptiles such as snakes and lizards do not have a backbone. These misconceptions can be challenged by showing children x-rays of a variety of animals. Find and collect resources that you might use in the classroom for research by your children.

Try this approach with your children and then reflect on what the children have learned and the extent to which they found this approach motivating and stimulating, so providing them with the opportunity to promote a love of learning and intellectual curiosity.

Try putting your children into ability groups based on their knowledge and understanding of this topic (Ofsted, 2013). This approach also has the advantage of enabling you to adapt teaching effectively to respond to the strengths and needs of all pupils, since the questions that they raise will be particular to them and will dispense with the need for you to provide teacher-prepared differentiated activities – the children will self-differentiate. Especially if you encourage them to raise questions to which they do not know the answer, the resultant learning will be authentic and challenging.

Case study

Raj, working with pupils in upper Key Stage 2, asked his children to raise questions about the skeleton, muscles and the heart and circulation system. He planned to split the class into groups of three. He then gave half the class the topic of skeletons and muscles and the other half the topic of the heart and circulation system. The idea was that following their research they would 'teach' their topic to other groups in the class. He started them off by giving them a KWHL grid (K – what we know or think we know, W – what we would like to find out, H – how we could find out and L (to be used at the end of the research) – what we have found out (learned)) to complete (Ward et al., 2008). He asked them to explore what they already knew about skeletons and muscles or the heart and circulation system. He knew that this was a good strategy for initially assessing their existing knowledge and identifying any misconceptions. He was fairly certain that what they would want to find out would include many things that he would want them to know by the end of the topic. Deciding to take a risk, once his children had researched their own questions, he challenged them to put together some activities to teach their peers about their topic. He encouraged them to think beyond a PowerPoint presentation.

Activity

Find out more about other animals, for example their skeletons or blood systems.

If animals are kept in your school, children could monitor the amount of food eaten and any changes in the weight of the animal over time.

Pupils could work scientifically by researching the gestation period of other animals and comparing them with humans, and by finding out and recording the length and mass of a baby as it grows.

Create a lesson plan that incorporates these ideas.

Curriculum links

Pupils might work scientifically by identifying and grouping animals with and without skeletons and observing and comparing their movement, exploring ideas about what would happen if humans did not have skeletons.

Research focus

Sharp et al. (2012, p.54) remind us that practical activities should be used when appropriate, but that there are instances like in this topic when alternative strategies should be used. They encourage the use of secondary sources of information such as pictures, videos and the use of models as well as analogy. Here there is an opportunity to embed ICT in science so that a range of secondary sources can be harnessed. While there are numerous websites that provide simulations, for example www.bbc.co.uk/schools/scienceclips/ ages/6_7/health_growth.shtml, you should be warned that not all resources are appropriate and worth investing the time that might be spent on them. However, you might want to consider selecting a range of sites with activities relevant to the topic under study and, rather than merely providing children with the opportunity to play or just visit these sites, you could challenge them to assess the value of the sites for themselves, therefore taking learning a step further and exposing children to basic scientific ideas in disguise! Such an approach takes learning to another level.

The blood and circulatory system

Blood vessels are tubes that carry blood around the body. Together the heart and blood vessels make up the blood system. The blood system is often called the circulatory system. The blood system transports important things around the body. It transports oxygen from the lungs to cells and food from the gut to cells. The blood system also removes waste materials: chemicals such as carbon dioxide from cells to the lungs and waste chemicals from the cells to the kidneys for removal from the body. The blood system also transports important chemicals like hormones, antibodies that help to fight off infection and blood proteins to all the cells of the body.

Small animals do not need a blood system because they can obtain the things they need by diffusion. They have a large surface area compared to their volume so it is easy for substances to diffuse in and out of the body from the surface of the animal. Larger animals cannot depend on diffusion for all the important things the body needs to sustain life because the bodies of large animals are too big. Instead, larger animals have a transportation system that consists of tubes and a pump to carry substances continuously around the body.

The heart, which is a pump that forces blood around the body, is at the centre of the human blood system. Tubes called blood vessels make up the rest of the blood system. There are two main types of blood vessels: arteries and veins. Arteries carry blood away from the heart. Veins carry blood back to the heart.

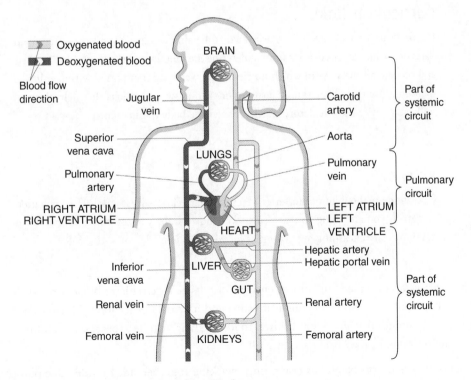

Figure 4.3 Human circulatory system (simplified)

When an artery reaches an organ it splits into smaller branches. The smaller branches are called capillaries. The capillaries then join to form veins. Chemicals like oxygen, food and carbon dioxide pass into and out of the blood in the capillaries. An analogy can be useful here: the blood could be thought of as consisting of billions of delivery vans that all carry packages of nutrients and oxygen to all the cells in the body (Roden et al., 2007, p.47). The circulation system only goes one way round.

The heart: a double circulation

The human heart is divided into two, the right and the left. Blood in the right half does not mix with the blood in the left. The right side of the heart pumps blood to the lungs and back to the heart again. Blood picks up oxygen in the lungs and deposits carbon dioxide. When blood picks up oxygen it is called oxygenated blood. The left-hand side of the heart pumps blood to the rest of the body and then back to the heart. As it travels around the body, blood gives its oxygen to the cells and becomes deoxygenated. Simultaneously, carbon dioxide, a waste product, passes into the blood to be taken back to the lungs. The blood passes through the heart twice on one circulation of the body. The heart is an amazing part of the blood and circulation system. The heart forces the blood around the body, but it could not do its job without the help of arteries, veins and capillaries that enable the flow of blood through the body, and valves that control the flow of blood.

Curriculum links

Pupils in upper Key Stage 2 are expected to be able to identify and name the main parts of the human circulatory system, describe the functions of the heart, blood vessels and blood, and the ways in which nutrients and water are transported within animals, including humans. They should also explore and answer questions that help them to understand how the circulatory system enables the body to function.

Activity

Find out more about how the arteries, veins, capillaries and valves work in the circulation system. If you are going to teach this topic, how might you use this information to develop creative learning opportunities for your children?

The heart is a pump made up almost entirely of muscle. It circulates blood around the body. The heart never stops during a life-time and normally beats about 70 times per minute. Although it is good for children to locate their own heartbeat, some children who are overweight may find this difficult.

Essentially the heart operates as two pumps working together side by side. One pumps oxygenated blood around the body and the other pumps deoxygenated blood back to the heart and to the lungs. Each side of the heart has two chambers.

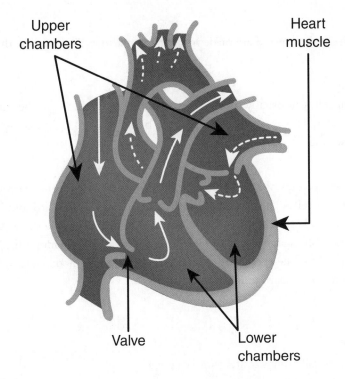

Figure 4.4 The heart

Blood

Blood, which has two very important functions, is a liquid vital for life. Blood transports important things from one part of the body to all other parts and it helps to protect from disease. The human body contains about five litres of blood. It looks like a red liquid, but it is a mixture that has a number of important ingredients. Blood consists of a yellow liquid called plasma which can be seen when whole blood is separated. Plasma has a number of chemicals dissolved in it such as food in the form of sugars, amino acids, vitamins and minerals; chemical waste like urea; blood proteins like antibodies and hormones, the chemicals that control things like growth. In addition to plasma, blood also contains three main types of blood cells, each of which has an important role in the maintainance of a healthy body:

- red cells – red cells have no nucleus; they contain a red pigment called haemoglobin;

- white cells – two main types: lymphocytes and phagocytes;

- platelets – tiny bits of cells.

Red cells

Each drop of blood contains about a million red cells. Made in the bone marrow, red cells are filled with haemoglobin and carry oxygen. Haemoglobin combines with oxygen to form oxyhaemoglobin. Red cells transport oxygen to all other cells in the body. Red cells also carry carbon dioxide, but most carbon dioxide is carried in plasma.

White cells

White cells fight disease and are made in the bone marrow. They protect the body from germs.

Blood clotting

If you cut yourself, you usually bleed. Shortly after this, the blood in the cut thickens and begins to clot. This is another way that the blood helps to fight disease by sealing off the open wound.

Platelets

Important in the process of blood clotting and also made in the bone marrow, platelets are small pieces of cells. The clot on the surface of the wound starts to solidify. This forms a scab which keeps the cut clean. Eventually the skin beneath the wound heals and the scab falls off. Some people suffer from a disease called haemophilia. This means that they do not have the chemicals in their blood that allow blood clots to form. You might be interested to learn more about this.

Activity

Look at the following websites with a colleague.

Heart and circulation system:

www.bbc.co.uk/bitesize/ks2/science/living_things/circulation/play/

www.bbc.co.uk/bitesize/ks2/science/living_things/circulation/

www.aboutkidshealth.ca/en/justforkids/body/pages/heart.aspx

Growth:

www.bbc.co.uk/schools/scienceclips/ages/6_7/health_growth_fs.shtml

Skeleton:

www.childrensuniversity.manchester.ac.uk/media/services/
thechildrensuniversityofmanchester/flash/skeleton.swf

Muscles:

www.bbc.co.uk/science/humanbody/body/factfiles/workinpairs/biceps_animation.shtml

Changes at puberty:

www.bbc.co.uk/science/humanbody/body/interactives/lifecycle/teenagers/

www.beinggirl.co.uk/my-body-wellness/puberty-body-development/

www.childline.org.uk/explore/mybody/pages/pubertygirls.aspx

www.childline.org.uk/EXPLORE/MYBODY/Pages/PubertyBoys.aspx

The heart:

www.aboutkidshealth.ca/en/howthebodyworks/introductiontotheheart/theheartbeat/pages/bloodflowthroughtheheart.aspx

Evaluate the above resources. Would you use them to inform your own subject knowledge and planning for teaching? Would you use them in your teaching of the topic under study? If not, why not? If you would use them, how would you organise their use with your class?

Which websites would you recommend to student colleagues and why?

Beware, though, that while models, simulations and analogies are useful, as Sharp et al. warn, they can have their limitations; children can take them too far. Models of the human body, for example, can be useful to see things that might otherwise be impossible to see, but when concrete models are used, teachers need to point out their limitations (Sharp et al., 2012, p.34).

Activity: Discussion

Discussion is an important strategy in learning and can be a particularly powerful tool in science.

Visit the Primary Science Teach Trust website to look at a continuing professional development (CPD) unit called Discussions in Primary Science (DiPS) at:

www.pstt.org.uk/ext/cpd/dips/why-talk-science.htm

How do your responses to the questions asked compare with those in the survey of teachers?

What is your view of the role of discussion in the teaching of science?

Case study: Developing scientific thinking through role-play or role-play in science education

Jack and Joe, two Teach First participants, were working with their mentor in the Reception classes of a large three-form entry school in North Kent. They were keen to build on their children's natural curiosity about themselves and others and other animals. They planned that over term three they would focus on developing science, particularly in relation to the role-play area which they changed frequently. Role-play is a very important aspect of Early Years education as, if it is planned carefully, it can provide a link between more teacher-directed aspects of the curriculum and the opportunities for child-initiated activity. They decided that they would change the theme of the role-play area each week, but that each different theme would link to an aspect of science, for example ourselves (humans) and other animals, and the needs of people and animals to survive. They knew, through carrying out their observations during child-initiated time, that their children loved dressing up and involving themselves in role-play as an extension of their formal learning. They decided that they would include the following as role-play areas:

- a hospital – a number of baby and other dolls and teddies were provided which could be patients; they also had simple dressing-up outfits, so that both boys and girls could pretend to be doctors and nurses, as well as pretend stethoscopes and thermometers, etc.;
- a vet's surgery or animal hospital – a variety of soft animal toys such as teddies, cats, dogs, rabbits, squirrels, etc. were provided to be patients along with stethoscopes, etc.;
- a kitchen for the preparation of food – pans, bowls, plates, plastic food items, etc. were provided.

Case study: Cross-curricular science in upper Key Stage 2

Malcolm, a School Direct student, wanted to reinforce some key ideas with his Year 6 class. He planned to do this in two ways. Firstly, after his class had learned about the heart and circulation system, he organised his class into groups to role-play the cardiovascular system.

Secondly, linked to health and physical education (PE), he wanted his class to undertake an investigation to find the effect of rest and exercise on the heart rate. He made use of the box of resources provided to all primary schools, 'In the Zone' by the Wellcome Trust.

Research focus: Science as a human endeavour – William Harvey

William Harvey, sometimes called the father of the heart and circulatory system, was born in Folkestone in Kent in 1578. He was educated at what is now known as King's School in Canterbury between 1588 and 1592. He gained a BA degree from Cambridge University before studying medicine at the University of Padua in Italy where he received a doctorate in 1602 during the reign of Queen Elizabeth I. The development of understanding in science usually starts with the current understanding and what is already known and understood. Harvey built on the then

→

understanding of his tutor Hieronymus Fabricius, who was fascinated by anatomy. Fabricius recognised that the veins in the human body had one-way valves, but did not understand their function. Harvey developed the understanding of the part played by valves in the circulation of blood through the body. He described how blood is pumped around the body by the heart. When he returned to England in 1602 he became a physician. He married Elizabeth Browne, a daughter of Elizabeth I's physician, in 1604. In 1607, he became a fellow of the Royal College of Physicians and later was appointed physician to St Bartholomew's Hospital. In 1618, he became physician to James I and later to James' son, Charles I. The development of scientific understanding at that time was helped by the interest that both kings took in Harvey's work about the heart and circulatory system.

Harvey's work was ground breaking at the time but, not unusually for developments in understanding, initially his ideas were not popular. A popular idea at the time was that the lungs were responsible for moving the blood around throughout the body. Harvey challenged these ideas and pursued his own theories. He died in 1657.

Visit www.sciencemuseum.org.uk/broughttolife/people/williamharvey.aspx for more information about the life of William Harvey.

Activity

Find out more about:

- the life and work of William Harvey;

- medical practice during the sixteenth and early seventeenth centuries at the time when Harvey was involved in medical research into the workings of the human body.

Consider the opportunities for cross-curricular work with this focus as a starting point. Here is a fantastic opportunity to make cross-curricular links, as life in the Elizabethan era has been a popular topic for study in primary history. Medical science at the time was in its infancy; some procedures used then would now be considered highly unethical. There is an opportunity here for upper Key Stage 2 children to find out about this aspect of medical history and to debate the issues.

Self-assessment questions

1. What teaching and learning strategies will you employ in the teaching of this topic to avoid the filling in of worksheets or didactic teaching?
2. How would you organise your class into groups for work of this kind to maximise the opportunities for learning of all children in your class?

(Continued)

(Continued)

3. What differences are there in the support systems of a) simple animals like the amoeba b) invertebrates and c) vertebrates?
4. Explain how the bones and muscles work together to move a vertebrate around.
5. What are the main functions of the heart and circulation system?

Further reading

Gregory, A. (2001) *Harvey's heart: The discovery of blood circulation.* Cambridge: Icon Books.

Harlen, W. (ed) (2010) *Principles and big ideas of science education.* Hatfield: ASE. Available at: www.ase.org.uk/bookshop/books-for-subject-leaders/ (accessed 11/6/14).

Loxley, P., Dawes, L., Nicholls, L. and Dore, B. (2014) *Teaching primary science: Promoting enjoyment and developing understanding*, 2nd edition. Chapter 15, pages 246–248 and 252–254. Abingdon: Routledge.

References

Department for Education (2013) *Science programmes of study: Key Stages 1 and 2.* London: DfE.

Howells, K. (2012) An introduction to physical education, in Driscoll, P., Lambirth, A. and Roden, J. (eds) *The primary curriculum: A creative approach.* London: SAGE.

Ofsted (2013) *Maintaining curiosity: A survey into science education in schools.* Manchester: Ofsted.

Roden, J., Ward, H. and Ritchie, H. (2007) *Extending knowledge in practice: Primary science.* Exeter: Learning Matters.

Sharp, J., Peacock, G., Smith, R., Johnsey, R., Simon, S., Cross, A. and Harris, D. (2012) *Primary science: Teaching theory and practice*, 6th edition. Exeter: Learning Matters.

5 Variety of life: the characteristics of living things, variation and classification

Learning outcomes

By reading this chapter you will develop:

- your understanding of key scientific concepts that underpin the teaching of variation and the classification of living things;
- effective pedagogic strategies for teaching about variety of life and classification.

Teachers' Standards

2. **Promote good progress and outcomes by pupils**

- be aware of pupils' capabilities and their prior knowledge, and plan to build on these

3. **Demonstrate good science subject and curriculum knowledge**

- have a secure knowledge of science, foster and maintain pupils' interest in science, and address misunderstandings.

4. **Plan and teach well-structured lessons**

- promote a love of learning and children's intellectual curiosity
- reflect systematically on approaches to teaching.

Introduction

There is an incredible variety of things living in and on the Earth and the huge diversity of life on Earth is difficult for many to fully appreciate. This is particularly true for those children who live in urban areas and have little opportunity to visit the natural world at first hand. For these children it is essential that provision is made for basic experience in school. There is a wealth of visual material available for the study of living things in more distant environments. This can play a huge role but can never really replace first-hand, well-planned as well as unplanned opportunistic experiences. Going outside is hugely motivating and exciting, and arouses curiosity. This can be enhanced even further by the provision of well-planned learning experiences based on the natural interest of children that starts from exploration in the natural world.

Learning in and through the environment has always been a feature of good provision in primary and Early Years education. Although many children and adults do spend some leisure time in the natural world, merely enjoying the outdoors, in itself, will not necessarily lead to learning about living things in their environment. The patterns of life in many environments are often intricate. It is not always easy to make sense of these and to fully appreciate the wide range of living things and the complexities of life that are there to be enjoyed.

Exploration of and learning about living things in the environment can be much enhanced by careful planning, but this must be informed by a very good knowledge of living things and how they are grouped scientifically. The concepts related to the variety of life and classification are not inherently difficult or confusing, but are often thought to be so. Basically what is needed is for you to take a systematic approach that reflects the scientific organisation of all life on Earth.

Curriculum links

In the Early Years, science forms part of Understanding the World. This aims to help children get to know about the place where they live and about all aspects of the environment through observation of things within it. Quite rightly, the very youngest children need to start with things in their immediate environment, such as trees, which is extended as they gain experience in a variety of environments as they get older. This is the start of noticing similarities and differences in the places they visit leading ultimately to understanding different habitats. However, in order for them to notice things that are significant, and to see similarities and differences, children's work must be supported by the adults around them. For more information see:

http://earlyyearsmatters.co.uk/index.php/learning-and-development/knowledge-and-understanding-of-the-world-kuw/

www.earlyyearsmatters.co.uk/wp-content/uploads/2011/03/eyfs_know_understand_world(1).pdf

The 2014 science National Curriculum places heavy emphasis on learning about living things, including first-hand experience in the outdoor environment, throughout the primary years. The main focus in Key Stage 1 is on pupils experiencing and observing the natural world around them, and on encouraging curiosity and question raising, using elements of scientific enquiry and secondary sources to answer those questions. These themes continue through into Key Stage 2. The introduction and use of simple scientific language for pupils to communicate what they have found out, not only to their peers but to a range of audiences, is also encouraged (DfE, 2013, p.5).

Older pupils at Key Stage 2 need to continue to raise and attempt to answer questions about habitats and the interdependence of living things in a variety of ways. The important thing is that learning should be through first-hand observation starting outdoors. Asking questions is, of course, a requirement of spoken English within the National Curriculum but it also helps to meet the requirements in developing vocabulary and building knowledge, including giving well-structured descriptions and explanations and exploring ideas. Linking with English in this way improves learning in both subjects and echoes the latest recommendations from Ofsted (2013).

Key scientific concepts

- Characteristics of living things

- Variety of life

- Variation and classification

- Evolution

Characteristics of living things

Living and non-living things

Very young children, exploring the world around them, come across things that are living, things that are not living and things that have never been alive. The world must be very confusing for them as they try to make sense of these concepts. Understandably, many very young children often think that anything that moves, such as fire or cars, must be alive and that their teddy bears are alive. This confusion is easy to understand.

Research focus: Children's ideas about living things

Much of the available research into this topic is dated, but it is likely many children today will hold similar ideas to those identified in the past. Commonly held ideas include thinking that something is alive if it moves. Alternatively, if it moves by itself it is alive, but if it is moved by something else it is not alive. This might explain why some children do not consider plants or fungi to be alive. Others think that if something makes light or noise it is alive and is not alive unless it is doing something. Some children believe that cars are alive explaining that, because they need fuel and use energy to make them start and continue to move and get rid of waste materials into the atmosphere, they must be alive. Others believe that their toys are alive because they look like animals and children might talk to them so they must be alive, but they do not feed, reproduce or do any of the other seven processes of life which is the test for life. Adding to the confusion is the fact that many plants, including some trees, appear to be dead in the winter. As children get older they must receive learning experiences that systematically challenge these early ideas (Leeds National Curriculum Science Support Project, 1992).

Activity

Look at the following websites. Although the research is quite old now, such ideas still appear to be held today. It is likely that you held some of the above misconceptions when you were very young. A summary of the findings of the Leeds National Curriculum Science Support Project (1992) can be found at:

(Continued)

(Continued)

www.learner.org/courses/essential/life/support/1_Livingthings.pdf

www.learner.org/courses/essential/life/session1/ideas.html

Reflect on your own past and present understanding of living and non-living things. It is likely that you held misconceptions in the past. Think about your current understanding of things that are alive. Look at the summary of research into children's ideas. What are the implications for your planning of the ideas that your children might hold before you teach this topic?

Look at the above websites before you start to teach this topic. How many of the ideas do your children hold?

Living things have self-sustaining processes that keep them alive. When these stop the living thing dies. Non-living things are inanimate and do not have self-sustaining processes. Anything that is living is called an organism. Organisms have a number of characteristics not found in inanimate, never alive things. Living organisms include plants, animals and other groups such as micro-organisms and fungi. All living things:

- grow – as the living thing gets bigger, cells divide and new cells are formed;

- move – although sometimes they do not seem to;

- reproduce – they are able to produce more living things of the same kind as themselves; all living things reproduce either sexually or asexually;

- respond to stimuli – they are sensitive; they detect changes in their surroundings and respond to them;

- feed – take in and use food; food is a form of energy that is used for growth and maintenance of the living thing;

- respire – they get energy from food;

- excrete – get rid of waste.

Case study: Introducing Nursery children to living things in the environment

Rachel, a student on her final placement on an undergraduate Teacher Education programme, was working with a small group of Nursery age children. Although it was February and the weather was cold, wet and windy, she was determined to take her children out into the outdoor area to look for small living animals in their habitats. She wanted to open their eyes to the variety of life that lives, often unnoticed, in their familiar outdoor area.

→

Before changing them into their coats and wellies, they revisited what they had learned the day before. They looked at some model animals and tried to remember what each presented animal was. After correctly identifying a butterfly, she asked 'Are all butterflies blue?' thereby extending their thought and ideas. She then introduced a laminated sheet showing pictures of small creatures including, for example, a butterfly, a slug, a snail, a woodlouse and a spider. This provided a very good visual stimulus for the planned learning. They discussed the differences between the animals shown on the sheet and talked about the number of legs they had and the fact that they were not all insects, as she knew that many children might well hold this misconception. Outside, armed with their simple identification sheets and large magnifying glasses, she allowed freedom for the children to explore the areas looking for small creatures, all the time encouraging them to look under logs, etc. to see what they could find. Next, she gently directed them to areas where she knew that some creatures were located. Once back inside, they talked about which creatures they had seen outside.

Curriculum links

Children noticing things and adults structuring learning in this way is fundamental to the EYFS area of Understanding the World. Later, in Key Stage 1, Year 2 pupils are expected to explore and compare the differences between things that are living, things that are dead and things that have never been alive. It would be appropriate to include sorting and classifying activities, ideally of real objects or alternatively of pictures of objects. Such activities are the start of learning to classify things, which is a key skill involved in working scientifically.

Variation and classification

Life on Earth began about 3.8 billion years ago. Despite a number of theories that attempt to explain how life on Earth came about, exactly how this happened is unknown. However incredible it might seem, it is generally believed that all life evolved from simple single-cell prokaryotic cells, such as bacteria, followed by more complex multicellular organisms that evolved over a billion years later. It is only in the last 570 million years that the more familiar kinds of life began to evolve. According to this school of thought, the process started with arthropods, followed by fish 530 million years ago, and later land plants and forests. Mammals did not evolve until even later. In terms of the history of the Earth, human beings are relative newcomers with Homo sapiens evolving only 200,000 years ago. Fossil records show that before man, other animals such as dinosaurs lived on the Earth. Subsequently life on Earth evolved so that today there is a wide variety and huge diversity in living things. Evidence of life and the evolution of living things can be found in fossil records.

Classification

Today there are a huge variety of living things in the world. Plants and animals as living things may look very different, but all have some things in common: they all exhibit the seven characteristics of living things. Living things differ in the way they look, where they live and how they behave. All living things can be divided up into groups. Individual members of each group have similar characteristics to other members of the same group. At a macro level, all plants share similar characteristics, but individual plants within the larger group have differences. Similarly, all animals have basic similarities, but different animals have differences. There are obvious differences between plants and animals. If a small number of animals are compared it is easy to pick out how they are the same and how they are different. These are the beginnings of classification.

Think about some animals that live in and around water, for example a swan, otter, water vole and duck. Swans and ducks have feathers; water voles and otters have fur. We can split these into two groups based on simple, easily observable differences. Swans and ducks are both birds; they have feathers, but there are many observable differences between swans and ducks so these can be split into two groups. Similarly, haddock and salmon are both fish; they have gills and scales, but there are many differences between them: they belong to different subgroups of 'fish'. Even very young children can sort small numbers of animals into groups based on observable features and can be asked to explain the basis for their groupings.

A group of plants or animals that share similar characteristics belong to the same species. Species are groups of animals or plants that can produce fertile offspring. Variation between living things can be of two types:

- variation between different species;

- variation between members of the same species.

The characteristics of individual animals or plants can be used to identify them. Even very young children can, and should be encouraged to, look regularly for similarities between animals or plants, or parts of plants.

Curriculum links

Fundamental to the programme of study at Key Stage 1 are the life processes common to living things with which pupils should become familiar. Habitats will be dealt with in the next chapter, but before that, children must be introduced to living things in their environment. Teachers need to introduce and reinforce the meaning of relevant scientific vocabulary at an early age so that, in time, children will come to be familiar with and to understand the terms and it will not be difficult for them to progress further in their learning.

Keys

Individual characteristics of living things and the similarities and differences between
them help to sort animals and plants into groups. The use of keys for identification
purposes is based on these similarities and differences. It is very easy to separate a plant
from an animal based on their similarities and differences, but it can be more difficult
to separate one type of plant from another or one type of animal from another. Children
of all ages can be taught how to use keys and older children should construct simple
keys for themselves or for use by younger children. There are a number of different
types of keys used for identification purposes. Keys sometimes are based on 'yes' 'no'
questions, as in the example below. Subsequent questions lead the user to the name of
individual living things (see Figure 5.1):

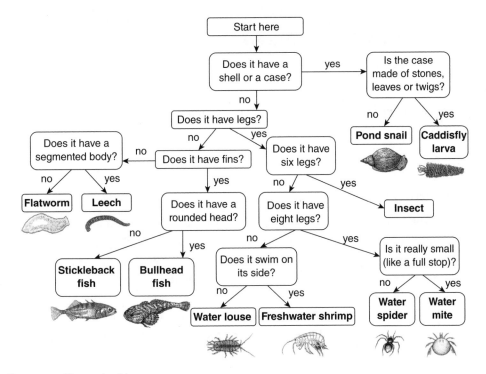

Figure 5.1 River animal key

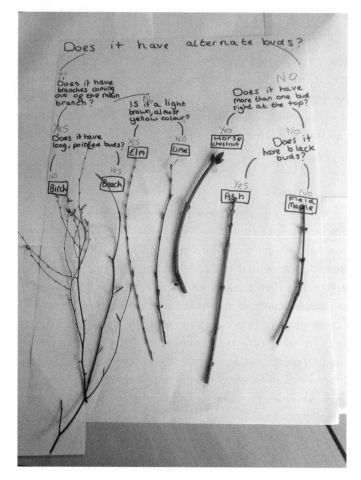

Figure 5.2 Example of a branching key made as a result of observation of winter twigs

Another type of key works in the same way but contains statements rather than questions.

Curriculum links

When working scientifically, pupils of all ages should be asked to sort and classify things regularly, perhaps recording their findings in a chart. They should be asked to justify their groupings. Lower Key Stage 2 pupils could use classification keys to help group, identify and name a variety of living things in their local and wider environment. Pupils in upper Key Stage 2 should be taught to describe how living things are classified into broad groups according to common observable characteristics and based on similarities and differences, including micro-organisms, plants and animals, and how these can be subdivided. Further, they should give reasons for classifying plants and animals based on specific characteristics and should ideally do all this work through first-hand experience. Older Key Stage 2 children should classify animals into commonly found invertebrates, such as insects, spiders, snails, worms, and vertebrates, including amphibians, reptiles, birds and mammals. They should discuss reasons why living things are placed in one group and not another.

If they did this at different times of year they would come to recognise that environments can change and that this can sometimes pose dangers to living things. Pupils of all ages can be asked to use keys to identify some animals and plants in the immediate environment. They could research unfamiliar animals and plants from a broad range of other habitats and decide where they belong in the classification system.

Research focus: Science as a human endeavour

Based on observable characteristics, all known similar living things have been put into groups. Taxonomy is the study of how living things are classified. Aristotle, a Greek philosopher (384–322 BC), was the first to classify living things systematically and produced the first classification system. He first separated living things on the basis of whether they were bloodless. Next he separated them into groups based on how they moved, on land or through water. He then split each category into subgroups. Later, Carl Linnaeus (1707–78), a native of Sweden, spent his life developing and refining a classification system for life on Earth based on the observable features of living things. His way of classifying living things is still used today. All living things can be separated into five groups based on observable features, which are called kingdoms:

- bacteria (Monera);

- protists (Protista);

- plants (Plantae);

- fungi (Fungi);

- animals (Animalia).

Each kingdom contains subgroups. Although the Linnaeus way of grouping living things is still used today, many now also recognise three 'domains' that are a higher taxon than kingdoms: archaea, bacteria and eukarya (for discussion about this see, for example, Dawson, undated – the small section entitled 'Five Kingdoms or Three Domains?' may help explain the current uncertainties!).

Curriculum links: Famous scientists

In the past, Aristotle and Linnaeus both made significant contributions to scientific thinking and the way that scientists work scientifically. Upper Key Stage 2 pupils should know something of their work.

How might you incorporate a study of these famous scientists?

Linnaeus gave each living thing two Latin names. This is called binomial nomenclature. Identification books of trees or birds or insects, etc. usually include the Latin names for the individuals that belong to the group, for example the Latin or scientific name for the English oak tree is Quercus robur, and for the lion it is Panthera leo. Quercus is the **genus** name for the English oak and always has a capital letter. The **species** name is always written in lower case. Experience suggests that children, when introduced to them, love the scientific names of plants and animals and enjoy using them. However, genus and species are only the last categories of classification of living things.

Linnaeus started with the two major kingdoms, Plant and Animal, and then subdivided them into sub-classifications for each kingdom, i.e. Kingdom, Phylum, Class, Order, Family, Genus and Species. Today further subcategories have been added, so for the well-known plant we call dandelion, we have:

Kingdom: Plantae

Division: Magnoliophyta

Class: Magnoliopsisda

Subclass: Asteridae

Order: Asterales

Family: Asteraceae

Genus: *Taraxacum*

Species: *officinale*

And for the African elephant:

Kingdom: Animalia

Phylum: Chordata

Superclass: Tetrapoda

Class: Mammalia

Subclass: Theria

Order: Proboscidea

Family: Elephantidae

Genus: *Loxodonta*

Species: *africana*

Note that the last two, i.e. the genus and species, should be italicised, the rest are not italicised and, traditionally, plants have 'Divisions' whereas animals have 'Phyla'.

The fact that animals and plants belong, simultaneously, to different groups makes classification quite confusing for those who are not aware of this.

The animal kingdom

The animal kingdom consists of two subgroups:

- invertebrates – animals without backbones;

- vertebrates – animals with backbones.

Invertebrates: animals without backbones

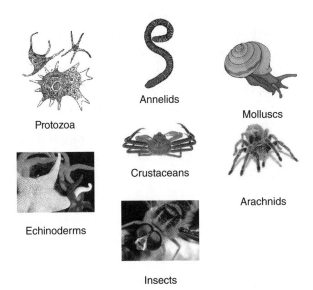

Protozoa

Annelids

Molluscs

Echinoderms

Crustaceans

Arachnids

Insects

Figure 5.3 Invertebrates – animals without backbones

Invertebrates make up 98 per cent of animal species and do not have a hard internal skeleton. Invertebrates are spilt into further groups each having distinctive characteristics in common.

- Cnidarians – most live in the sea and have a sac-like body with one opening and tentacles. They have stinging cells around their mouth. They paralyse their prey and push the prey into their mouth. Sea anemones and jellyfish belong to this group.

- Flatworms – have a flat body with the mouth at one end. Some live in water, but most are parasites of animals.

- Roundworms – have a long thread-like body and do not have segments. Some live in soil, but many are parasites of plants and animals.

- Segmented worms – have a long tube-like body divided into segments. Earthworms are found in soil, but most segmented worms live in the sea.

- Arthropods – have an exoskeleton and jointed legs. Examples of arthropods include crustaceans (for example, crabs, lobsters, shrimps and woodlice); myriapods (for example, millipedes and centipedes); insects (butterflies, moths, bees and wasps) and arachnids (spiders).

- Molluscs – have a soft body and a muscular foot. Many have one or two shells, for example, snails and cockles.

- Echinoderms – have spiny skins and a pattern of five parts, for example starfish and sea urchins.

The invertebrates deserve a special mention because there is often confusion about this group of animals, with a common lack of understanding of the subgroups within the invertebrates. The arthropods cause particular difficulty. Many people in everyday life might describe invertebrates as 'bugs' or 'mini-beasts' not realising that there are different subgroups. Some might even call all small creatures that live in and around the soil 'insects'. It is important that teachers and others who work with children understand that the arthropod group can be split further.

- Crustaceans – often have a chalky exoskeleton which protects them from predators. Nearly all crustaceans live in water. They breathe oxygen using gills. They have more than four pairs of legs but fewer than 20 pairs of legs, and have two pairs of antennae.

- Myriapods – have a segmented body and many pairs of legs. They have long bodies with many segments. Millipedes have two pairs of legs on each segment. They are herbivores and move slowly. They can often be found feeding in leaf litter. Centipedes have one pair of legs per segment. They are fast moving carnivores. They have powerful jaws and paralyse their prey before feeding.

- Insects – are the largest group belonging to the arthropods. They have three separate body parts: head, thorax and abdomen. They have three pairs of legs and two pairs of wings. They breathe through holes in the sides of the body called spiracles. Insects often pass through different stages in their lives, for example butterflies hatch from eggs as caterpillars that metamorphose into a chrysalis before changing into the adult butterfly.

- Arachnids – have a body in two parts and have four pairs of legs and no wings for example spiders and scorpions. They have no antennae. They paralyse their prey with poison.

It is important that you remember these animal groups when teaching this topic formally and informally as it is very easy to reinforce common misconceptions.

Vertebrates: animals with backbones

All vertebrates have an internal skeleton that is made of bone or cartilage. There are five main groups.

- **Fish** – live in water and are cold blooded. They are covered in scales. Fish breathe oxygen dissolved in water through gills. Fish are streamlined and use fins for moving through the water.

- **Amphibians** – have smooth, moist skin and are cold blooded. Females release eggs and males release sperm into water so fertilisation is external. Fertilised eggs hatch into the larval form (tadpoles) that live in water. Tadpoles breathe through gills. On land, adult amphibians breathe using their lungs, but in water they can breathe through their skin. Frogs, toads, newts and salamanders are amphibians.

- **Reptiles** – have dry scaly skin and are cold blooded. Reptiles can live in very arid conditions because their skins are able to retain moisture which stops them from drying out in high temperatures. They breathe air through lungs. Fertilisation takes place inside the female's body. Reptiles lay eggs with leathery shells. Crocodiles, snakes and lizards are reptiles.

- **Birds** – have feathers and wings and are warm blooded. This means that they can regulate their body temperature and keep it constant no matter what the outside temperature. Most birds are able to fly. Their beaks are adapted to different kinds of food. They do not have teeth. They lay eggs with hard shells.

- **Mammals** – have fur or hair and are warm blooded. Like birds they can regulate their body temperature. Mammals breathe through lungs. Fertilisation is internal. Female mammals suckle their young, which feed on milk produced by mammary glands.

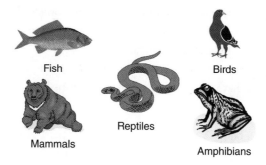

Figure 5.4 Vertebrates – animals with backbones

Each of these subgroups can be split further.

Curriculum links

In Year 1 pupils are expected to be able to name a variety of common wild and garden plants, including deciduous and evergreen trees, and identify and name a variety of common animals, including fish, amphibians, reptiles, birds and mammals (DfE, 2013). Pupils in Key Stage 2 could raise and answer questions about plants and animals in different habitats. They could observe and compare a wide selection of animals and plants and put vertebrate and invertebrate animals into their scientific groupings as above.

Pupils in upper Key Stage 2 in Year 5 should be taught to describe the life cycles of a mammal, an amphibian, an insect and a bird. This is an area of science that has frequently been taught through worksheet-based activities in the past. Similarly, they are expected to be able to describe the life process of reproduction in some plants and animals. Both these provide opportunities for pupils to undertake a series of observations over time, recording changes in the living things systematically and possibly recording their observations in drawings.

Plants

There are two kinds of plants. Some, like mosses, liverworts and ferns, make spores that grow into new plants. Others, like flowering plants and conifers, make seeds that grow into new plants.

The plant kingdom

The plant kingdom consists of four subgroups.

- Mosses and liverworts – live in damp places. They have very thin leaves that lose water easily in dry weather. They do not have stems, roots or seeds. Instead of seeds they make spores that are dispersed by the wind to make new plants.

- Ferns – have strong stems, roots and leaves. Fern leaves have a waxy surface that stops them from dehydrating. Spores are made on the underside of the leaves.

- Conifers – do not have flowers, but make seeds inside their cones. Most conifers are evergreen and keep their leaves all year round. Leaves are like needles that stop dehydration.

- Flowering plants – have flowers that contain reproductive organs. Pollen is carried by the wind or insects from one plant to another. Seeds form after fertilisation and grow into new plants.

Each of these subgroups can be split further.

Bacteria

Bacteria are simple cells with no organised nucleus. They are very small, are found everywhere, for example in water, in soil, in air and in and on animals, and have different shapes. They can be seen through a microscope.

Curriculum links

Lower Key Stage 2 pupils are expected to be able to recognise that living things can be grouped in a variety of ways and should explore and use classification keys to help group, identify and name a variety of living things in their local and wider environment. However, as we have already seen, these skills can be and should be introduced much earlier. Building on this in upper Key Stage 2, pupils in Year 6 need to know that living things are classified into broad groups according to common observable characteristics and based on similarities and differences, including micro-organisms, plants and animals. They should give reasons for classifying plants and animals based on specific characteristics. Non-statutory guidance suggests that the major groups of animals and plants can be subdivided.

However, as stated before, although the classification system of living things is based on similarities and differences, when exploring their environment children are bound to encounter and ask questions about other living things outside the stated statutory groups. It is very important that you are clear in your own mind about the overall classification of living things so that you do not add to the confusion that clearly exists.

Protists

Protists have a nucleus in their cells and live in water or in other organisms. Some protists are made up of a single cell. Algae, many celled organisms, belong to this group. Algae are often found in the sea or ponds. Algae, like plants, make their own food using chlorophyll. Spirogyra and seaweeds are protists.

Fungi

Fungi do not contain chlorophyll and cannot make their own food. Many fungi feed on dead and decaying matter. They produce spores that grow into new fungi. Some fungi are parasites and live inside other organisms. Mushrooms, toadstools, bread mould and yeast are fungi. Some fungi are poisonous.

Case study: Micro-organisms in upper Key Stage 2

Selina, a second year undergraduate student, knew that children really enjoy learning about micro-organisms and was planning a scheme of work for her class in Key Stage 2. Children are often surprised to find that, for example, some microbes can be harmful while others are friendly.

She reviewed the following websites which provide a wealth of information and potential activities for inclusion in plans for teaching this topic.

The British Society for Antimicrobial Chemotherapy: http://bsac.org.uk/science-fair/

DCFS e.bug (linked to the old curriculum): www.e-bug.eu/lang_eng/primary_pack/downloads/UK%20Junior%20Pack%20Complete.pdf

The Children's University of Manchester:
www.childrensuniversity.manchester.ac.uk/interactives/science/microorganisms

As a result of her research she set up a circus of activities that included exploring the passing of germs using hand-gel and glitter, friendly and unfriendly bacteria and microbes in our local environment, using bakers' yeast and making yoghurt. Children were asked to make observations and raise questions that led to further investigations including how much of a bacterium culture is needed to make a perfect yoghurt. Really strong links were made to healthy eating, the need for a balanced diet and links to the design and technology curriculum.

Inheritance

Living things reproduce in two ways: sexually and asexually. Offspring often look very like their parents because they inherit genes from their parents. Sexual reproduction allows genes from different individuals to mix with those of others. Genes are located in the nucleus of egg cells in the female and in the nucleus of sperm cells in males.

When eggs are fertilised, the nucleus of the egg joins with the nucleus of the sperm and new individuals are produced. Each individual will have half the genes of each parent. This gives the new individual a different mix of genes and these determine the particular characteristics of the individual.

Curriculum links

Although the study of genetics is fascinating, this is not a statutory requirement for teaching at Key Stages 1 or 2. However, the idea of characteristics of individual species is important and children need to look for similarities and differences between different kinds of organisms and within the same kind of organism. 'Ourselves' is a popular topic for study in the EYFS and Key Stage 1. Although teachers need to approach this topic with sensitivity, looking at similarities between ourselves as humans can be very productive in helping children to notice small differences, and developing their observation skills is an important aspect of working scientifically. Upper Key Stage 2 pupils are expected to know about different types of reproduction.

Case study: Variation in 'ourselves' as living things in the EYFS and Key Stage 1

Georgie and Sarah were working together to ensure continuity and progression in their children's learning from Reception to Year 1. They were keen for their children to look for similarities between themselves as living things and for them to notice changes as they grow. They asked their children to make simple observations and comparisons focusing on hair colour and eye colour. They did this first of all in their own classes, then they put groups of children from each class together to see if they could notice physical changes between children from different aged classes. The children in Reception merely counted how many children had, for example, blue eyes or brown eyes and they talked about how many different colours of eyes were found in their class. Next they looked at the size of feet by putting their feet into paint and making a footprint on a piece of sugar paper. They did the same with their hands. Instead of merely making an attractive display of random hand and feet prints which is common practice, Sarah, wanting to make the activity more scientific, arranged for the children to put the size of feet in order before they were stuck on the wall. The older children were able to measure their hands and feet using non-standard measures and made simple Carroll diagrams of eye colour and hair colour. In this way they were able to link aspects of mathematics to science effectively while carrying out simple surveys through observation.

Curriculum links: Working scientifically – 'Ourselves' as a topic with Key Stage 2 children

The topic of Ourselves offers numerous opportunities for children to undertake simple comparative surveys, for example where the learning intention is linked to making comparative statements, with questions such as:

- Does the person with the widest hand span have the biggest grab?

- Is there a relationship between chest size and lung capacity?

- Can the person with the longest legs jump the furthest?

- Does the tallest person have the longest arms (or legs)?

Activity

Choose one of the above and think through how you would plan for your children to carry out a simple survey, allowing them to have choices such as what question to ask, what resources they would need, what data they would collect and how they might record the data collected. For example:

- What equipment might you need to have available?

- What questions would you ask of your children to prompt them to plan and carry out a worthwhile comparison?

- What data could your children collect and how might they record this?

- How could your children be organised to communicate their findings to others at the end of their comparative investigations?

- Might there be the opportunity to communicate their findings to audiences outside their class? If so, to whom, when and how?

Thinking about your class, how many other possible comparative surveys can you add to this list?

How does this approach contribute to the learning of your children?

Evolution

Evolution encompasses the change of living things over time. Many organisms have changed over time to suit their environment. This is called adaptation: living things adapt to suit conditions they live in. As living things adapt to their environment the adaptations help them to survive better than individuals without those adaptations. Small changes happen slowly over time as successful adaptations are passed to offspring through genes. Successful adaptations make the animals or plants more likely to survive into future generations. Some animals and plants were once common on the Earth and are now extinct. This is possibly because changes happened relatively quickly in their environment and there was not enough time for successful adaptations to be made to those living things.

All living things compete with others to survive. This includes competition with other individuals within the same species so that not all individuals will survive. This is called survival of the fittest, which is a difficult concept for children to understand. Survival of the fittest relates to individuals that are best suited to the environment in which they live. Adaptations that help a living thing to survive a particular environment are passed on to successive generations through genes passed on through sexual reproduction. Individuals without those adaptations are less likely to survive. Life can be harsh. There are many factors, such as competition for food, competition for space, predators, local conditions such as drought or flood and climatic change, that stop offspring surviving to future generations. Some animals and plants produce large numbers of offspring so that there is a better chance of some surviving through to the next and subsequent generations. However, relatively few individuals survive into adulthood, but those that do are the ones that are best adapted to the environment.

Activity

Charles Darwin's work is well known. See the BBC website:

www.bbc.co.uk/history/historic_figures/darwin_charles.shtml

Find out about Darwin's work.

Think about how his observations of birds, or reptiles that he encountered on his travels, informed scientific thinking at the time.

How could you use this information in your teaching?

Examples for teaching about animal adaptation frequently draw on Darwin's observations of animal differences on his travels around the world. In particular the way that finches had different characteristics on different islands, for example the shape of their beaks that adapted to the particular diet available on different islands in the group.

Reflection

Computers, tablets and mobile phones are increasingly being used as research tools by children in primary schools. How might you use available downloadable and other resources, for example from the BBC's Natural History Unit, the Royal Society for the Protection of Birds (RSPB) or the Woodland Trust, to provide your children with the opportunity to learn about the adaptations of animals and plants nearer to home?

Activity

Following learning about adaptation and how Darwin's finches, or birds in their local environment, are specially adapted to live in their particular habitat, children could explore making models of alien birds.

The fossil record

Fossils provide insight into the history of life on Earth, giving information about how creatures evolved through geological time. Fossils are the preserved remains of plants and animals whose bodies were buried in sediment under ancient seas, lakes and rivers. Over time the sediment became sedimentary rock such as limestone and sandstone. The fossil record is important because it provides evidence of transition over time from one species to another. According to the Encyclopaedia Britannica (www.britannica.com/EBchecked/topic/214564/fossil-record) the fossil record provides a history of life though fossils which are the remains or imprints of organisms from earlier geological periods that have been preserved in sedimentary rocks. In a few cases the original substance of the hard parts of the organism is preserved, but more often the original components have been replaced by minerals deposited from water seeping through the rock. Occasionally the original material is simply removed, while nothing is deposited in its place; in this case, all that remains is a mould of the shape of the plant or animal.

Figure 5.5 Examples of fossils in rock

The soft parts of the body of animals usually decayed after death leaving the hard parts, such as teeth, shells and bones, preserved as the sediment hardened to rock. Fossils provide evidence of plant and other life as well as animals.

Recent finds include one of footprints that are 800,000 years old on the Norfolk coast which has led to speculation by scientists that these are footprints of the earliest known humans in Northern Europe. See www.bbc.co.uk/news/science-environment-26025763

Curriculum links: Dinosaurs and fossils

Children are fascinated by dinosaurs and fossils. Dinosaurs are often included as a topic in Key Stage 1 but this is often treated superficially and is very limited. Very young children have little or no sense of time. It is very difficult for children to appreciate the time scale involved in a topic of this kind to the extent that children often question whether their teachers were alive when the dinosaurs were on the Earth! Popular media confuse the situation even more.

The information in the 2014 statutory science programmes of study is also confusing since it seems to suggest that fossils are formed when things that have lived are trapped within rocks, which, without care, might promote misconceptions.

Case study: Building on previous learning in Year 6

Danny was aware of the fact that his Year 6 children had studied dinosaurs when they were in Year 2 and also that the science National Curriculum 2014 makes no mention of them. He knew that they had looked at the different kinds of dinosaurs, their shapes and what they ate. They had been introduced to the idea that some dinosaurs were herbivores and others were carnivores, but they had no real understanding of the relative sizes of the various dinosaurs and very little understanding of fossils and how they were formed. He decided that he needed to find out just what their understanding was before planning the next stages in their learning.

Danny was aware of the potentially confusing wording in the National Curriculum programme of study. He decided that his Year 6 class would find out and share information about fossils and how they provide information about living things that inhabited the Earth millions of years ago. Also, because his Year 6 children needed to become cautious about evidence, he would challenge them to be cautious about the claims of the information they found on this topic. He decided to link this study with the ideas of the evolution of living things over time and the different ways that animals and plants are adapted to their environment and how this might lead to evolution.

Danny split his class into a number of groups. He asked one group to find out about the work of Mary Anning, who was a palaeontologist who collected and studied fossils, starting with the website www.nhm.ac.uk/nature-online/science-of-natural-history/biographies/mary-anning/

He asked another group to look at the work of Charles Darwin, paying particular attention to his observations on the slight differences in the same kinds of animals on the Galapagos Islands. A further group were asked to

→

research the life and work of the naturalist Alfred Wallace, starting with the Natural History Museum website www.nhm.ac.uk/nature-online/science-of-natural-history/biographies/wallace/

Later in the term he planned for his class to explore how particular animals and plants are adapted so that they could understand the idea of adaptation better.

Another group were asked to explore fossils starting with the American website www.agiweb.org/news/evolution/examplesofevolution.html and www.bgs.ac.uk/discoveringGeology/time/Fossilfocus/home.html

Later he planned for each group to report back to the others on their findings.

Self-assessment questions

1. What are the seven processes of living things?
2. What misconceptions might you encounter when teaching this topic? How might you challenge these?
3. What kind of keys can help children in their classification of living things?
4. How would you use the outdoors to further your children's understanding of the characteristics of living things?

Further reading

Brumby, M. (1982) Students' conceptions of the life concept. *Science Education*, 66: 613–22.

Department for Education (2012) *Statutory framework for the Early Years Foundation Stage 2012*. Runcorn: DfE. Available at: www.education.gov.uk/publications/standard/AllPublications/Page1/DFE-00023–2012 (accessed 11/6/14).

Driver, R. et al. (1992) Life and living processes. *Leeds National Curriculum support project, Part 2*. Leeds: Leeds City Council and the University of Leeds.

Howe, A., Davies, D., McMahon, K., Towler, L., Collier, C. and Scott, T. (2009) *Science 5–11 A guide for teachers*, 2nd edition. Chapter 11. Abingdon: Routledge.

Loxley, P., Dawes, L., Nicholls, L. and Dore, B. (2014 *Teaching primary science: Promoting enjoyment and developing understanding*, 2nd edition. Chapter 12. Abingdon: Routledge.

Osborne, J., Wadsworth, P. and Black, P. (1992) *Primary SPACE project: Life processes*. Liverpool: Liverpool University Press.

For information on Carl Linnaeus: www.nhm.ac.uk/nature-online/science-of-natural-history/biographies/linnaeus/

For information about the fossil record: www.nhm.ac.uk/nature-online/life/dinosaurs-other-extinct-creatures/darwinius-masillae/angela-milner-on-ida/

References

Dawson, S. (undated) *Creatures from the black lagoon: Lessons in the diversity and evolution of Eukaryotes.* Available at: www.ucmp.berkeley.edu/education/events/eukevol.html (accessed11/6/14).

Department for Education (2013) *Science programmes of study: Key stages 1 and 2.* London: DfE.

Driver, R. et al. (1992) Life and living processes. *Leeds National Curriculum support project, Part 2.* Leeds: Leeds City Council and the University of Leeds.

Leeds National Curriculum science support project (1992) *Children's ideas about living things research summary.* Available at: www.learner.org/courses/essential/life/support/1_Livingthings.pdf (accessed 11/6/14).

Ofsted, (2013) *Maintaining curiosity: a survey into science education in schools.* Manchester: Ofsted.

Ward, H., Roden, J., Hewlett, C. and Foreman, J. (2008) *Teaching science in the primary classroom: A practical guide.* London: SAGE.

6 Habitats

Learning outcomes

By reading this chapter you will develop:

- your understanding of key scientific concepts that underpin the teaching of habitats, the relationships between living things, food webs and food chains;
- effective pedagogic strategies for teaching in, through and about habitats, including the feeding relationship between living things.

Teachers' Standards

1. **Set high expectations which inspire, motivate and challenge pupils**
- set goals that stretch and challenge pupils of all backgrounds, abilities and dispositions.
2. **Promote good progress and outcomes by pupils**
- be aware of pupils' capabilities and their prior knowledge, and plan teaching to build on these.
3. **Demonstrate good science subject and curriculum knowledge**
- have a secure knowledge of science and the science curriculum, foster and maintain pupils' interest in the subject, and address misunderstandings.
4. **Plan and teach well-structured lessons**
- promote a love of learning and children's intellectual curiosity.

Introduction

The previous chapter considered living things and how they are classified and organised into groups based on their similarities and differences. This chapter builds on these ideas by considering how things live together and depend on each other in the places that they live in: their habitats. It is incredible to think how life on Earth has evolved and how different forms of life have colonised every part of the world from the coldest to the hottest places on Earth and everything in between.

Young children in the EYFS and older children alike can learn best about these concepts by exploring, at first hand, life in the outdoors, but also by finding out about living things and their interdependence through the use of excellent secondary sources of which there are many.

Key scientific concepts

- Habitats

- The interdependence of living things

- Living things in their habitats

- Food webs

- Food chains

Habitats

Animals, plants and other living things are adapted to the place in which they live. Basic needs of individual living organisms are met within their habitat. Often, a wide variety of different living things live together in the same habitat. The type of habitat determines the kinds of organisms that live within it. Habitats can be small, such as the bark of a tree, a small pond, part of an animal's skin or a piece of stale bread. Habitats can also be large, for example forests, grassland, mountains, seas or oceans. Habitats are affected by the physical geography and climate including how much light, water and food are available and the ambient temperature. Some habitats remain physically stable all day and through the year, but others are affected by daily or seasonal changes like the change of temperature from day to night or winter to summer, the variation in tides on the coast and seashore or grassland that is prone to flood in wet weather.

The physical conditions of a habitat affect the kinds of animals and plants that can successfully live in the habitat, for example the daily changes in the tides on the coast determine the kinds of plants and animals that live between high and low tide, their characteristics and how they are adapted to the harsh changing conditions. Here organisms need to be adapted not only to being submerged for hours in water, but also to be able to withstand the dry conditions when the tide goes out.

Living things that are well adapted to life in their habitat often depend on each other for survival. Special evolved features might help them to survive within particular habitats, for example some trees that live in drier conditions such as conifers have needles instead of leaves with a big surface area to retain moisture. Similarly, cacti tend to be short and stumpy with spines for leaves that help them to store water. Some birds migrate from one part of the world to another to escape harsher winter conditions. Some plants that live on walls and other dry areas have developed long penetrating roots and often grow flat to the surface instead of growing outwards.

The system of relationships between living things when they coexist within a habitat is called an ecosystem. Within an ecosystem there are patterns of feeding relationships between the plants and animals. Some feeding patterns are simple; others are complex. This chapter will look at these relationships.

Children may not be familiar with the range of habitats in their local surroundings. The challenge for you is to extend the understanding of your children so the relationships that exist between plants and animals in a variety of habitats, both big and small, are better understood. This is a tall order given that children who live both in densely populated urban areas and in rural areas spend much time indoors for a variety of reasons. The role of the school in extending children's experience of the living world has never been greater.

Curriculum links

Every time children go outside they are, usually unknowingly, seeing a variety of habitats: a wall, a gravestone, a flowerbed, a wood or forest, etc. Children need to have their awareness raised of the fact that there is a range of life around them all the time, some of which are so small that they are only seen with the aid of microscopes. Many of these are beyond study by most children in the primary years, but the National Curriculum does offer the opportunity for children to understand the basic concepts involved and to learn through raising questions about their local surroundings. Teaching at Key Stage 1 includes opportunities for pupils to know that most living things live in habitats to which they are suitably adapted. They need to know how different habitats provide for the basic needs of different kinds of animals and plants and how they depend on each other. Fundamental to the programme of study at Key Stage 1 are the life processes common to living things with which they should become familiar. These were dealt with in Chapter 5. Pupils should be introduced to the terms 'habitat' and 'micro-habitat'. The National Curriculum describes a habitat as a natural environment or home of a variety of plants and animals and micro-habitats, which are very small habitats. It is suggested that pupils could look at what animals live under stones, logs or in leaf litter as a starting point for the development of their understanding of habitats. They are required to raise and answer questions about the local environment to help them 0identify and study a variety of plants and animals within their habitat, observing how living things depend on each other, for example, plants serving as a source of food and shelter for animals. They should compare animals in familiar habitats with animals found in less familiar habitats, for example on the seashore, in woodland, in the ocean, in the rainforest (DfE, 2013).

Building on this knowledge pupils in Key Stage 2 should raise and answer questions about plants and animals in different habitats, observing and comparing a wide selection of animals and plants as they work scientifically, and putting vertebrate and invertebrate animals into their scientific groupings as above.

It is important that teachers plan their children's learning throughout EYFS and Key Stages 1 and 2 so that there is progression and not mere duplication of learning that has already taken place.

Activity

There are a range of activities that can help children to focus on specific aspects of the environment. Four such examples are as follows.

1. Cut up a colour chart such as a paint shade chart and provide each child with a different shade of the same colour. Each child has to, independently, find their colour in the natural environment and match the found object carefully to the colour chart.

2. Magic spot – take children on a walk to different environments. In silence, ask them to record observations while standing on a spot using all of the senses, when safe to do so. Ask the children to compare and contrast their observations.

3. Place a strip of double-sided sticky tape onto a strip of card and remove the paper strip to leave a sticky surface. Ask children to go to different small, dry habitats to create 'snapshots' of the environment by sticking any relevant materials on the strip such as leaf litter, flowers (take care over which ones are picked), seed cases, etc. Children can repeat this in a range of locations to help them to compare the environments by looking at the collected materials.

4. String trails – habitats such as a wood or manicured or uncut grassy area can provide a focus for the study of plants and animals within that habitat. Construct trails by using lengths of brightly coloured wool that create a path for children to follow. Should there be specific areas of interest in the path, place items such as a peg to indicate where children should stop to make observations and comparisons along the trail.

The interdependence of living things

Ultimately, all animals depend on plants which depend on sunlight so that they can produce their own food by photosynthesis. Animals eat plants and when animals and plants die other living things live by feeding off the dead and decomposing material. The whole process is very complex. However, it is possible to identify and study how this all works within a habitat through study of the feeding relationships that exist there.

Living things in their environment
Survival

Individuals of the same type within a habitat compete for the things that they need to survive. Plants compete for light, water, space and nutrients. Animals also need space, food, nutrients and a habitat to live in and reproduce and so also compete for these things. Only those who compete successfully will survive. Competition between individuals restricts the size of the population of living things in any habitat. Competition within a habitat takes two forms: competition between individuals of the same species and competition between different species.

Curriculum links

There are opportunities for observing competition in the indoor or outdoor classroom. Planting seeds and growing plants has high status in the 2014 National Curriculum. Children can observe what happens when many seeds are growing in the same space.

Observation of an untended cultivated area over time will show how quickly weeds establish themselves, colonise and squeeze out other plants. A weed is merely an unwanted plant, for example in a garden or vegetable patch. Seedlings and plants, if crowded together, compete for space and light, water and nutrients. Similarly, birds and other animals living together in a small habitat compete for available food. Sometimes this leads to fights. This is competition between different species. Children can undertake a survey of birds attracted to a bird table. They soon come to understand the term 'pecking order'. They compete both with other members of their 'family', but also with other species. This is sometimes called a struggle for survival.

Predators and prey

Animals and plants not only have to compete with their own kind and other species for survival, they are also at risk of things that might eat them. Animals that eat other animals are called predators. Predators such as hyenas often work in packs sharing their kill. Prey species often crowd together in herds to protect themselves. Usually, the weakest such as the old, young or sick animals are the first of the herd to be killed, which helps keep the numbers in check so that there is a reduction in competition between members of the herd. This means that weaker ones do not survive to reproduce. Individuals that are best adapted to their habitat will live to reproduce, passing their genes onto their offspring.

Living together with a large number of others is also a good thing because although some members of the group might be killed, some will survive. Some animals have a symbiotic relationship with others. Sometimes both animals benefit from a symbiotic relationship, for example between a bird and a crocodile in the tropical regions of Africa. Effectively, the bird flies into the mouth of the crocodile so that it can feed off the decaying bits of food stuck in the teeth thereby cleaning them. Sometimes, only one of the animals gains from a relationship leaving the other unharmed. Yet other relationships exist where one creature is a parasite and the other a host such as a tapeworm in, or head lice on, the body of a human animal, or fleas on mammals such as cats and dogs and ticks on the bodies of mammals such as goats, hedgehogs and sheep. Quite often the host suffers and may become sick and die. For more information see: www.bbc.co.uk/nature/adaptations/Symbiosis

Feeding relationships

Producers

Plants and many bacteria are called producers because they are living things that can produce their own food from simple substances. Within habitats there are feeding relationships. Many living things feed on plants or decaying plants or on other living organisms. These other members of the ecosystem depend on producers for their food.

Consumers

Animals are not able to produce their own food. They have to eat food so are called consumers. There are different kinds of consumers: primary, secondary, tertiary and decomposers.

- Primary consumers eat plants or bacteria; they are herbivores.

- Secondary consumers are carnivores; they eat herbivores.

- Tertiary consumers are carnivores; they eat secondary consumers.

- Decomposers are microbes that feed on dead and rotting material.

At each level, energy is transferred. The Sun is the ultimate source of energy which provides sunlight for photosynthesis (see Chapter 2). Energy from the Sun is transferred to plants and then transferred to herbivores when the plants are eaten. When herbivores are eaten by carnivores, energy is transferred to the carnivore. Energy transfer of this kind is known as a food chain.

Curriculum links

Key Stage 1 pupils should be able to identify and name a variety of common animals that are carnivores, herbivores and omnivores and to describe and compare the structure of a variety of common animals – fish, amphibians, reptiles, birds and mammals, including pets (DfE, 2013, p.7).

Upper Key Stage 2 children in Year 5 should compare life cycles of plants and animals in their local environment with other plants and animals around the world – in the rainforest, in the oceans, in desert areas and in prehistoric times – asking pertinent questions and suggesting reasons for similarities and differences. They could also observe changes in an animal over a period of time, for example hatching and rearing chicks, comparing how different animals reproduce and grow.

Year 5 pupils should be taught to describe the life cycles of a mammal, an amphibian, an insect and a bird. This is an area of science that has frequently been taught through worksheet-based activities in the past. Similarly, pupils are expected to be able to describe the life process of reproduction in some plants and animals. Both these provide opportunities for children to undertake a series of observations over time, recording changes in the living things systematically and possibly recording their observations in drawings.

Food chains

Food chains indicate what eats what within a habitat or community, for example:

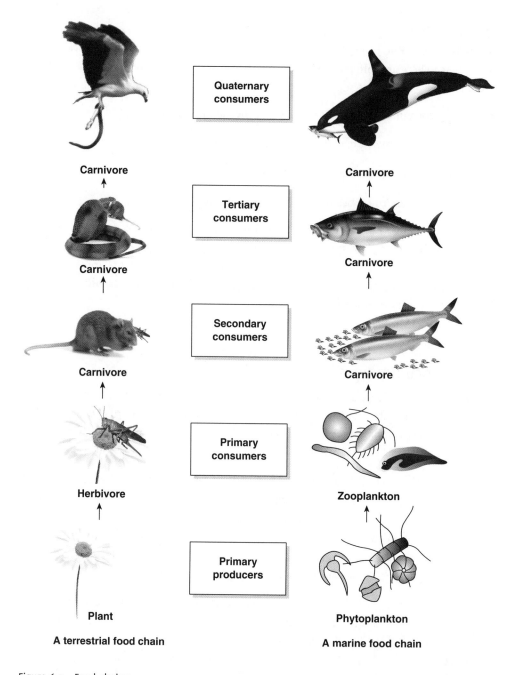

Figure 6.1   Food chains

seeds from cereal plants $\xrightarrow{\text{(eaten by)}}$ mouse $\xrightarrow{\text{(eaten by)}}$ red kite

(producer)   (primary consumer)   (carnivore)

grass   (eaten by) ⟶   hare   (eaten by) ⟶   fox

(producer)   (primary consumer – herbivore)   (secondary consumer – carnivore)

These are simple food webs. Food webs can be identified in all habitats.

Plant   (eaten by) ⟶   cricket   (eaten by) ⟶   mouse   (eaten by) ⟶   snake   (eaten by) ⟶   eagle

(producer)   (primary consumer – herbivore)   (secondary consumer – carnivore)   (tertiary consumer – carnivore)   (quaternary consumer – carnivore)

Other simple examples can be found on the Nature Detectives page of the Woodland Trust site at naturedetectives.org.uk

Food chains always start with the producer, which is usually a plant or parts of a plant such as seeds, flowers or dead leaves. In the diagrams, the arrows move from producer to subsequent consumers. When children are looking for mini-beasts in a habitat, for example in leaf litter below a tree in autumn, it is important that they look at not only what plants or parts of plants are in the habitat, but also what animals are there so that they can begin to start to identify food chains.

Curriculum links

Food chains along with food webs are important concepts for teaching at Key Stage 1 and Key Stage 2. Building on experiences where pupils have been introduced to a variety of habitats and have observed the animals and plants, older pupils could be asked to raise and carry out basic survey investigations to answer simple questions, for example about the conditions in which creatures like to live or about what they like to eat, etc. Using secondary sources they can be asked to identify the plants and animals that they find in any particular habitat and to research what eats what in order to construct simple food chains. They can then construct simple food webs to share with their peers. They could construct a simple food chain that includes humans (for example: grass → cow → human). They could describe the conditions in different habitats and micro-habitats (under a log, on a stony path, under bushes) and find out how the conditions affect the number and type(s) of plants and animals that live there (DfE, 2103). Additionally, they should be able to identify and name a variety of plants and animals in their habitats, including micro-habitats, and describe how animals obtain their food from plants and other animals, using the idea of a simple food chain. They should also be able to identify and name different sources of food.

Case study: Producers, predators, prey and food webs

Instead of teaching the ways that animals avoid predation directly, Luke, a School Direct student working with upper Key Stage 2 children, asked his class to undertake some research on animals in a distant habitat, i.e. forest, jungle and an arctic region. He then split the class up into groups and gave them a choice of animals to research from a list. He planned carefully so that children were given a choice from a list of animals he knew would fall into the above groups.

When children had researched individually, he collated some of the information based upon the above categories so that he could reinforce the idea of different strategies for survival. Then he asked them to think about and then find out how some animals are adapted in other ways to try to avoid being killed by predators. Prey try to avoid being killed by:

- moving faster;

- staying in large groups;

- having a bad taste so that predators avoid them;

- warning colours;

- camouflage;

- having markings that make them look like another scary animal.

Activity

Used with care, models can help children to understand the concept of food chains. Initially you could make a class set of badges or sticky labels with the names of different producers, consumers, predators and prey, for example dandelion, rabbit, fox, and corn, grasshopper, owl. Each child could wear one sticker or badge. Then in an open space, the children could be asked to find other components of their food chain. The children could be instructed to stand in order pointing to the next living thing in their chain and then to explain their food chain, the relationships and the movement of energy from one part of the chain to the next to another group of children forming a different food chain.

How could this idea be applied and extended to the teaching of more complex food webs? Could you plan the questions you would ask and the strategies you would use in implementing this idea?

How might the activity be used to assess your children's understanding of food chains and food webs?

Food webs

Food webs are more complex than food chains because they take account of the fact that many animals eat a varied diet. Food webs show the relationships between producers and consumers and often contain a number of food chains. Some people find food webs confusing and cannot remember in which direction the arrows in the web point. This is because it might be expected that the arrows would go from the thing eating to the thing being eaten rather than the other way round. The thing to remember is that, like the food chains, the arrows always start with the producers.

Figure 6.2 Food webs

Case study: Constructing feeding chains and webs with Year 6

Working with her Year 6 class, Abigail, a first year undergraduate student, planned to teach her children about feeding relationships and food webs. She found a fantastic interactive site for looking at ecosystems and finding out about some marine creatures and what they eat, etc. within an aquatic habitat – a coral reef. This was obviously, for most of the children, a habitat that they would not be able to explore at first hand. Therefore exploring the website could take them beyond their immediate experience.

After spending time familiarising herself with the website she asked her children to use the website, first to learn the names of the different organisms living together in the habitat and then, after identifying all the creatures, to find out what ate what within that habitat. She found that her children were highly interested, highly motivated and curious about working out the feeding relationships within the habitat and wanted to construct food chains and food webs from the information they had discovered for themselves.

When the class had finished their research and had constructed their food chains and food webs, she assessed their understanding by looking at the information provided in their diagrams, noticing in particular the direction of the arrows from one organism to another. She asked a focus group for assessment to explain, individually, the feeding relationships in their diagrams. This was also used as an opportunity to assess their use and understanding of the key vocabulary in this topic, i.e. habitat, food chain, food web, producer, consumer, predator and prey.

Research focus: Science as a human endeavour – famous scientists

In the past, Aristotle and Linnaeus made significant contributions to scientific thinking and the way that scientists work scientifically. More recent scientists such as David Attenborough and Jane Goodall have also been instrumental in contributing to and communicating with a range of audiences furthering their understanding of science and things scientific.

David Attenborough has been a well-known face on television over many years. There is a wealth of films and other material available for use in school.

Jane Goodall is a primatologist whose work in Africa has made her an expert on chimpanzees. See www.nationalgeographic.co.uk/explorers/bios/jane-goodall/

Information about both these scientists is easily available and could be used as a starting point for assessment of written work in English.

Curriculum links

Older Key Stage 2 children should know something of the work of David Attenborough and Jane Goodall. The English National Curriculum requires pupils to retrieve, record and present information from non-fiction.

Self-assessment questions

1. Explain what you understand by the term 'habitat'.
2. Give three examples of different habitats and explain the kinds of animals and plants that might be found in those habitats.
3. Using your answers to question 2 draw:

   a) a simple food chain
   b) a food web

to show the feeding relationships within the organisms in your diagrams.

Further reading

Department for Education (2012) *Statutory framework for the Early Years Foundation Stage 2012*. Runcorn: DfE. Available at: www.education.gov.uk/publications/standard/AllPublications/Page1/DFE-00023–2012 (accessed11/6/14).

Howe, A., Davies, D., McMahon, K., Towler, L., Collier, C. and Scott, T. (2009) *Science 5–11 A guide for teachers*, 2nd edition. Chapter 11. Abingdon: Routledge.

Loxley, P., Dawes, L., Nicholls, L. and Dore, B. (2014) *Teaching primary science: Promoting enjoyment and developing understanding*, 2nd edition. Chapter 12. Abingdon: Routledge.

Ofsted, (2013) *Maintaining curiosity: A survey into science education in schools*. Manchester: Ofsted.

Osborne, J., Wadsworth, P. and Black, P. (1992) *Primary SPACE project: Life processes*. Liverpool: Liverpool University Press.

Peacock, G., Sharp, J., Johnsey, R. and Wright, D. (2009) *Primary science: Knowledge and understanding*, 6th edition. Chapter 5. London: Learning Matters SAGE.

Wenham, M. and Ovens, P. (2010) *Understanding primary science*, 3rd edition. London: SAGE.

References

Department for Education (2013) *Science programmes of study: Key stages 1 and 2*. London: DfE.

7 Everyday materials: their uses, properties and changes of materials

Learning outcomes

By reading this chapter you will develop:

- your awareness of the properties of materials and how materials can be used;
- an understanding of the processes that can be used to assist the separation of materials;
- an ability to explain the differences between physical and chemical changes;
- an awareness of effective pedagogic strategies for teaching about materials.

Teachers' Standards

1. **Set high expectations which inspire, motivate and challenge pupils**

- set goals that stretch and challenge pupils of all backgrounds, abilities and dispositions.

3. **Demonstrate good science subject and curriculum knowledge**

- have a secure knowledge of science and the science curriculum, foster and maintain pupils' interest in the subject, and address misunderstandings.

4. **Plan and teach well-structured lessons**

- promote a love of learning and children's intellectual curiosity.

Introduction

Materials are genuinely amazing! Taught well this area of science enthuses, engages and excites children. But what do we mean by materials and how are they made? Let's start at the very beginning. Scientists have determined that the entire universe including the Earth is made up of a total of 92 elements. When we are talking about everything we can hear, smell, touch, taste and see, and some things that we can't, the fact that it takes only 92 different naturally occurring elements to create these things is mind blowing. Materials are made up of elements which are the building blocks of materials. Many elements are able to combine chemically with others in different ratios to form a whole host of molecules.

Atoms are some of the smallest units of matter. They are the smallest particle that can be divided by normal procedures. The word atom derives from two ancient Greek words meaning 'no-division'. It is widely known that hydrogen atoms and oxygen atoms together form molecules of water in a ratio of two hydrogen to one oxygen atom (H_2O). Hydrogen and oxygen are both gases at room temperature. When they combine chemically, a molecule of water is formed. Therefore, water is one material and not just a mixture of hydrogen and oxygen. Materials are formed by the chemical joining of molecules that are held together by weak or strong forces of attraction in a particular formation. Not all elements can be combined with other elements.

Although it may be difficult to believe, scientifically, gases and liquids as well as solids are materials. Children need to begin to understand this at a young age. Already we can appreciate that the topic of materials can appear fairly complex. If this complexity is not an issue for us then it can be for the children we teach. It is imperative, therefore, that we seek to adopt an approach to teaching materials that promotes curiosity at the same time as assisting understanding at an appropriate level.

Key scientific concepts

- Types of materials

- Physical properties of materials

- Molecular structure and states of matter

- Physical changes – melting and freezing, evaporation and condensation, sublimation and deposition – reversible changes

- Materials and their uses

- Chemical changes – irreversible changes

Types of materials

It has long been suggested that children have firmly held ideas around the topic of materials that often lead them to construct alternative frameworks and naïve constructs (Peacock et al., 2009, p.82). A classic example of this is often seen when teachers ask children to select, find or identify a 'material'. The usual response for children of all ages within the primary phase is to identify a piece of fabric. Here a vernacular misconception made from the children appreciating the term 'material' to be used in a particular context can be seen. Often this common misconception has an impact on the child's ability to form accurate constructs about what materials are and the different types there can be.

Research focus

Skamp (2009) undertook a research project with a group of primary teachers. He looked at the teaching of materials and their properties. His findings suggest that:

- primary teachers should focus initially on the **macro**scopic properties of matter;

- first-hand experiences of 'matter' need to predominate;

- most primary school children are not ready for the particulate model of matter as it is not an intuitive idea for them;

→

- some primary pupils are capable of fairly complex thinking and therefore are capable of thinking in a micro-particulate manner.

It was suggested, however, that the formal introduction of particulate ideas will not hinder primary pupils' conceptual development.

The abstract nature of the particle model of matter can be assisted through the use of concrete models and analogies.

Activity

With the above in mind consider the following questions.

- How should the materials theme be introduced to young children?

- Why do you think first-hand experience is important?

- What models or analogies could you use to promote children's understanding of the particle model?

Activity: Physical properties of materials

When considering the properties of materials, being mindful of the terminology and its meaning is imperative. Below is a selection of vocabulary that can be used to help describe the physical properties of materials. Look at the following words.

Table 7.1   Materials vocabulary

Hard	Soft	Stretchy	Stiff	Shiny
Dull	Rough	Smooth	Waterproof Non-waterproof	Absorbent Non-absorbent
Opaque	Transparent	Translucent	Malleable	Flowing

Consider how you would define them. Once you have done this, consider how you would explain each word as a concept to children in the primary phase. It may be helpful to consider how your explanations would progress in complexity for more able children – but don't forget to ask them how they would describe and explain their ideas to you first!

Case study: Describing vocabulary

Gurpreet had already achieved a foundation degree in early childhood studies and was undertaking a part-time Primary Education Progression Route course to enable her to achieve a full BA (Hons) degree. She has already

→

worked in various Early Years settings and is passionate about the role of play in learning. During her course she undertook a placement in a Year 1 class. The class was using the story of *Elmer* by David Mckee as their theme for the term. Gurpreet was keen to engage the children in a session that involved explorative play and observation. Working in small groups she gave children a papier-mâché elephant and squares of different materials. She asked them to stick the squares of the materials onto their elephant using PVA glue. As they were sticking the squares down, as a form of assessment the children were asked to talk about the properties of the materials, with adults on hand to record the words that were being used, thereby extending a common 'art'-based activity into science. These were collected in and discussed at the end of the session.

Figure 7.1   Papier-mâché elephant

In a following lesson, Gurpreet provided children with a printed-out copy of the words used. She put a few further, slightly trickier words onto stickers. Children were encouraged to match up the stickers with the different squares of the materials on their elephants. During this activity, Gurpreet held several mini-plenaries where she discussed the meaning of each word, but particularly the tricky words such as dull and opaque. Once complete the children were asked to name their elephant. For subsequent science sessions on materials the elephants came out onto the tables and were added to with new materials and new words.

Questions to consider:

Why might this be an effective strategy to promote and extend the vocabulary that the children were using?

How could this practice be adapted to suit the needs of an older class?

Curriculum links

Materials are all around us. The importance of this area of the curriculum is recognised at all key stages. Younger children need to begin to recognise the different materials in their world through exploration and that not all the materials belonging to the same group, for example plastic materials, either look the same or have exactly the same properties. Sorting materials into groups and being asked to explain why they have grouped materials in this way helps children to grow in their appreciation of the wealth of different materials around them. Going on 'trails' to find particular materials or setting out a table with different types of the same material can help children to understand better. Activities using 'feely bags', with objects that children cannot recognise immediately by touch, can help children to describe and extend their vocabulary by having to tell others about the properties of the material in the bag through touch.

Sorting and classifying is fundamental to science across scientific disciplines at all ages through the primary years. Just as in the case of animals and plants, materials belong to different groups and identifying similarities between materials is as important as recognising differences. While younger children need to sort fewer objects with obvious differences at first, older children should be given more objects with less obvious differences to sort and classify.

Older children need to recognise the difference between physical and chemical changes in materials. Helping children to developing specific vocabulary and the scientific meaning of particular words is an important role for every teacher in the EYFS and primary classroom.

Molecular structure and states of matter

There are three key states of matter of which children need to become aware. Table 7.2 identifies their key qualities.

Curriculum links

Pupils are required to explore states of matter during lower and upper Key Stage 2. They are required to know about the properties of these states of matter. In order for children to develop a secure understanding of these states it is imperative that they are given time to observe changes and opportunities to sort materials into groups. Through observation children should be able to develop an understanding of the key facets of each stage.

Table 7.2 States of matter

State	Image	Key characteristics
Solid	Sand — Wood	Solids have a fixed shape and volume. They cannot be compressed, for example bricks, pennies, a piece of wood, a block of aluminium metal, a piece of wax. Particles in a solid are tightly packed and vibrate around a fixed point. N.B. Many young children think sand is a liquid because it can be 'poured'.
Liquid		Liquids have no fixed shape. They can be easily poured. They take the shape of the containers that they are in. They vary in viscosity. The viscosity of the liquid impacts on the rate at which it spreads when not in a container; it also impacts on the area the liquid assumes once spread. Molecules in a liquid are further apart than in a solid. They slip and slide over each other as they move and gain energy as they are heated.
Gas		Gases have no fixed shape. Most gases cannot be seen in their natural form. Gases take the shape of the container they are in. Molecules can be spread more widely apart compared to solids and liquids. Particles move fast and collide with the walls of their container and with each other.

Tricky substances

There are some materials that can prove to be fairly tricky for children to classify. Materials such as toothpaste, shaving foam, sand, cotton wool, sponge, play-dough and even fabrics can cause all sorts of cognitive conflict. All these are explored regularly in the Early Years classroom. Confusion is largely due to the fact that most of the tricky substances are mixtures. Toothpaste, for example, is a mixture of both a solid and a liquid. With these materials children require expert teaching to aid their classification. Undertaking an elicitation activity to ascertain children's understanding of the classification of these substances and others like them will prove an invaluable assessment activity. This will show the children's understanding of the properties of solids, liquids and gases, even if they misclassify them, and the activity can be used as a super starting point for discussion which involves speaking, listening and challenging ideas to stimulate thought.

Physical changes

Although not all materials do so, some can go through the various physical changes of state. A solid can become a liquid, a liquid can become a solid and so on. There are key processes that are involved as Figure 7.2 highlights.

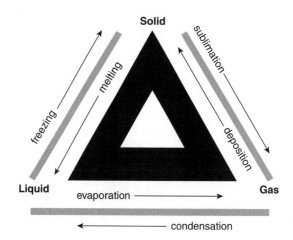

Figure 7.2 Physical changes of state

Melting and freezing

Particles in a solid are held firmly together, often with a high concentration of particles being crammed together. In solids, particles move ever so slightly around a fixed point, because of the forces of attraction between them, but this does not affect the shape or structure of the object. When a solid is given energy through transfer from a heat source the particles start to vibrate faster. The process eventually weakens the core structure of the object causing it to expand. The forces between the particles become weaker.

As this process continues the particles begin to break free from the structure. Initially the particles are still loosely connected; however, there is an increase in movement. Here the solid has changed into a liquid. When heat energy is applied the attraction between the particles is lessened allowing the particles to break apart. This is the process of melting. The temperature at which an object changes to a liquid is referred to as the melting point. When a liquid is cooled the energy of the particles lessens. The transition between a liquid becoming a solid is known as freezing. Freezing occurs when the liquid's temperature is lowered below its freezing point. For most substances the melting point and freezing point are the same temperature. However, each different material has its own melting point, for example ice melts to water at 0° C but metals need a much higher temperature to change them from a solid to a liquid. It is important that children come to understand that this is the case.

Young children can become familiar with these processes. Through a range of contexts such as *The Snowman* by Raymond Briggs to the experience of battling with an ice cream on the beach on a summer day, this process is embedded within the child's experience. Developing a conceptual framework for this area, however, can be more complex. It is often hard for the children to appreciate that a heat source is needed for this physical change as in most cases the heat source is not obvious. In the examples of the snowman and ice cream, as well as many others like them, it is the invisible air around them that provides the source of heat for melting. Children also need to meet this idea through observing other materials that melt.

Although they are not true solids, the process of 'melting' can be observed through common everyday school activities like, for example, when margarine or jelly is put into a microwave oven or hot water is poured over them. It is important to stress that when jelly is put in hot water, initially it can be seen to melt on the bottom of the container, then it diffuses through the liquid as the mixture is stirred.

Similarly, there are opportunities for children to understand the terms solid and liquid when a mixture of cornflour and water is squeezed in the hand as the 'gloop' seems to solidify as it is squeezed and then seems to melt as it is released and runs through the hand. As a primary teacher it is important to ensure that children do not misappropriate this concept and believe it to apply to all materials as, in many cases, materials when heated undergo a chemical rather than a physical change.

Evaporating and condensing

Evaporation happens when the particles of a liquid have enough energy to escape from the liquid's surface to form a vapour. This phenomenon is observable by children through everyday experiences. Observing themselves or clothes being washed and being allowed to dry, or puddles forming on rainy days and then seemingly disappearing through evaporation, is a constant in a child's life. Evaporation can occur at all temperatures, but happens more rapidly as the temperature rises. Liquids begin to evaporate considerably before the boiling point is reached. The rate of evaporation increases with the rise of temperature. It is important to note, however, that the rate of clothes drying and puddles disappearing can also be influenced by the weather. Puddles disappear and clothes dry more quickly on windy days compared to still days of the same temperature.

Evaporation itself cannot be observed and therefore it is difficult for children to understand the process. Evaporation happens in all sorts of scenarios from an obviously wet context such as the drying of the clothes and the puddles disappearing to some less obvious, such as the drying out of cakes, fruit in a fruit bowl or sandcastles over time. Children need to recognise the process of evaporation in a wide range of contexts.

Water is not the only liquid that will evaporate. A helpful way to introduce the process of evaporation is by observing what happens when perfume is placed on a warm hand. Children can actually feel this process for themselves. Additionally, children can observe this process through the sense of smell being able to detect diffusion of the perfume once it has vaporised into a gas. Diffusion is the spreading of particles within a particular space, in this case, the perfume through air. When chemical particles such as perfume are released into a room they mix with the air particles and spread to fill the room. This process is also apparent when a bag containing a chopped onion is opened and left for a short time.

Given the right temperature, a gas can condense. This means that when the gas vapour cools, the gas changes state to a liquid. An obvious example is water vapour condensing on a window pane forming condensation in the morning because of a drop in temperature overnight.

Activity

Figure 7.3 Model of water cycle

When looking at evaporation it is useful for the children to explore the water cycle. Models like the one in Figure 7.3 allow the children to explore the water cycle on a micro scale. There are cheaper alternatives, however! Try placing a half-full bottle of water in a warm place, for example next to a radiator, then put it into a fridge. With luck, water droplets form in the top half of the bottle replicating the water cycle. Resources such as these can be used effectively throughout the primary phase. In Early Years settings these resources can be used as small world play things. In older years the models can be useful observational tools to aid children's curiosity and exploration.

Sublimation and deposition

Sublimation and deposition are not processes that are explored within the primary phase. This said, it is important to be mindful of them. In its simplest form sublimation is the process of a solid changing to a gas without first becoming a liquid. Deposition is the opposite process whereby a gas becomes a solid without first being a liquid. A common example of deposition is the process of water vapour turning to snow in clouds.

Case study: Chocolate

Olumide, a mature part-time PGCE student, formerly had his own baking business and has a passion for all things to do with cookery. Using his experience he carefully planned a unit looking at changes of state using Roald Dahl's *Charlie and the Chocolate Factory* as his context. The children looked at a section of the book that described the Wonka bar and the properties of its chocolate. The children spent time looking at the properties of chocolate to find out which chocolate they thought was closest to Willie Wonka's secret recipe.

Figure 7.4 Heat and cool pack

Using heat and cool packs like those pictured in Figure 7.4 that were found at the school, Olumide asked the children to microwave these and place them in clear plastic bags. Returning to their tables the children placed different types of chocolate on the heat packs. Through observation, the children explored the rate of melting of white, milk and dark chocolate. They made notes about their observations.

Through discussion and using their notes, the children raised a whole host of questions that could be used as a starting point for investigations looking at changes of state. Obvious questions surrounding melting and cooling of the chocolate were asked.

- Will the white chocolate always melt the fastest?

- Why does the dark chocolate take so long to melt?

- How can we turn the chocolate back to a solid more quickly?

However, because the children raised the questions themselves, they had ownership over the questions and, therefore, over finding out the answers!

Later on in future sessions the class went on to explore through child-directed investigations. Interestingly, however, children realised that as the chocolate melted the chocolate smell in the room intensified. The children had observed evaporation and diffusion in a real context. Children raised real questions and were allowed to explore. The children made fascinating discoveries about the rate of diffusion in relation to heat and distance. They realised that the greater the heat source, the quicker the rate of evaporation which was in turn responsible for the increase in the rate of diffusion. The children concluded that Willie Wonka must have used chocolate like the one that was quickest to evaporate and therefore fastest to diffuse the smell of chocolate. It was their opinion that Willie Wonka would want the chocolate that would diffuse the smell of chocolate around his factory the quickest.

Activity

Thinking about the case study above:

Why do you think that the children were genuinely curious during this activity? How many reasons can you identify?

Why may it be beneficial to look at the physical changes of materials within contexts?

Dissolving

Just like melting, solidifying, evaporation and condensation, dissolving is a physical process and is reversible. When a material is mixed with a liquid three things might happen: the material might dissolve, it might not dissolve or it might mix with the liquid to form a suspension or an emulsion. Chemicals such as salt, sugar or copper sulphate* or potassium permanganate* (*not to be used in primary school) dissolve to form a solution. Substances that dissolve in this way are called solutes. The liquid in which they dissolve is called the solvent and the resulting mixture is called a solution. This process can be confusing for many. Solutions may not be colourless as in the case of copper sulphate or potassium permanganate solution, but they are transparent. Unless you have a saturated solution, i.e. one where so much solute has been added no more can dissolve, you cannot see the solute in the solution. A solution is not cloudy. Everyday experiences like 'dissolving' an aspirin in water should not be termed as such, unless the resulting solution is transparent. If it is cloudy, some particles are held in suspension in the liquid.

Substances that dissolve in a liquid can be recovered through the process of evaporation. This may be easier said than done, however, which leads to confusion, for example if you mix instant coffee and sugar with hot water, the coffee particles and the sugar dissolve in the hot water. The water could be evaporated off, but then the remaining coffee and sugar mixture would be pretty difficult to separate from each other. This leads to the thought that since they cannot be separated, a chemical changed has occurred. Similarly, when powder paint is mixed with water, while some of the paint colours the water, most of the paint is held in suspension in the water. The solid particles will settle to the bottom, over time, to leave a coloured transparent liquid above. The solid particles can be recovered, but it does not look the same as it did before it was mixed with the water. However, it has not undergone a chemical change; the paint is still the same chemically. The point here is that teachers often teach children about physical change in terms of whether the original substances can be got back. Clearly, this question can cause children to come to the wrong conclusion. This should be avoided.

Some materials when mixed with a liquid form an emulsion, for example when oil and water are mixed together they form an emulsion. Oil is less dense than water. When they are shaken together, they form an emulsion which then separates out with the oil floating on the water.

Milk is an emulsion. Some materials such as minerals and vitamins are dissolved in the liquid part of milk, but the fat particles are too big to dissolve in the liquid and 'hang' or suspend in the liquid, or float on the top of the liquid, as they are less dense than the liquid. Milk is a mixture of materials that can be separated to make other products.

Curriculum links

Upper Key Stage 2 pupils should be taught to group together everyday materials on the basis of their properties, including hardness, solubility, transparency, conductivity (electrical and thermal) and response to magnets. They need to know that some materials will dissolve in liquid to form a solution, and to describe how to recover a substance from a solution. They should also be taught to use their knowledge of solids, liquids and gases to decide how mixtures might be separated, including through filtering, sieving and evaporating. They should give reasons, based on evidence, for the particular uses of materials including wood, metals and plastics.

Materials and their uses

Engineers are scientists who seek to apply science often in a practical way. One of the first noted female engineers was a woman called Mary Anderson. Mary was a skilled engineer who wanted to apply her knowledge of the properties of materials in order to solve an issue of great importance and it is thanks to her knowledge of materials and their properties that many of us benefit still today. In November 1903 Mary invented the first ever patented window cleaning device. While visiting New York in the snow, Mary saw car drivers opening their side windows in order to see to carry on with their journey. You can imagine how less than satisfactory this was. In addition there were significant dangers with this approach. Mary invented a rubber blade that could clear rain, sleet and snow from the windscreen that was operated by the driver from within the car. Mary's invention was fitted as standard in all American cars by 1916. Knowledge of the materials has significant benefit to the way we live.

Research focus: design and technology

Davies and Rogers (2000) undertook a resource project looking at trainee teachers' perceptions of science and design and technology. They advocated that combining these two subject disciplines could significantly strengthen the teaching and learning in these areas. They discovered, however, that:

- many primary teachers lacked the confidence to cover two areas simultaneously;

- primary teachers were often simply confused about the nature of, and relationship between, science and design and technology;

- many student teachers in England and Wales then entering training were in primary education themselves as children from the 1980s onwards – this had an impact on their understanding of the relationship between science and design and technology as they had not experienced a curriculum that joined these two disciplines together;

- most student teachers had experienced a more innovative model of design and technology education than in science.

Key questions to consider

How would you define or explain the relationship between primary science and design and technology? Why may this be important?

What may the benefits of combining science and design and technology?

What is a mixture?

Of the many mixtures in the world around us, some are naturally formed while others have been made. A mixture is simply formed when two or more different materials are mixed together and no chemical reaction occurs. There are numerous common examples including sherbet dip dabs, washing powders and mixed spices. Often mixtures can be separated by undertaking various processes. Some of the processes involved in the physical change of materials can assist separation.

Although there are a whole host of processes that can aid the separation of mixtures, it is important to realise that not all mixtures can be separated. When children make a mixture with powder paint and water, once the water has evaporated they are not left with powder in its original form. When exploring the separation of mixtures children always need to be prepared to discover that it is not possible to separate all of them.

Sieving

Sieving is one of the easiest methods to separate out a mixture. A sieve is a simple tool made from wire or plastic. Sieves are made with various different gauge sizes to enable the sifting and separating of relatively large solid particles of different sizes.

Figure 7.5 Sieve trays

Archaeologists use sieve trays like the ones in Figure 7.5 to separate out the components from their digs. Children can easily engage with this activity. Traditionally teachers have laboured putting together a mixture of sand, mud, stone, marbles and paper clips for children to separate out into the mixture's constituent parts. Although this activity provides children with the opportunity of engaging in separating techniques including sieving, the context is less than inspiring. It is important that teachers ensure that a used context is meaningful. Instead of separating an 'artificially' produced mixture, it might be far better for children to dig soil samples in a range of settings and seek to separate these using appropriate techniques. This may mean that some methods are lost as, for example, not all soil samples will provide results for magnetic sorting. For an example of how this can be better achieved see the case study below. However, it might also be beneficial for children to undertake both activities so that the underlying principle is reinforced in a number of different contexts.

Filtering

Mixtures that combine liquids and solids can often be separated through the process of filtering. The mixture is passed through a filter. In the primary phase this is often in the form of filter paper or layers of other absorbent paper like kitchen roll. A filter paper is merely a sieve with much smaller holes through which some particles can pass while others cannot. The fluid able to pass through the filter is known as the filtrate. Solids that are larger than the pore size of the filter are collected. It is possible, however, for the filtrate to still contain fine particles – especially if children poke pencils into the filter paper to make the mixture filter faster! Further processes, even finer filters, are required to remove these.

Curriculum links: Evaporation

In the primary phase it is important for children to explore the process of simple evaporation. It is commonplace for children in upper Key Stage 2 to explore how they can separate a solution made of salt and water using evaporation.

Magnetic separation

Magnets can be used effectively to separate materials. Metal elements such as iron ore, nickel and cobalt are all magnetic. Magnets can be naturally occurring, permanent or can be created, such as electromagnets. A permanent magnet is made from magnetic metals. In these metals the atoms are aligned creating a North and South Pole which in turn create a magnetic field. Permanent magnets display these properties at all times. Electromagnets are made from a coil of wire wrapped around a ferromagnetic core with an electric current passing through it. Magnets can be made in the classroom by stroking a large iron nail many times in the same direction with a permanent magnet.

Curriculum links

Key to children having a secure understanding of how materials can be separated is for them to be aware of the properties of the materials that they are trying to separate. In early Key Stage 1 children are encouraged to identify and classify different properties of materials. Children at this stage need to be provided with opportunities for collaboration and talk when seeking to identify key features. When children are confident about the properties of materials they should be able to identify the separating processes required.

Case study: Instant rice

Natalie, a second year undergraduate student, wanted her class to undertake a practical science investigation involving separating materials. She was keen to explore a real life context that enabled the pupils to develop a broad array of subject knowledge regarding the materials and their properties. She decided to include observation of the contents of a packet of a supermarket's value instant rice. She asked the children to devise investigations to help sort out the materials into their various parts. The children were surprised to note that in the list of ingredients of the instant rice, 20 per cent of the packet was listed as salt.

The children already knew how to separate a solution of salt and water having looked at this in a previous session. Following their new investigations that involved a range of processes, the children were asked to present their findings. The children were animated in their oral reports and shared their amazement that they had almost been able to get the equivalent of 20 per cent of the contents back in the form of salt. This science investigation enabled Natalie to make cross-curricular links with design and technology as the children went on to design healthy meals.

Questions to consider

This scenario enables most of the separating processes to be used. How could Natalie use cereal flakes to look at magnetic separation?

What were the children learning?

Why is it important for a context to be meaningful?

Chemical changes – irreversible changes

When heated, some materials like wax, chocolate, butter, lard and metals change state. Change of state is a reversible physical process. Instead of changing state when heated, other materials like plastic, wood or other fuels such as gas, coal or oil burn. Burning, or more accurately, combustion, is a chemical change and is not reversible. This is a little confusing as some things that burn, such as wood and coal, often leave ash as a residue. Other fuels, like household gas, wax and other hydrocarbons, burn to leave no residue. Fuels consist mainly of carbon which when burnt produces carbon dioxide, which is a colourless gas. Fuels burn when they react with oxygen in the air:

$$\text{carbon} + \text{oxygen} \rightarrow \text{carbon dioxide}$$

Children should, whenever possible, undertake practical activities for themselves. However, sometimes this is not possible for health and safety reasons. Although children can become restless if they are unoccupied for periods of time, demonstrations are sometimes better than no observation at all. A number of illustrative demonstrations which involve change over time related to chemical change are possible. The role of the children would be to observe changes and record data over time through use of a chart or a series of drawings. They could describe what is happening over time during the demonstration and so provide written evidence of learning while simultaneously avoiding 'idle hands'.

The first activity involves watching a burning simple hydrocarbon, such as paraffin oil or methylated spirits in an oil burner. These are easily obtained from local suppliers. Initially the level of the oil is recorded on the outside of the container. The wick is lit and the change in the level of the oil is recorded over time. At the end of the activity, children should be asked to explain where the liquid has gone.

Similarly, the changes in weight over time of a tea light burning can be measured using simple scales and recorded in a table.

When asked to explain what is happening in these two scenarios, many observers will say that the oil and the wax have evaporated. Indeed, some of the wax in the tea light may have evaporated, but this does not explain why most of the wax seems to have disappeared. The fact that evaporation does not explain what is happening is more convincing in the case of the oil burner as the oil's surface is not, at any time, exposed to the air. The explanation lies in the fact that the wick transports the fuel, i.e. the wax or the oil, to its surface. When lit, the wax or oil burns on the surface of the wick until all the liquid has burned and the flame goes out. In the case of the wax, the lighted wick first has to change the state of the wax from solid to liquid (which is a physical process), after which the liquid wax is burned as explained above. The burning of a candle or tea light, therefore, is a two-step process: firstly the wax melts (physical change) and then the liquid wax burns (a chemical change).

It is not obvious that a chemical change is taking place in the case of combustion, because of the lack of any obvious changes. Children often consider a chemical 'reaction' to involve the mixing of materials, sometimes with gases and smells involved. You need to extend your children's understanding of chemical change to include less obvious chemical reactions. Naïve ideas relate to children thinking that chemical changes take place very rapidly, but in nature, slow chemical changes are very common. Rotting and decay are examples of slow chemical change. Although apples nowadays do not go brown when cut in half as quickly as they used to, apples left in a fruit bowl will rot over time. Leaves on the floor of woods and forests decay over time. These too are examples of slow chemical changes. Chemical changes happen inside plants and in the bodies of animals. Chemical changes are important in cookery. Toasting bread, cooking cakes in an oven and making meringues out of egg whites and sugar are examples of chemical change. Teachers can take the opportunity to reinforce the ideas of chemical change when undertaking such activities with children in the classroom.

Chemical changes are usually irreversible, yet there are some chemical changes that are reversible. Primary age children do not need to know about those chemical changes that are reversible. Some ideas should be left for later!

Burning is a chemical change that involves the production of water and carbon dioxide through the chemical combination of oxygen from the air with the carbon in the fuel. The products, the materials produced as a result of combustion, are different chemically to the materials before combustion, i.e. carbon and oxygen, through the process of combustion producing carbon dioxide and water.

Other chemical changes involve more obvious mixing of materials. For example, when sodium bicarbonate (bicarbonate of soda, an alkali) is mixed with citric acid in the presence of water, an obvious chemical change takes place. If a teaspoon of sodium bicarbonate and one teaspoon of citric acid is mixed with 5 ml of water, an endothermic chemical change takes place. If these materials are placed together in a sealed plastic bag, a number of observations can be made. The mixture effervesces – a gas is produced. The plastic bag expands as the chemical change takes place. The liquid at the bottom of the bag feels very cold as the chemical changes take place. There are a number of observations that children can make here. Firstly, younger children can just observe that the materials in the bag bubble, that the bag gets full of a gas, which they often describe as 'air', and that the liquid gets cold. However, older children can use this illustrative activity as a starting point for more careful investigation involving a series of measurements like, for example, the drop in temperature over time, the amount of gas produced over time or the effect of changing the proportions of the initial materials. In a very simple way, they would be investigating the rate of reaction of the chemical change, which is quite a sophisticated idea, but very relevant and authentic for older Key Stage 2 children. Older children could also investigate whether other 'mixtures' behave in the same way, for example vinegar and sodium bicarbonate or sodium bicarbonate and tartaric acid. The main point to remember is that these activities help children to understand the more difficult ideas about chemical change. In all cases, the products, i.e. what is left at the end of the chemical change, are not the same chemically as the materials that were put together at the start. The original materials have changed chemically to form different materials. These changes are irreversible.

Curriculum links: Chemical changes

Primary children are sometimes asked to simulate a volcanic eruption using the chemical changes that occur when vinegar and sodium bicarbonate are mixed together in a 'model' volcano. Children love this activity and find it very exciting. However, this is not really a very good model to represent lava erupting from a real volcano. This can lead to misconceptions. Neither are the chemical changes involved explained to children to help them to understand what actually is happening. This, of course, is a missed opportunity. Another common activity that involves chemical change is placing yeast, warm water and sugar in a plastic bottle sealed with a balloon. Over time, a chemical change takes place that results in the formation of a gas, carbon dioxide, which inflates the balloon. Again this is an interesting activity that children find amusing, but this again must be used as a vehicle for helping children to understand the difference between physical and chemical change.

In upper Key Stage 2, pupils are expected to be able to explain that some changes in materials result in the formation of new materials, and that this kind of change is not usually reversible, including changes associated with burning and the action of acid on bicarbonate of soda.

Children in upper Key Stage 2 can investigate burning and other chemical changes in the classroom (Roden et al., 2007, pp120–21). Although you might feel anxious about the health and safety aspects of these activities, they can be carried out safely given careful risk assessment, good supervision and good classroom management.

The science National Curriculum requires that pupils should demonstrate that dissolving, mixing and changes of state are reversible changes. They should also be able to explain that some changes result in the formation of new materials, and that this kind of change is not usually reversible, including change associated with burning and the action of acid on bicarbonate of soda (DfE, 2013, p.28).

Of course, more able children should be provided with the opportunity to exceed this basic requirement.

Activity

Reflect on your understanding of the ideas within this chapter. Have your ideas changed as a result of reading the chapter? If so, how?

How will the ideas presented in this chapter affect the way that you teach about materials in the future?

Self-assessment questions

1. What is a material?
2. What is a mixture?
3. What are the different ways of separating a mixture?
4. Explain the differences between physical and chemical changes.
5. Give three examples of physical change.
6. Give three examples of chemical change.

Further reading

Archer, J. (2014) An introduction to design and technology, in Driscoll, P. Lambirth, A. and Roden, J. (eds) *The primary curriculum: A creative approach*, 2nd edition. London: SAGE.

Brunton, P. and Thornton, L. (2010) *Science in the Early Years*. Chapter 6 'Materials'. London: SAGE.

Peacock, G., Sharp, J., Johnsey, R. and Wright, D. (2009) *Primary science: Knowledge and understanding*, 6th edition. Chapter 6 'Materials'. London: Learning Matters SAGE.

Roden, J. (2014) An Introduction to Science, in Driscoll, P. Lambirth, A. and Roden, J. (eds) *The primary curriculum: A creative approach*, 2nd edition. London: SAGE.

References

Davies, R. and Rogers, M. (2000) Pre-service primary teachers' planning for science and technology activities: Influences and constraints. *Research in Science & Technological Education*, 18(2): 215–25.

Department for Education (2013) Science programmes of study: Key stages 1 and 2. London: DfE.

Peacock, G., Sharp, J., Johnsey, R. and Wright, D. (2009) *Primary science knowledge and understanding*, 4th edition. Chapter 6 'Materials'. *London:* Learning Matters SAGE.

Roden, J., Ward, H. and Ritchie, H. (2007) *Extending knowledge in practice: Primary science*. Part 3 'Materials and their properties'. London: Learning Matters SAGE

Skamp, K. (2009) Atoms and molecules in primary science: What are teachers to do? *Australian Journal of Education in Chemistry*, 69: 5–10.

8 Forces

Learning outcomes

By reading this chapter you will develop:

- an understanding of key scientific concepts that underpin the teaching of forces and their effects;
- effective pedagogic strategies for teaching about forces and their effects.

Teachers' Standards

1. **Set high expectations which inspire, motivate and challenge pupils**
- set goals that stretch and challenge pupils of all backgrounds, abilities and dispositions.

2. **Promote good progress and outcomes by pupils**
- be aware of pupils' capabilities and their prior knowledge, and plan teaching to build on these.

3. **Demonstrate good science subject and curriculum knowledge**
- have a secure knowledge of science and the science curriculum, foster and maintain pupils' interest in the subject, and address misunderstandings.

4. **Plan and teach well-structured lessons**
- promote a love of learning and children's intellectual curiosity.

Introduction

The effects of forces can be seen all around us, but forces themselves cannot be seen. Things move because of the effects of forces, things change shape and direction as a result of forces and things stay still because of the effects of forces. There are a number of misunderstandings about forces that lead many to shy away from teaching this topic. These include a lack of understanding about what a force is and what a force does, but are also related to the use of scientific words used differently in everyday life and in science. This 'misuse' of scientific vocabulary is deep rooted and needs to be understood if children are to realise that this is the case.

You will find implicit and explicit reference to forces in other chapters such as the movement of the planets around the Sun; the forces of attraction in solids, liquids and gases; the movement of fingers when playing a computer game or working a tablet phone; the movement of the blood around the body by the heart, which is a sophisticated pump; or the movement of a snail over a surface. Life as we know it would not exist if it were not for forces and their effects. Forces permeate our lives and it is part of your role as an effective teacher of science to raise children's awareness of the forces that are evident all around us. While forces are invisible, the effects of forces can be seen all around us.

Key scientific concepts

- What is a force?

- Forces and their effects

- Balanced and unbalanced forces

- Forces and motion – some basic ideas

- Magnetic forces

- The effect of gravity on unsupported objects

- Levers, pulleys and gears

What is a force?

Forces are simply pushes and pulls. Individual things exert forces on objects and the objects, reciprocally, exert forces back. Some forces are 'balanced' and others are 'unbalanced'. Things stay still when the forces acting on them are balanced. Things move when the forces acting on them are unbalanced. Balanced forces keep things such as cathedrals from crashing to the ground, support bridges in place over rivers, keep the stems of plants firm and erect, and keep our drinks in our cups without spilling. Unbalanced forces, on the other hand, cause movement such as the force of a kick on the ball in a football match or the push on a stone in curling.

Everyday synonymous usage of words like power, might, and energy confuse the issue. Teachers need to reinforce the term 'force' when children use other words incorrectly in their place. Children's understanding of forces is not helped by terms like 'police force' or people being 'forced to do things' that they do not want to do and, of course, ideas drawn from science fiction 'let the force be with you'.

Forces and their effects

Forces are involved in everyday actions: pulling, pushing, squashing, twisting, squeezing and bending. The effects of these forces are clearly visible. Forces are very important in physical education and sport. While watching or engaging in sport we do not usually think about the forces involved, but we can see or sometimes feel the effects of forces, particularly in contact sports such as rugby, boxing or wrestling. Learning about the science through cross-curricular links with physical education can be very productive. Merely raising the awareness of children to the involvement of forces and asking them to think about and identify the pushes and pulls and the outcomes of those pushes and pulls can do much to help them to understand about forces and their effects at an early age. Indeed, this is a fantastic opportunity to help children to realise the relevance of science in their everyday lives.

Very few children will be unaware of the effects of the forces of the wind, the waves and floods on life during the storms in the winter of 2013/2014. During that period, there were many spectacular and obvious opportunities, throughout England, for teachers to relate the almost everyday happenings to the effects of forces. Less spectacular, but nevertheless just as potentially useful from a learning point of view, are the everyday actions that involve forces from play in the home corner, play on equipment in the school grounds or recreation grounds, or climbing a tree. Talking to children about these as they occur in informal as well as formal teaching sessions can really help children to understand better the role of forces in their lives. This is important.

Forces and motion – some basic ideas

Forces make things start to move, keep them moving, keep things still and change the shape, speed or direction of an object. Isaac Newton played a key role in the development of scientific thinking about forces. The unit of force, the newton (N) was named after him. In the classroom, forces can be measured using a range of newton meters, some of which can measure pulls and others that can measure push. Children should be introduced to the measurement of forces at an early age through exploration, firstly by noticing the extension of elastic bands or simple springs used to lift different objects and then by using newton meters, even though they may not understand the scales on them. Many newton meters have transparent covers which can help children to understand how newton meters work through observing how these simple measuring instruments measure forces through the compression and extension of a spring.

Forces need to be considered in pairs. Scientists believe that all objects exert forces of attraction on each other. Some of course are very small, negligible in size, and cannot be measured, but are still important. There are forces of attraction between the Moon and the Earth that hold the two bodies in motion.

You need to be familiar with scientific terms associated with forces. The following words in the study of forces have a particular meaning.

- Weak and strong forces or bonds exist within chemical molecules that hold the material together.

- Surface tension is a force between individual liquid particles at its surface. Pond skaters and water boatmen are able to hunt for prey on the surface of water because of this force. Surface tension is the force that can support a fine sewing needle. The downward force of the pond skater or fine needle is balanced by the surface tension at the surface of the water.

- Weight is a force. On Earth people and other objects have weight because of gravity that has the effect of pulling everything towards the centre of the Earth.

- Mass is not a force even though on Earth the weight of an object when measured is the same as the mass. The mass is the 'amount of stuff' in an object and is measured in kilogrammes (kg). Weight is a measure of the force of an object acting downwards and is measured in newtons (N), or sometimes kilogramme force or gramme force.

- Magnetism is a force – opposite poles of a magnet attract each other; similar poles repel.

- Friction is a force between moving surfaces. Other words for this force include air resistance, drag, water resistance and fluid resistance.

- Upthrust is a force that is involved in floating and sinking. This happens when an object in a liquid displaces some liquid when it is fully or partially immersed.

Research focus

Archimedes was significant in developing scientific understanding of forces. He was interested in hydrostatics, levers and pulleys among many other things. He also developed siege engines which were used in warfare during earlier times. You may have heard about the device known as the Archimedean Screw, which is used today to raise water for irrigation purposes in dry, Middle Eastern countries. The word 'eureka' is often attributed to Archimedes. It is said that he made the exclamation as he suddenly understood, while he was bathing, about buoyancy and about the volume of water displaced by a submerged body. This is now known as the Archimedes principle.

Curriculum links

Forces are a fundamental part of many basic Early Years activities in the home, Nursery and Reception class. Water play and many activities in the home corner involve forces as well as other play that involves anything that moves, such as pull-along toys or cars that need to be pushed to make them move. Changes in shape require the use of forces such as the manipulation of play-dough or clay. These activities and others such as free play with magnets can be used to introduce scientific language and to highlight the effects of a force – that is, of course, if the practitioner is aware of the opportunities presented within teacher-directed or child-initiated activities.

Forces are not part of the statutory programme of study at Key Stage 1, but clearly, if the foundations for learning about forces and their effects have been laid carefully in the Early Years then there should be some continuation of this through Key Stage 1. Discontinuity could hamper pupils' later learning about this topic. If you are working in Key Stage 1 there will always be opportunities to reinforce the ideas of forces almost every day because of the possibilities through cross-curricular links, particularly in physical education and outdoor play on large apparatus and when children are swimming or playing games such as football, netball, rounders or contact sports.

Magnetic forces

Like other planets, the Earth is a huge natural magnet with a North and South Pole.

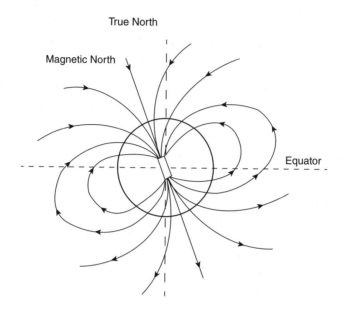

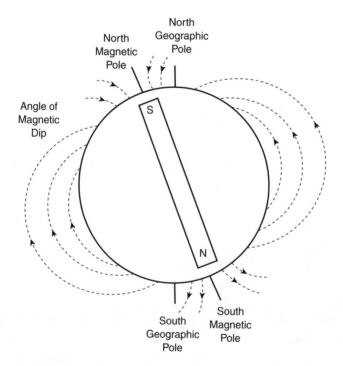

Figure 8.1   Magnetic forces

In the past, people used to use the stars and the position of the Sun to locate themselves, but this was obviously difficult when the Sun or stars were not visible. Under these conditions, natural magnets called lodestones were used as simple compasses by the Chinese and Vikings so that they could find north. Later, the Tudors learned how to make simple compasses out of a steel needle by stroking it with a lodestone (Peacock et al., 2009, p.115).

Compasses can be used to detect magnetic fields. A simple compass is just a magnetic needle suspended on a point that can turn to show the position of north and the path of magnetic fields. Simple compasses can be made quite easily in the classroom. See, for example, http://members.scouts.org.uk/documents/rollsroyce/Making%20a%20compass.pdf or www.bbc.co.uk/science/0/23033112 or www.magnet.fsu.edu/education/teachers/resources/documents/worksheets/make-a-compass.pdf

Although we would want to discourage the use of worksheets, these links provide good starting points for planning teaching around magnets and some interesting illustrative activities for your children to raise their own investigative questions.

All magnets have poles although not all magnets are rectangular. Magnets can be round with holes in the middle, or square or other shapes. Magnets are made from metals like iron, and nickel. These metals can be magnetised. When they are magnetised they exert a magnetic field. Things called domains are distributed randomly inside an unmagnetised piece of iron or steel. When the metal is made into a magnet, either by stroking it with a permanent magnet or by putting it in a magnetic or electrical field, the domains become aligned. Each domain is like a mini-magnet inside the material.

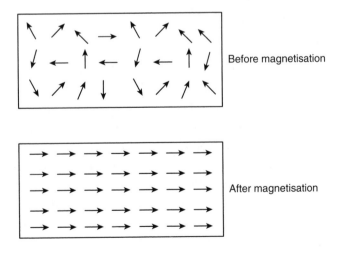

Figure 8.2 Domains in a magnetic material before and after magnetisation

Temporary and permanent magnets

It is easy to make a magnet and it is easy to destroy a magnet through rough handing or by storing it incorrectly. Rough handling leads to the domains of the magnet becoming misaligned rather than in uniformed lines. So although a magnet might be called 'permanent' it might still lose its magnetic properties quite easily. Permanent magnets can be made from hard metals like steel by the metal being stroked by a permanent magnet as described above. The stroking puts the domains into lines as described above. Permanent magnets can also be made by putting them in a device called a solenoid or by winding a wire around the magnet and passing an electric current through the wire. The longer the time the current passes through the wire, the stronger the magnet.

Temporary magnets can be made out of soft metals such as iron rods or bars. The magnetism only lasts while the current is switched on. This property is used widely in industry, for example in the sorting of magnetic and non-magnetic materials in recycling centres. Permanent magnets have a wide range of uses including in electric turbines and motors and more recently in computers.

Magnetic materials

Some materials will be attracted to a magnet. These are called magnetic materials. Some materials are not attracted to a magnet. These are called non-magnetic materials. Many children will think that all metals will be attracted to a magnet, but this is not the case. When given the chance, children will discover for themselves that some metals are not magnetic, perhaps by going on a trail around the school to find metals that are attracted to a magnet. Of course, this can be done more formally, but this is not quite the same!

Curriculum links

In lower Key Stage 2, pupils' understanding of forces is extended in relation to magnetic forces and the forces involved in movement. Pupils are required to compare how things move on different surfaces, which builds perfectly on the concrete experiences in earlier years. The requirements are that pupils notice that some forces need contact between two objects, but that magnetic forces can act at a distance. Observation of magnets and how they attract and repel each other and other materials links well to the requirements about materials and provides an opportunity not only for raising questions, but also for numerous ways of working scientifically linked to exploring magnetic materials and the properties of magnets themselves, collecting, recording and interpreting data, and drawing conclusions (DfE, 2013).

Air resistance, water resistance and friction

All three of these terms represent similar concepts. They are forces that oppose the direction of movement. They are slowing-down forces. Air is a mixture of gases. When things pass through air, in any direction, their motion is opposed by the air acting in the opposite direction resisting the movement, for example a parachutist falling from an aeroplane or a cyclist peddling along a road.

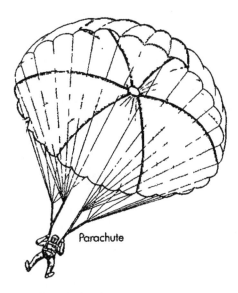

Parachute

Figure 8.3   A parachutist falling through the air

Air resistance can be easily felt by children running with large pieces of card held in front of them, but not obscuring their vision for health and safety reasons. Similarly, when things pass through water, their motion is opposed by water acting in the opposite direction. The reason why ducks can propel themselves through water is because of water resistance. As the duck paddles backwards the effect of the opposing force of the water on the duck propels the duck forward. Friction is the name of the force that acts between solids that are moving against each other in opposite directions.

Figure 8.4   A duck paddling through water

Friction is a force between solid objects. When you rub your hands together or push yourself off on a skate board or bicycle, you can feel the effect of friction resisting the movement where the two solids are in contact with each other. When you rub your hands together, the opposing forces create heat; the smoother the surface, the less the effect of friction. Rubbing oil onto your hands reduces the friction between your hands. Cyclists or cars may skid on an icy or oily road because the ice or oil reduces the friction between the tyres and the road.

Curriculum links

Friction can be measured in the classroom. A popular investigation with upper Key Stage 2 children is one where they investigate which shoe has the best grip. Essentially, children use a newton meter to drag a shoe along a surface, measuring the force needed to move each shoe, which are then compared.

The effect of gravity on unsupported objects

Both Galileo and Newton were interested in what happens to unsupported objects. After making observations, they tried to explain what they were witnessing. Newton is said to have watched an apple fall from a tree and, famously, Galileo performed investigations of falling objects from the leaning tower of Pisa. When an object is dropped from a height it falls to the ground as a result of the force due to gravity. Peacock et al. (2009) explain this phenomenon very clearly. They explain that when children are investigating the effects of gravity on an object, teachers need to understand that gravity, reaction forces and friction all come into play (Peacock et al., 2009, p.142). If an object does not slip down a slope, the three forces will be balanced, but if the force due to gravity (weight) that acts downwards along the surface of the slope can overcome the friction, the object will slip. These ideas are quite difficult, but children in the primary phase are not required to explain about forces in these terms.

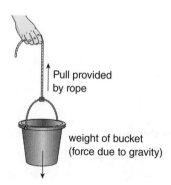

Pull provided by rope

weight of bucket (force due to gravity)

Figure 8.5 Forces acting on an object

Curriculum links

Children often investigate the effects of the force due to gravity in school – often without this being made explicit. Early Years children often put cars on ramps to see how far they travel or to compare how fast they move down the ramp. Speed is not part of the science National Curriculum until beyond the end of upper Key Stage 2, but nevertheless children are interested in speed and making things go faster. Similarly, children are interested in dropping objects such as balls, parachutes or spinners from different heights. Again, they could rank the speed of drop. This could be achieved by filming using a mobile phone or tablet. The number of film cells recorded could be counted and these could be ranked and compared. In this way the time taken for different objects to drop could be compared.

Like Aristotle, children often think that heavier objects fall faster than lighter ones. However, Galileo in the seventeenth century believed that everything falls at the same rate and performed experiments to investigate his ideas further. Children can easily investigate how things fall through the air. At first these might include noticing the effect of air resistance on a sheet of A4 paper held horizontally and dropped from a height. Next they can observe the decrease in the time taken to drop when the same piece of paper is screwed up and dropped. This is a good way to teach about the effects of gravity on an unsupported object while also learning about the slowing-down force of air resistance as the paper drops. Indeed, it is excellent if children can learn about the effects through a range of activities that could also include making and testing spinners, paper aeroplanes and parachutes. Undertaking these activities can help children to understand the ideas of air resistance, but also tend to reinforce ideas about heavier objects falling faster.

The idea that heavier objects fall through the air faster than lighter ones can be challenged through practical activity. Children can be provided with a number of canisters such as film canisters of the same size and asked to plan and carry out an investigation to find out if heavier objects take less time to drop to the floor than lighter ones. They can then load each canister with a different weight of, for example, modelling dough and investigate the time of drop for each.

Using ramps is always popular. Younger children can undertake a simple investigation using a toy 'tipper' truck that can be loaded with different amounts of a material such as modelling clay or marbles. Similarly, older children in Key Stage 2 can investigate how far unopened tins of food of various sizes and weights can move down a movable ramp. This can extend learning from earlier years and provides an authentic experience which is so important for older learners as the outcome of the investigation is not at all obvious.

Figure 8.6   A loaded small toy truck on a ramp

Figure 8.7   Tin cans on a ramp

Curriculum links: Upper Key Stage 2

Building on work in earlier years, pupils in upper Key Stage 2 should explore the effects of gravity on unsupported objects. They should be able to explain that they fall to the Earth because of the force of gravity acting between the Earth and the falling object. They should explore and learn about the effects of air resistance, water resistance and friction that act between moving surfaces.

Floating and sinking

Floating and sinking is something that almost every child will investigate through child-initiated play in the Early Years classroom. Typically, they will play in a water tray filled with many water play toys. There is huge potential here for learning about floating and sinking using their play and exploration as a starting point. Merely reducing the number or type of water toys in the water tray at any one time can lead to more systematic learning, especially if an adult joins in with the play and asks questions about what is being observed or 'what happens if' type questions during the play. There are lots of opportunities for speaking and listening and discussion which is such an important part of learning in science (Brunton and Thornton, 2010; Newton, 2002), as well as being important in English. However, to optimise learning, the adults working with the children need to understand the science involved if they are to provide more teacher-directed exploration that will challenge the children's ideas about floating and sinking and push their learning beyond knowing about the kinds of materials that can float and those that sink – even more so if the exploratory play tradition is extended in to Key Stage 1 and beyond, as it is in some enlightened schools where exploration forms the starting point for much science in the primary school.

It is easy to understand that children will think that light things float and heavy things sink. Even adults presented with a large block of ice and ask to predict what will happen if the block is placed in a tank full of water will often immediately say it will sink. They often change their minds quite quickly on reflection or when their idea is challenged by peers, but nevertheless the idea that heavy things sink is deep rooted and problematic.

Reflecting on the ideas of floating and sinking and with simple exploration of trying to make things that float sink and things that sink such as modelling clay float can help a great deal. Older children can think about these concepts without practical exploration, but for many, practical experience is necessary.

Activity

How can children be best supported by adults in Early Years settings when exploring floating and sinking?

What are the implications for supporting teaching and learning in Key Stage 1 and Key Stage 2?

Research focus: Ideas about floating and sinking in a primary school

Mandy, a mature student, undertook a small-scale research project into an aspect of children's learning in science as part of her chosen Enhanced Studies course within her PGCE training. Previously, she had been employed as a teaching assistant before joining the programme. She had worked with primary children undertaking science in school, but was keen to extend her understanding of children's learning in the subject further. Previously, she had been fascinated by very young children involved in teacher-led and child-initiated water play. Consequently, she decided to focus on the area of floating and sinking for her research across the primary age phase in an urban primary school. The research involved a similar starting point, providing children with an opportunity to draw on previous experiences to predict whether certain objects would sink or float in water.

The review of literature revealed that this topic had been of much interest to previous researchers. Mandy used the ideas and identified misconceptions to inform her study. Typically, children were said to think that big and heavy objects sink and that light objects float, and even that some small things made of a particular material would float while a larger piece of the same material would sink. All this indicated that they had no idea that it is both size and weight, i.e. the density of an object, which is significant in whether an object floats or sinks. In her own research, Mandy provided children with a number of real objects to predict whether they would float or sink in water. Across the 5–11 age range, 37 out of 42 children predicted that how heavy an object was would determine whether it would float or sink. One Year 2 child wrote: sinking – 'it is heavy things that go down to the bottom'; floating – 'when light things float on top'. One Year 3 child wrote: 'sinking is when somthink (sic) that doesent (sic) stay on the top of the water because its heavy'. What is floating? 'floating is where there is somthink (sic) light that stays up when it gos (sic) in the water'. However, there was an observed difference of opinion among Reception children. Some suggested that light things like clay sank and foil was heavy so would float. One Year 1 child said 'submarines are under water because they are heavy' and another that 'a hammer sinks because it is heavy', therefore suggesting how children begin to build up their ideas. Shape was another factor identified by Reception and Year 1 children. Older children thought things with holes in them would sink so that, for example, foil and a paper clip would sink. Properties of materials were also important for some children in Years 2, 3 and 5: for example, plastic spades, dolls and cups would float. One Year 3 child thought that 'water is weak, so heavy things sink'.

Mandy identified differences in ideas by year groups. While all children thought weight was significant, younger children thought that shape and size were of more importance, but for older children, ideas about the properties of water and forces were thought to support the weight of objects. Overall, the study revealed that there was a distinct improvement in correct predictions from the younger children through to the older ones although this was not evident in all objects. Her research suggested that primary aged children had started to form the basis of some of the scientific understanding of why objects sink and float due to the concept of its size, weight and, in Years 5 and 6, the application of forces.

Activity

Could you devise a small-scale research project to investigate children's ideas about a science concept? How might research of this kind inform your planning? Similarly, how might it inform your assessment of individual children?

The reason why something floats or sinks is linked not only to its weight, but also to its volume. Things that float have the force that acts downwards as a result of gravity balanced by the equal and opposite upward force of the water acting in the opposite direction. When things sink, the force on the object as a result of the effect of gravity on the mass is greater than the upward force of the water on the object. The forces are unbalanced and the object sinks. The relationship between the weight of an object and its size is called density. However, we would not usually teach about density in the primary classroom unless children were capable of understanding this concept.

Upthrust

The upward force on an object in water is called upthrust, or sometimes buoyancy. Gravity has the effect of pulling things down. An object that floats has its weight, the force acting downwards, balanced by the force of upthrust acting upwards.

When an object floats, the upthrust is equal to the weight of the object. When an object sinks, the weight acting downwards is greater than the upthrust. Upthrust can be measured by suspending an object that will sink from a newton meter.

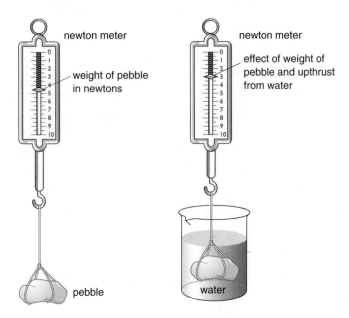

Figure 8.8 An object suspended in air then in water

Firstly, the weight of the object is measured in air. Then the object is suspended under the surface of the water and the reading on the newton meter is noted. If the new reading is subtracted from the original weight of the object, the upthrust can be calculated:

Weight of the object in newtons − weight of the object in water = upthrust

If an object floats, the upthrust is equal to the weight of the object. These forces are balanced.

NB The upthrust on a submerged object remains the same no matter what the depth. Upthrust is not the same as water pressure.

Curriculum links

Air resistance, water resistance and friction have been part of the upper Key Stage 2 science curriculum for many years, but the inclusion of mechanisms including levers, pulleys and gears that allow a force to have a greater effect is new at this level and brings new demands on the teacher's knowledge.

Activity

When given the opportunity, young children love exploring and using newton meters. This is even more so when water is involved. Just present your children with a number of newton meters of different strengths and observe what they do and what investigations this leads to – lots of active learning without the need for detailed advanced planning for learning.

Try out an activity like this with your children using a simple stimulus. Observe carefully what they do, what they say, what questions they ask, and then try to encourage them to plan and carry out some simple investigations of their own to answer their questions about forces. Use the evidence you collect to assess your children's use of vocabulary and their level of skill in observation and asking questions. Do they use scientific vocabulary in the correct way? Do they understand the meaning of the vocabulary they use? How well do they observe? What kinds of questions do they ask?

Use your collected evidence to plan the next steps in your children's learning in terms of their use of vocabulary, their understanding of the scientific ideas under study, and in terms of working scientifically.

How would you record this information for communication to others including colleagues and parents?

Levers, pulleys and gears

Basically, levers, pulleys and gears are simple machines. A simple machine usually has a number of parts that work together to perform an operation more easily than humans. In everyday life we might think of an automatic washing machine or dishwasher as a machine, but the term extends further than these modern labour-saving devices.

Levers

A lever is a simple bar that turns around a fixed point called a fulcrum. Think about a crowbar and what you might use it for.

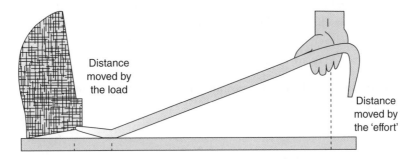

Figure 8.9   A simple crowbar lifting a stone

A crowbar makes it easier to do an otherwise very difficult job such as lifting a stone. The crowbar works by exerting a downward force on the 'long-end' to create movement at the tip of the 'short-end'. The result is that the paving stone is lifted at the point where the force was exerted making it easier to lift the whole. The small force exerted on the crowbar is magnified to lift the larger load at the other end. This is much easier than trying to lift the stone by hand. The load, in this case the stone, is overcome by the smaller force, the effort, at the other end. The lever had a positive 'mechanical

Figure 8.10   A trebuchet: when a heavy weight at the short end is dropped the rocks at the other end are launched from a rope bag

advantage', which is a more sophisticated name for the relationship between the forces involved in the 'effort' and the 'load' when work is made easier. Obviously, except for the most able or the most interested, primary children do not need to know about this term, but do need to know the simple principles in terms of forces involved in action (the push) and the reaction (the lifting of the stone). Levers work on the principle that the distance travelled by the 'effort' is greater than the distance travelled by the load. Try this out for yourself! The trebuchet, a medieval siege engine, is a machine which consists of a simple lever. You can see that the distance from the pivot, or fulcrum, of the two parts of the lever are unequal.

Nutcrackers are also simple levers. Examine one and try to work out how they work in terms of forces.

Figure 8.11   A pair of nutcrackers

Pulleys

Pulleys, too, are simple machines that have been used for many purposes in a range of industries for many years. Pulleys have been used to make work easier for a very long time, probably for as long as humans have tried to make work easier for themselves. In the past, pulleys were very important in the movement of goods on the docks and on board ships. They were important, too, in corn mills where sacks of corn had to be lifted from the delivery carts on the road to the upper floors of the flour mills where the process of turning corn into flour began. Archimedes was interested in this aspect of science. A basic pulley is simply a rope that passes over the groove in a wheel secured between two supports:

Figure 8.12   A simple pulley system

The load is attached to one end of the rope and is lifted by one or more men pulling on the other end of the rope. The men exert a downwards force on the rope and the load moves upwards. This simple idea was used to work pile drivers or hammers for driving poles into the ground. Basic pulleys that consist of only one wheel make the lifting of the load easier, not by magnifying the force as in the case of levers, but by the load being pulled upwards rather than being lifted. Cranes also make use of this simple technology.

More complex pulley systems involve more than one grooved wheel (pulley) where one rope is threaded between the pulleys.

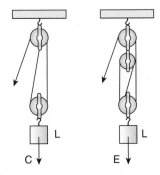

Figure 8.13 Pulley system using two and three pulleys

In this case the force is magnified so that the load lifted does not feel as heavy as it would with a single pulley system. The more complex pulley system magnifies the lifting force. The system is said to have a mechanical advantage. The mechanical advantage is the amount by which a machine increases the force. It is calculated by dividing the load by the effort. Therefore a small effort can lift a much larger load.

Pulleys in action

Pulleys are used today in shipping to move large loads. They are involved in simple lift systems like the dumbwaiters that are used to move food or bed linen from one level of a building to another. They make the job of moving things up and down much easier than having to carry them from one floor to another. More complicated lifts use a series of pulleys to raise and lower passengers in the compartment. Car mechanics use a simple pulley called a block and tackle to lift engines. Flags are raised and lowered using a pulley system, venetian blinds often have a pulley to raise and lower them and conveyor belts frequently use the same technology. Cranes use a very large pulley. Rock climbers use pulleys to help them scale the sides of mountains. They are essential for the safety of the climbers.

Curriculum links

Large-scale pulleys for use outdoors in the Nursery or Reception class can also be used with older children. Of course older children can set up smaller pulley systems for themselves and investigate the force needed to lift fixed weights using one, two and three or more pulley systems. Although these can be very fiddly to set up, such investigations are well worth the effort and can provide authentic investigations that are so much more interesting for children than merely carrying out illustrative activities to which they often already know the answer. In this way curiosity can be fostered (Ofsted, 2013), which is so important as formal teaching of this topic can be so boring.

Activity: Levers and pulleys

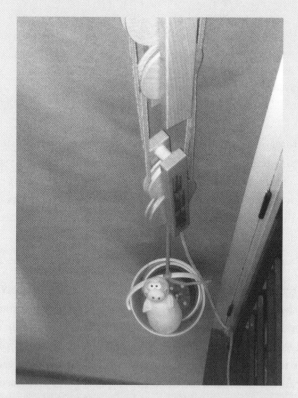

Figure 8.14 A large-scale pulley system lifting a toy pig in a bucket

Why is it important to set the study of pulleys in an everyday context?

Look around your school to find examples of levers and pulleys in action.

Case study

Mark, a Teach First participant, was working on the topic of forces with his Year 5 class in a school on the east coast of England. His careful planning in relation to rides at a fairground served as a hook to immerse the children in the significance that forces play on our favourite rides. He was surprised by the children's own enthusiasm to push their learning further than had been originally planned by exploring the more complex forces of centrifugal and centripetal force. To consolidate learning further the children visited a theme park. Here they had the opportunity to meet a park engineer and learn about the forces that designers encounter not only when building rides but also when testing and running them. The children were able to observe, at first-hand, the importance of gravity and friction by building small scale models of one of the theme park's most famous rides and testing the effect that these forces had on the rollercoaster carriages.

Reflection

You may not be able to take your children to a theme park, but reflect on how you might reinforce similar ideas in PE or on large apparatus in school or at a local playground.

Self-assessment questions

1. Explain what you understand by the term 'force'.
2. What do you understand by the terms:

- air resistance;
- friction;
- upthrust?

3. Explain the forces involved in moving a rowing boat through water.
4. Where might you find pulleys in use in everyday life?
5. Why is it important to set the teaching of ideas about scientific and technological applications in a real-life context?
6. Think about your class or a class known to you and about everyday events and routines that regularly involve forces to move things or to keep them still. How could you reinforce some of the scientific ideas met within this chapter in your general teaching?
7. How could you plan to stretch your more able pupils in their learning about forces and their effects?

Further reading

Brunton, P. and Thornton, L. (2010) *Science in the Early Years*. Chapter 7 'Forces'. London: SAGE.

Brunton, P. and Thornton, L. (2010) *Science in the Early Years*. Chapter 9 'Magnets and magnetism'. London: SAGE.

Brunton, P. and Thornton, L. (2010) *Science in the Early Years*. Chapter 8 'Air and water'. London: SAGE.

Peacock, G., Sharp, J., Johnsey, R. and Wright, D. (2009) *Primary science: Knowledge and understanding*, 6th edition. Chapter 8 'Electricity and magnetism'. London: Learning Matters SAGE.

Peacock, G., Sharp, J., Johnsey, R. and Wright, D. (2009) *Primary science: Knowledge and understanding*, 6th edition. Chapter 10 'Forces and motion'. London: Learning Matters SAGE

Wenham, M. and Ovens, P. (2010) *Understanding primary science*, 3rd edition. Part 4 'Physical processes'. London: SAGE.

References

Brunton, P. and Thornton, L. (2010) *Science in the Early Years: Building firm foundations from birth to five*. Chapter 10 'Electricity'. London: SAGE.

Department for Education (2013) *Science programmes of study: Key stages 1 and 2*. London: DfE.

Newton, D.P. (2002) *Talking sense in science*. London: Routledge.

Ofsted (2013) *Maintaining curiosity: A survey into science education in schools*. Manchester: Ofsted.

Peacock, G., Sharp, J., Johnsey, R. and Wright, D. (2009) *Primary science: Knowledge and understanding*. 6th edition. London: Learning Matters SAGE.

9 Earth, space and rocks

Learning outcomes

By reading this chapter you will develop:

- an awareness of the solar system and how it works;
- your understanding of the planets and the rotations of the Earth, Sun and Moon;
- your understanding of effective pedagogic strategies for teaching the topics of Earth and space.

Teachers' Standards

2. Promote good progress and outcomes by pupils

- demonstrate knowledge and understanding of how pupils learn and how this impacts on teaching.

3. Demonstrate good science subject and curriculum knowledge

- have a secure knowledge of science and maintain pupils' interest in the subject.

Key scientific concepts

- The movement of the Earth and other planets relative to the Sun in the solar system

- The movement of the Moon relative to the Earth

- The Sun, Moon and Earth as spherical bodies

- Day and night

- Seasonal change

- Rocks and their formation

Introduction

Space: the final frontier! Space is a fascinating topic. Children of all ages can be inspired by the study of Earth and space. There are so many unknowns in relation to space and so much still to discover. Children can feel particular kinship with the scientists who are exploring space. Unlike some areas of established science, there is still a sense of mystery and discovery about space that can unite the professional scientist and the primary child.

Learning about the Earth and space can fill children with a genuine sense of awe and wonder. Children are exposed to mind-blowing and -bending information. For example, did you know the following?

- Neptune's winds reach 2,100 kmh.

- There could be over a septillion stars in the universe.

- About 99.86 per cent of the mass of the Solar System is made up of the Sun.

- It would take you roughly 35,000 years to reach the nearest star next to the Sun.

- There are more stars in the universe than all of the grains of sand on Earth.

- You would need 1,100 years to circle the largest known star in the universe.

Space is truly fascinating! In addition to this, space, and in particular the genre of science-fiction, captures the interests and imagination of children. This said, however, space can be a tricky topic. Sharp and Sharp (2007) reported a gender gap in favour of boys in relation to interest and attainment levels. When teaching about Earth and space it is vital that the teacher uses pedagogical tools in order to capture the imagination of all learners.

How stars and planets are formed

The solar system has fascinating origins. Scientists suggest that it was formed 4.5 billion years ago from huge clouds of dust and gas. It is suggested that this dust came from an exploded star. These dust clouds are known as nebulae and each one is different. Each one contains the individual components such as iron or oxygen that go to form the planets and the stars. Gravity works on a nebula to draw this dust back together. Over the period of millions of years objects such as stars and planets are created. Earth began as a rocky ball. It then attracted further fragments of the exploded star to itself. As the Earth grew so did its gravitational pull, which meant it became larger. At the heart of the nebula the Sun was forming from a ball of hydrogen. The pressure and temperature of this ball became so great that the hydrogen atoms became fused together. As the Sun first ignited it formed a great gust of solar wind that created order by pushing all of the remaining dust and gas to the outer reaches of the nebula.

Case study: Learning about Earth and space in the Reception class

Ellie, a Teach First participant, was working with 'Moonbeams' class in a large three-form entry primary school. Joint planning was undertaken with her two fellow Reception teacher colleagues and their teaching assistants. Planning started from the children's interest and was tailored to meet the needs of each particular class. In the first half of term 4, the chosen topic was Earth in space and the start of the topic coincided with a visit to the school from a planetarium. Ellie decided to make an attractive role-play area for her children as they had expressed an interest in going into space.

→

Figure 9.1   Role-play display area

Ellie also hung blow-up plastic planets from the ceiling of her classroom. When asked why she had included Pluto, since it was no longer considered to be a planet, she said that all the songs that she had found on the internet aimed at this topic for younger children also included Pluto. She had taken this as an opportunity to talk to her class about Pluto and why it should not really be in the song.

Figure 9.2   Classroom display of the solar system

In the role-play area she included some audio material so that her children could experience some of the sounds that they might hear in the spaceship. A 'space ship log book' was provided inside the spaceship along with a 'check list' to be completed before every blast off. Also inside the spaceship, Ellie had included relevant written key vocabulary such as up, down, right, left, blast off, rocket, satellite, control panel, alien, flying saucer, etc. Outside the space ship, Ellie planned over the course of the coming week to link both the teacher-directed activities and the choosing table activities to the topic. The writing task linked to the visit by the planetarium. Ellie had provided children with a table full of words written on cards for choosing to support the written task. She supported them in their writing by asking questions to stimulate thought.

Figure 9.3   Child completing a writing task

When assessing each child's written work, she also looked at the photographs, taken at the time for recording purposes, to gauge how her children were holding their pencils as well as looking at the content of their work. Other activities gave the children the opportunity to make models of space rockets through the use of shapes. Linked to mathematics and construction materials like multilink and Lego, the children were asked to consider how many blocks they needed for their rockets and how many they were adding. All the children were totally engaged and interested in all aspects of the topic. This was very impressive practice!

Curriculum links

Although Earth in space does not appear in the statutory orders until upper Key Stage 2, and does not appear at all, specifically, in the EYFS statutory orders, young children are fascinated in all things to do with space. There are many fiction books and TV and animated films that take this as a theme that aim to interest this age range. Although these may well introduce unwelcome ideas about, for example, aliens and life on other planets, it is good to balance these with more accepted ideas at a young age. The capabilities of very young children are often underestimated. They live in both the fantasy and the real world and seem to have no trouble slipping between the two, even if their ideas are formed from both. Clearly there is a need to help them to understand a more scientific view of Earth in space in an educational setting.

The solar system

The solar system is a wonderful thing of which planet Earth is a part alongside seven other planets, various dwarf planets and countless stars. The solar system has been charted by astronomers and star-gazers alike for thousands of years. Currently it is largely agreed that there are eight planets in our solar system. These being (in order from closest to furthest from the Sun):

1. Mercury

2. Venus

3. Earth

4. Mars

5. Jupiter

6. Saturn

7. Uranus

8. Neptune.

Activity

Different people use a range of tools and techniques to assist the remembering of this order like mnemonics such as: **My Very Educated Mother Just Served Up Nachos.**

Make up your own mnemonic to help you to remember. Why not try this for the properties of the different bodies in the solar system.

The Sun, a medium-sized star at the centre of our solar system, is bigger than any of the planets. The Sun is over 100 times wider than planet Earth stretching a vast 864,949 miles. The Sun is so great that it would take one million planet Earths to equate to the same mass as the Sun. The sheer mass of the Sun creates the tremendous gravitational pull that ensures that all of the planets in the solar system are kept in their regular orbits, even Neptune which, at its closest proximity, is 2.7 billion miles away from the Sun.

Figure 9.4 The solar system

Every planet in the solar system is unique. Each of the planets has features in common with the others. One simple example is that they all have a north and south pole. Each planet has an axis which is an imagined line connecting the two poles together. Every planet rotates on its axis regardless of how quickly or slowly this is achieved. The time it takes to complete a full rotation is called the planet's rotation period. For most planets, with the exception of Mercury and Venus, the full rotation period closely equates to the length of its day.

Each planet revolves around the Sun, spinning on its axis as it does so. The time it takes for the planet to complete a full orbit around the Sun is the planet's year. The length of each 'year' differs from planet to planet. Neptune's year is equivalent to 164.79 Earth years. The orbital paths that planets take around the Sun differ in shape.

Case study: The solar system

Jane, a PGCE part-time student, has a passion for craft. Before starting on her PGCE course she had been involved in various educational creative arts projects, both here in the UK and in the USA. She was confident in her creative abilities and so drew on these to develop her class's understanding of the scale of the solar system. She had identified that many of the children did not fully appreciate the scale of the planets. It became clear through the children's talk that they thought the planets were of a similar size. It became apparent that this was largely due to the inflatable planets that were suspended from the ceiling in the classroom. She provided the children with the scale below. Some children needed this chart explained to them; others were capable of the challenge of being asked to work it out for themselves. In small groups the children created scale models of the Sun and the planets.

Table 9.1 The scale of the planets

	Real diameter (km)	Diameter (rounded to the nearest thousand)	Scaled diameter (1cm = 10,000km)	Earth metres
Sun	1,392,000	1,392,000	139.2cm	109
Mercury	4,878	5,000	0.5cm	0.38
Venus	12,104	12,000	1.2cm	0.95
Earth	12,756	13,000	1.3cm	1
Mars	6,794	7,000	0.7cm	0.53
Jupiter	142,796	143,000	14.3cm	11
Saturn	120,660	121,000	12.1cm	9
Uranus	51,118	51,000	5.1cm	4
Neptune	49,523	50,000	5.0cm	4

Aware that this was a science session, Jane planned for the use and development of the children's ability to observe and raise questions. Asking the children to leave their labelled models of the Sun and the planets in the middle of the table, Jane asked the children to create a list of observations. As a class they went through the process of converting their observations into questions. Unsurprisingly, a common question was 'Why is the Sun so much bigger than any of the planets?' All of the questions were collated and led into a child-initiated session where they sought to use secondary sources to answer their questions that derived from their observations.

Activity

Reflect on why it is important to include process skills as part of your learning intentions when teaching science.

What do you think are the benefits of children generating their own questions as a starting point for research?

Case study: Year 6 children working on the topic of Earth and space

Claire, a School Direct student working with a Year 6 class, sought to introduce the topic the Earth, Moon and Sun. She first established what the children did and did not already know about the Earth, Moon and Sun using

→

some true/false cards. They were then asked to raise questions. Questions that were asked by the children included the following.

- If all the planets fell out of orbit, where would we go?
- Why do we see the Moon in the day?
- Will the Sun ever go out?
- What would happen if the Moon hit the Earth?
- Why does the Moon sometimes turn orange?
- Who first landed on the Moon?
- How does an eclipse happen?
- What would happen if the Moon stopped orbiting the Earth?
- What would happen if the Sun shrunk?
- Why does the Moon look bigger on some days and not on others?
- How do we see the Moon when it is so far away?

The aim of the lesson was to have children draw a diagram of the Sun, Moon and Earth and their respective orbits. During the lesson, Claire showed the children cut-out pictures of the Sun, Moon and Earth put together with split pins to allow each to move. The following week they made their own and these became the basis of a wall display.

Figure 9.5   Children's work on the solar system

What makes the planets, planets?

There is a potential risk of confusion for some student teachers as well as children regarding the number of planets, not least because of the common misconception surrounding the planetary status of Pluto. It is therefore important for you to understand and to be able to define what is meant by the term 'planet'.

What exactly counts as a 'planet' has changed over the course of history. Changes over time have reflected the scientific understanding of different periods in time. In Ancient Greece (800 BC) the Moon and the stars along with Mercury, Venus, Mars, Jupiter and Saturn were all classified as planets. You will notice that this list does not include all the now known planets in our solar system. This was because they were not visible to the naked eye. Interestingly Ancient Greeks did not consider the Earth to be a planet because they thought of the Earth as a sacred object around which all of cosmos rotated. It was not until the seventeenth century that astronomers agreed that the planets including the Earth rotated around the Sun and that the Moon was not a planet.

Pluto, discovered in 1930, was at that time attributed the title of the ninth planet, a status that was retained until 2006. However, Pluto is significantly smaller than Mercury, the next smallest planet. Pluto's make-up is extremely different to planets such as Mercury, Venus, Earth, Mars, the gas giants (Jupiter, Saturn) and the ice giants (Uranus, Neptune). Pluto also has a huge satellite which is nearly half the size of Pluto and shares Pluto's orbit. This is why Pluto is now no longer considered to be one of the planets.

Technical advances in tools to assist space discovery began to highlight very small, very distant objects in the early 1990s which led a team of astronomers in 2005 to announce that they had found the tenth planet that had similar characteristics but was even bigger than Pluto. This find indicated that there was a real need to be able to define and identify a planet.

The International Astronomical Union (IAU), a worldwide organisation of astronomers, took on the challenge of classifying the planets. In 2006 a new category, dwarf planet, was established. The table below helps us sort planets and dwarf planets on the basis of their characteristics.

Table 9.2 Planet characteristics – what makes a planet and dwarf planet according to the IAU definition

	Planet	Dwarf planet
Is in orbit around the Sun	Yes	Yes
Has sufficient mass to assume a nearly round shape	Yes	Yes
Is not a satellite (like the Moon)	Yes	Yes
Has cleared the neighbourhood around its orbit – it has become gravitationally dominant – there are no objects larger than it around it	Yes	
Has *not* cleared the neighbourhood around its orbit		Yes

Curriculum links

Year 5 programme of study:

Pupils should be taught to:

- describe the Sun, Earth and Moon as approximately spherical bodies.

Activity

Look at the curriculum link above. Why may the classification tool of spherical bodies help children to learn about this topic?

What misconceptions could occur as a result of teaching this point?

Why may it be helpful for children to be aware of other features of planets?

The Sun, Earth and Moon being approximately spherical bodies

Like all other topics in science it is essential for primary teachers to seek to elicit children's prior knowledge and understanding. The nature of this particular topic often results in there being a really diverse range of children's ideas derived from experts, enthusiasts as well as novices. Recent educational research has explored a range of assessment techniques that are particularly useful when teaching the topics of Earth and space.

Research focus: Eliciting children's understanding of the planets

Bryce and Blown (2013) undertook an international study to find out about children's knowledge and understanding of the Earth, Sun and Moon. They discovered that:

- most young children have a scientific grasp of the shape of the Earth, Sun and Moon by the time they leave primary school;

- the majority of older children have a scientific understanding of the relative sizes of the Earth, Sun and Moon by the time they leave secondary school;

- the creation of a super concept, such as the shape of the Earth, can be enhanced if factors including physical shape, habitation, identity, ground and sky are explored together; simply by encouraging children to draw on their current understanding of the Earth made through simple experiences and observations, their ability to develop a big understanding of the complexity of the Earth should be enhanced;

→

- children's understanding of the Earth, Sun and Moon can be enhanced if they are encouraged to support the development of their Earth concept drawing on a wide range of information.

The study also demonstrated that the following are effective tools for eliciting children's understanding of the Earth, Sun and Moon:

- giving children the opportunity to share their ideas orally;

- giving children opportunities to draw and discuss their ideas;

- enabling children to model their ideas about the Earth, Sun and Moon in play-dough and drawing.

Activity

Reflect on why it might be important to explore children's ideas.

Why might the modelling dough approach be a particularly effective means to elicit children's ideas?

Will it always be beneficial to explore children's ideas?

The movement of the planets

In 1543 Copernicus published his ideas about the planets revolving around the Sun. This monumental discovery enabled Kepler to identify the orbits of the planets. Through his careful observations Kepler was able to develop three orbital laws.

1. Each planet's orbit around the Sun is an ellipse.

2. Planets move at different speeds depending on the point the planet is at in its orbit – the closer the planet is to the Sun the faster the orbit, the further away the planet is from the Sun the slower the orbit.

3. The period it takes for a planet to orbit the Sun increases with the radius of its orbit – the further the planet is away from the Sun the longer the orbit will take. We know this to be true as Mercury, which is the closest planet to the Sun, takes 88 days to complete a full orbit, Earth takes roughly 365 days to complete a full rotation and Saturn, the sixth furthest planet from the Sun, takes a total of 10,759 days.

Kepler's laws assisted Newton to define motion. Newton discovered that all motion, be it an apple falling from a tree or a planet orbiting the Sun, falls under three basic principles. Newton's three laws are as follows.

1. An object at rest will remain in rest as will an object in motion remain in motion at the same speed and in the same direction unless it is made to change by other forces acting upon it.

2. This law states that the acceleration of an object depends on the mass of the object and the amount of force applied (Force = Mass and Acceleration).

3. For every action there is an equal and opposite reaction.

Newton's laws helps to explain how a planet moves. For example, the orbits and rotations of the planets are as a result of force being applied and the larger the planet the greater the amount of force that is required to assist the orbit. Newton also developed his universal law of gravitation through his studies on motion. He proposed that all matter exerts a gravitational attraction that draws all other matter towards its centre. The strength of the attraction is dependent on the mass of the object: the Sun has greater gravitational attraction than Earth, which in turn has more than an apple. This attraction weakens with distance. Planets furthest from the Sun will not be influenced by the same levels of attraction as those that are closest.

Newton's laws of motion and gravitational attraction help us to understand the Earth's orbit around the Sun. Earth would continue to travel through the universe in the same direction at the same speed; however, the Sun exerts a constant pull on our planet. This force draws the Earth's path back toward the Sun, pulling the planet into an elliptical orbit.

Day and night

The concept of day and night can be tricky for young children. Often children hold alternative frameworks as to how we get day and night. Some children misappropriate knowledge from everyday life. A common example of this is children believing that the sunrise and sunset is like a basketball going up and down. Some children may believe historic misconceptions learned during their studies. An example of this is the Ancient Egyptians believing that it was a scarab beetle rolling the Sun into place just as a dung beetle rolls its food. It is therefore important to ascertain what children know, understand and believe about a topic in order that you can help the development of new understanding.

We have already said that the planet spins on its axis, which is the imaginary line that goes through the middle of the Earth from the South to North Poles. The Earth's axis is titled at an angle of 23.5 degrees. The Earth takes approximately 24 hours to complete an entire rotation. As the Earth spins, different parts of the Earth are facing in different directions. During the daytime when it is light, a given area on the Earth's surface is facing towards the Sun. During the night when it is dark, that area of the Earth is in shadow and is facing space.

During the day the Sun appears to be passing through the sky. This happens because the Earth is spinning on its axis. The Sun appears to move from east to west. This movement is due to the Earth spinning towards the east. We start facing the Sun on an easterly spin meaning that the west is the last to face towards the Sun during the day. Similarly, when we enter night, due to the spinning of the Earth on its axis, we do so from east to west.

Figure 9.6 Day and night

The phases of the Moon

The moon is a satellite that orbits around the earth due to the Earth's field of gravitational attraction.

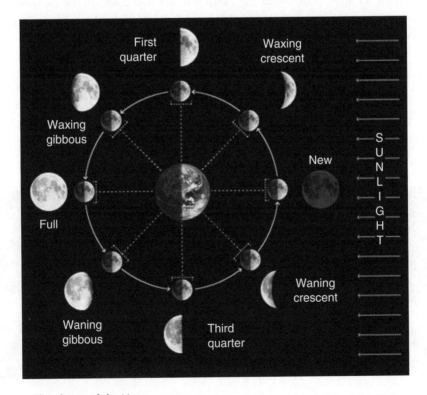

Figure 9.7 The phases of the Moon

The Moon goes on a cyclical rotation around the Earth. A new Moon occurs when the Moon is positioned between the Earth and Sun. The three objects are in approximate alignment. The entire back side of the Moon, not visible to us on Earth, is illuminated. A full Moon occurs when the Earth, Moon and Sun are in approximate alignment but the Moon is on the opposite side of the Earth. The entire sunlit part of the Moon is facing Earth, creating the full Moon. Half-Moons, better known as first quarter and third quarter Moons occur when the Moon is at a 90 degree angle in relation to the Earth and Sun. Only half of the Moon is illuminated and half is in shadow; on Earth we can see the half that is being illuminated.

After the new Moon has occurred the visible sunlit portion increases but this is less than half, so it is a waxing crescent. After the first quarter, the sunlit portion is still increasing, but now it is more than half, so it is a waxing gibbous. After the full Moon when maximum illumination has occurred, the light progressively decreases. This results in the waning gibbous phase. Subsequent to the third quarter is the waning crescent, which wanes until the light is completely gone and we start back where we began with a new Moon.

Seasonal changes

Teachers and children often hold numerous misconceptions about the cause of seasonal change. Many wrongly believe that the Earth is closer to the Sun in the summer and give this as the explanation as to why it is hotter. Similarly, children often believe that during winter the Earth is furthest away from the Sun. Both ideas are untrue.

The Earth's orbit around the Sun is an ellipse and, because of the Earth's rotation, there is a time when the Earth is closer to the Sun and a time when it is further away from the Sun. However, when, in the Earth's rotation, it is close to the Sun the northern hemisphere can be experiencing winter while the southern hemisphere experiences summer.

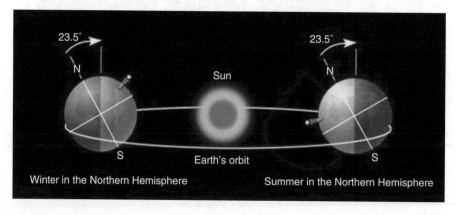

Figure 9.8 Seasonal changes

The explanation for the change in the seasons relates to the fact that the Earth tilts on its axis. As the Earth orbits the Sun, its tilted axis always points in the same direction. Over the course of the year different parts of the Earth's surface come into direct contact with the Sun's rays. At times it is the North Pole that tilts to face the Sun, and this tilt reaches its height during June, and at other times it is the South Pole's turn to tilt toward the Sun, and this tilt normally reaches its height around December.

Case study: Recording over time

Fahim, a first-year undergraduate student, undertook a placement consisting of a day a week in school within a Year 1 class over the course of an academic year. He was placed with the school's science co-ordinator. Being aware of some of the recommendations of the new National Curriculum, Fahim's mentor was keen for him to engage the children in a longitudinal enquiry about changes in the seasons over time.

Located within a context of a 'time capsule', on a weekly basis Fahim worked with small groups of children to create 'evidence bags' for their time capsule. The contents varied from week to week and were guided by the children. Fahim sought to capture the children's observations of the school environment during different seasons. He used a range of methods including photos, paintings, drawings, annotated artefacts (for example, leaves and twigs) stuck on paper with labels, paper and written discussions.

At the end of the placement Fahim and the children opened the capsule and ordered the evidence bags from the beginning of the year to the end. The children discussed what they had observed. Through this simple but clever activity Fahim was able to encourage children to observe the characteristics of the seasons.

After this, Fahim and the children discussed the four different seasons' features. Using four large labelled hoops, Fahim and the children sorted the evidence bags into Spring, Summer, Autumn and Winter groups. Here Fahim has begun to introduce the process of classification on a simple level.

Rocks

A significant proportion of the Earth's mass is formed out of rocks. There are many different types of rocks providing a great variety of tone, texture, shape and size. Rocks can be taught in an interesting way that captures the interest of young children. Rocks are all around us. They are in the buildings where we live, work and play. They are found at the beach, in the country and around the town. They are used to commemorate events, such as in the use of granite for gravestones, to celebrate, for example in the use of malachite in the FIFA World Cup trophy, as well as to decorate, for example to create opulent effects as is the case with marble. Using our environment to explore rocks *in situ* can provide a wonderful starting point for learning. When children observe, draw, touch and wax-rub the rocks in their local environment they are immediately hooked and want to find out more about these rocks.

The three types of rock

There are three distinct groups of rock: igneous, sedimentary and metamorphic. Each has its own distinct characteristics that help us to sort and classify them.

Igneous rocks

Igneous rocks are created when molten rock cools and solidifies. Rock under the Earth's surface can be exposed to significant pressure and temperatures. Molten rock known as magma can make its way to the Earth's surface and can erupt from volcanoes forced upwards as a result of high pressure below. Magma can cool above or below the Earth's surface. Where the solidification of magma takes place determines the type of rock that is formed. When magma is allowed to cool slowly under the Earth's surface, crystals can form and a coarse igneous rock is created. When the magma cools nearer to the Earth's surface the crystals are often smaller and a finer-grained rock is produced.

Sedimentary rocks

Sedimentary rocks are created on the Earth's surface. They are formed from fragments of rocks that have broken away by wind or rain to create dust. This often finds itself being taken down a river or stream creating a silt layer at the bottom of the river or stream bed. In addition plant and animal materials as well as minerals combine with the rock fragments to make the sedimentary rocks. Sedimentary rocks are formed over thousands of years. As layer upon layer is built up so the pressure on the sediment below increases, pushing the sediment together and creating the rock. Over time the river or stream may disappear and the sediment that has built up in layers over the years and has been placed under pressure is now part of a sedimentary rock. The layers of matter often produce distinct layers that are still visible in the rock.

Metamorphic rocks

Metamorphic rocks are a combination of both igneous and sedimentary rocks. When these rocks are subjected to great pressure and intense heat they can come together to form a new rock. Metamorphism is the process of creating a denser more compact rock out of the two other types of rock.

How fossils are made

Fossils can be formed in a few ways. One of the most common ways is connected to the formation of rocks. When plants or animals die they can fall to the ground and get covered by sediment. If the plant or animal dies near to a body of water the animal or plant can form a layer in the rock which is quickly covered by other layers of sediment. Over several thousands of years the landscape changes and where water once was it may have disappeared. If this happens the rock is exposed and can be broken up by the elements. As rocks are broken up by natural or artificial means they can reveal their hidden treasures: layers of animals and plants that tell us about the planet's historic past.

Soils

Soil is a natural mixture made from broken-down rocks and minerals, and decayed leaf litter. This soil can have been mixed for thousands of years by special mini-beasts. There are distinct layers that go to make up soil. Each layer is known as a horizon and has particular characteristics that help us to differentiate it from the other layers.

Horizon O – is the top layer. This layer is made from living and decomposed materials such as leaf litter. This layer is fairly thin and dark in colour.

Horizon A – is located just below horizon O. This layer is also made from decomposed matter. In this layer many plants take root. This layer is more commonly referred to as the topsoil.

Horizon B – is often referred to as the subsoil. This layer has less organic matter in it and has a high proportion of clay and mineral deposits. This layer is lighter in colour than the layers above.

Horizon C – This layer mostly consists of unbroken rock. An alternative name for this layer is the regolith, which comes from two root Greek words that mean blanket and rock.

Activity: Soil samples

Children should be encouraged to take soil samples and observe and identify the different layers. Using simple metal piping hammered into the ground, pulling these up and pushing the contents out with a wooden dowel is fairly accessible even for schools on the tightest of budgets. Alternatively, children could construct soil profiles representing each of the layers, regardless of the composition of the soil in the school grounds.

Try this activity for yourself.

How many different layers can you identify in your soil sample?

What problems did you encounter?

How might these be planned for when carrying out similar work with children?

Self-assessment questions

1. List the eight planets starting with the planet closest to the Sun.
2. Why is it important for children to appreciate the scale of the planets in relation to the Sun?
3. What are the different phases of the Moon and what happens to make them occur?
4. How do we get the four different seasons?
5. What are the different types of rocks and how are they formed?

Further reading

Howe, A., Davis, D., McMahon, K., Towler, L. and Scott, T. (2006) *Science 5–11: A guide for teachers*. Chapter 7 'The Earth and Beyond'. London: David Fulton.

Peacock, G., Sharp, J., Johnsey, R. and Wright, D. (2009) *Primary science: Knowledge and understanding*, 6th edition. Chapter 13 'The earth and beyond'. London: Learning Matters SAGE.

References

Bryce, G. K. and Blown E. J. (2013) Children's concepts of the shape and size of the Earth, Sun and Moon. *International Journal of Science Education*, 35(3): 388–446.

Sharp, J. and Sharp, J. (2007) Beyond shape and gravity: Children's ideas about the Earth in space reconsidered. *Research Papers in Education*, 22(3): 363–401.

10 Light, sound and electricity

Learning outcomes

By reading this chapter you will develop:

- an awareness of the properties of light, sound and electricity;
- an understanding of effective pedagogic strategies for teaching about light, sound and electricity.

Teachers' Standards

1. **Set high expectations which inspire, motivate and challenge pupils**
- set goals that stretch and challenge pupils of all backgrounds, abilities and dispositions.
2. **Demonstrate good science subject and curriculum knowledge**
- have a secure knowledge of science and the science curriculum, foster and maintain pupils' interest in the subject, and address misunderstandings.
3. **Plan and teach well-structured lessons**
- promote a love of learning and children's intellectual curiosity.

Key scientific concepts

- How sound and light travel

- How we see

- Seeing and materials and their properties

- Reflection and refraction

- Sound insulation

- Frequency and pitch

- Amplitude and volume

- Electrical symbols

- How electricity flows

- Creating circuits

Introduction

Energy is all around us and is involved in everything we as humans do. Energy takes many forms. It is important to note that energy is never created, nor destroyed; it is merely transferred. All energy finds its origins in the formation of the Earth. Since this time energy has been transferred from one form to another.

These transfers are rarely perfect. For example, when turning on the light in a room you are turning electrical energy into light energy. If you touch the light you can feel that it is hot and sometimes you can hear a faint buzzing sound. During this transfer, although the greatest amount of energy transferred is in the form of light, small amounts of heat and sound, which are also forms of energy, also result.

What is light?

Light is a form of energy and originates from both natural and artificial sources. The form of light we are often familiar with is the light we can see. This is known as visible light. Visible light forms only a small part of the electromagnetic spectrum. The electromagnetic spectrum is made up of various types of light waves. Figure 10.1 shows the entire spectrum.

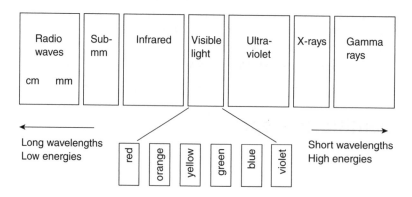

Figure 10.1 The electromagnetic spectrum

Each type of light is made of little bits of energy known as photons. Most photons are produced when atoms within an object begin to heat up. The heat excites the electrons inside atoms and they gain extra energy. This energy is released as a photon. When an object is increasingly heated the amount of photons released is also increased. What objects can you think of that are heated and release photons thus producing light?

Research focus: White light, a spectrum of visible colours

In 1665 an Italian Jesuit named Francesco Maria Grimaldi conducted a simple investigation. Grimaldi allowed light to enter a room through a small aperture and travel onto a screen. He made predictions regarding the size of the projected images. He was surprised when he discovered that the projections were larger than he expected. He was even more surprised to discover that the light was no longer white but was split into two or three colours. Grimaldi named his new discovery diffraction.

Inspired by this discovery, in 1662 Newton undertook an experiment in which he passed sunlight through a prism. He observed that the light split into different coloured beams. He realised that white light must therefore consist of different rays each having their own different colour. Newton also perceived that white light can be separated because each of the different colours can be deviated from each other as they each have different rates of travel. Newton believed that light was made up of different particles and it was these that were changed when passed through a prism.

Dutch mathematician Huygens in 1678, however, disproved Newton's particle theory. By looking at the laws of reflection and refraction he was able to support his thinking that light moved in waves.

Curriculum links

Light is a topic that formed part of the science National Curriculum at Key Stage 1 from 1989 onwards. The fact that it no longer appears in Key Stage 1 in the new curriculum is short-sighted. Building on their experiences of light in the EYFS for many years, Year 1 children have thoroughly enjoyed activities such as playing with torches, shining torches on shiny things and dull things, making comparisons between these, putting layers of different materials over the torch to see if they can still see the light, not forgetting looking at images in shiny spoons and themselves in mirrors, including mirrors that distort the images. The loss of light as a topic for study at Key Stage 1 is a tragedy.

In the 2014 National Curriculum, light is a topic that is explored in both lower and upper Key Stage 2. Pupils in lower Key Stage 2 should be taught that they need light in order to see things and that dark is the absence of light. They should notice that light is reflected from surfaces, that light from the Sun can be dangerous and that there are ways to protect their eyes. In terms of shadows, pupils should recognise that shadows are formed when the light from a source is blocked by a solid object. They should find patterns in the way that the size of a shadow changes.

Children should be encouraged to explore the properties of light, sources of light, what light makes possible and what happens when lights are not around. In upper Key Stage 2 children should explore how light travels and how light helps us to see. They should recognise that light appears to travel in straight lines and use this idea to explain that objects are seen because they give out or reflect light into the eye. Pupils should also be able to explain that we see things because light travels from light sources to our eyes or from light sources to objects and then to our eyes. Within both phases in Key Stage 2, pupils should discover what happens when light is blocked and how shadows are formed, with upper Key Stage 2 pupils using the idea that light travels in straight lines to explain why shadows have the same shape as the objects cast on them.

Travelling light

Light is incredible. How it travels is nothing short of amazing. Light waves travel in straight lines. Unlike sound waves, light waves do not need to travel through matter or material. Light can travel through a vacuum. Light is the fastest form of energy, travelling at a speed of approximately 186,000 miles per second. A significant consequence of this is that we often see something before we can hear it. A good example of this is exploding fireworks. We can see the great splashes of colour exploding in the sky before we hear the almighty bang. Light is measured in lux, which is the measurement of the intensity of the light when it hits or passes through an object. A lumen is a single unit of measurement that describes how bright a source is. The Sun provides a greater illumination than a firework so it will have a greater lux measurement.

How we see

The human eye plays a pivotal role in sight. Light rays bounce off, or more accurately, are reflected by an object and enter the eye via the pupil. The pupil is a hole that appears black. It is black because the light passes straight through it. Around the pupil there is a circle of muscle that controls the pupil's size; the darker the setting the larger the pupil, the lighter the setting the smaller the pupil. This response occurs in order to protect the nerve cells located at the back of the eye.

Light has to enter the pupil in order that we can see. The light entering the eye gets bent slightly. The bent light rays meet and focus upon the retina. To ensure that the image received is as defined and as focused as possible the lens changes shape. Muscles that surround the lens assist it to widen in order that we can see objects that are further away and to contract in order that we may see objects that are close by. This phenomenon can be observed quite easily.

Our eye converts the light into millions upon millions of impulses that are sent to different parts of the brain via the nerves. The brain co-ordinates the messages from the impulses to provide the meticulous images that we see.

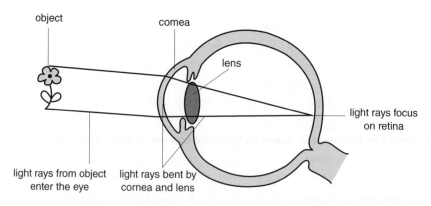

Figure 10.2 The human eye

The light sensitive cells found within the retina are known as rods and cones. There are three different types of cone cells with each one being responsive to red, blue or green light. When these cells fire off their impulses to the brain, the brain is able to combine them which enables us to see all of the colours of the rainbow. The amazing thing is that the image that is formed on the retina is actually inverted and it is the brain that corrects this so that we see the right way up.

Reflection and refraction

When light travelling in straight lines comes into contact with a surface, it can be bounced back or reflected. When light comes into contact with rough surfaces, the light is scattered and bounces in all directions. When light hits smooth and flat surfaces, it bounces back or is reflected back at an angle equal to the angle at which it hit the surface.

Light and colour

Light is a form of energy. Most of the light on our planet comes from the Sun. Light comes from other places too – electric lights, candle flames and even some types of animals.

Lines and Shadows

Light always travels in a straight line. If light hits an object that is opaque, it can only shine past it, not around it. This makes a shadow where the light cannot reach.

Light shines in straight lines. Shadows happen because rays of light cannot bend around objects.

Light can turn a corner if it reflects (bounces) off a surface, such as a mirror.

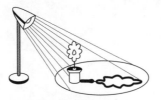

You can make light turn a corner. If you shine a lamp or torch at a mirror, the light will bounce off it.

The speed of light

When you flick a light switch, light seems to fill the room instantly. This is because light travels very fast.

It takes eight minutes for light to travel from the Sun to the Earth.

Figure 10.3 Diagrams to show light being reflected and scattered

The angle at which the light hits the object is known as the angle of incidence. The angle at which the light returns is referred to as the angle of reflection. Objects like mirrors are made from materials that are exceptionally smooth and flat. They reflect light in a way that enables us to see ourselves in them.

Refraction is simply a term associated with the bending of light. The rate at which light travels depends on what material it is travelling through. When light travels from one transparent material to another, such as when it travels through air then water, the light wave is slowed down and the light wave bends.

Case study: Observing light

Hamish, a School Direct student, wanted to help his Year 4 class explore some of the properties of light using everyday materials. Before the children arrived at school he spent the early morning setting up several observational scenarios. The first scenario involved plastic food pots containing different coloured water with a tea light behind set on a large piece of white paper.

Figure 10.4   Food pots containing coloured water with tea light behind

When the children observed this scenario they were able to ask questions around the properties of light and how we see colour.

The second scenario was similar, but this time the pots contained different liquids including water, vegetable oil, baby oil, treacle, malt vinegar, distilled vinegar and bubble bath.

Figure 10.5 Light travelling through liquids of different viscosity

Here the children saw the impact of transparent, translucent and opaque materials on the travelling of light.

The next scenario involved lots of plastic food pots full of water. These were placed clustered around a tea light at various points from the light source.

Figure 10.6 Light refracted through liquids

The children were encouraged to explore and play with the pots. As they moved the pots they observed how the light was bent and focused into clear rays of light. The children were seeing refraction at first hand.

Finally the children were given a large sweet tin one-third full of sand with a candle placed on top. Initially, children were encouraged to make observations. Next, the children placed flat mirrors around the edge of the tin and again made lists of observations. The final stage involved the children placing a further row of concave mirrors in the tin and recording observations.

Figure 10.7   Light reflected off smooth shiny surfaces

The children observed the phenomenon of reflection in different settings. Hamish asked the children to collate observations and use them to generate questions that could be a starting point for an observation. Hamish collected the children's questions in and used them when creating his medium-term plan. Each week the children worked together to try to answer a question raised by the class. In these sessions the child who asked the original question was invited to sit in the teacher's chair while the rest of the children reported back the findings they had gathered during their work in small groups.

Case study: Year 3 children exploring light

Leanne, Becca and Matt, three third year undergraduate students, were working with a Year 3 class in a challenging school for a morning. Their brief was to engage children with activities starting with a stimulus and to encourage them to raise questions that they could then investigate. This short period of time allowed the students to experience teaching in a way that they had not been able to before.

Immediately after the experience Becca said that she had:

> mainly learned that a science teacher should approach investigative science with key questions and possible investigations already in mind so that you could maybe guide the children if they seem unsure where to begin with designing their own investigation following observation of a stimulus. I found it hard to help pupils explain why they had certain ideas They sometimes said things that they knew or thought they knew and could not take the idea any further. It was then difficult to design investigations to combat these.

All three students learned much from this experience that they then applied in their final teaching placement. After final practice, Leanne said:

> The experience had a positive impact on my final practice as it enabled me to teach science more confidently and to feel more secure in the understanding of how I could captivate the children's interest by beginning with a stimulus. Building on this, I then used assessment to establish what the children's next steps could be. This led to a focus on the planning process of an investigation as the children were not secure in their understanding of this and therefore could not get the most from the activities.

Shadows

We have established that light waves travel in straight lines. Transparent materials such as glass allow light to travel through them. Materials such as tissue paper or 'frosted' glass allow some through; however, this light gets diffused and is scattered. These materials are known as translucent. Finally, opaque materials such as bricks block light and do not allow light to pass through them. Light travelling in straight lines cannot bend round opaque objects to find alternative routes. When the light is blocked a shadow is formed. Darkness is the absence of light.

What is sound?

Sound is all around us. We experience it most of the time in our everyday lives. Through sound we can identify the difference between a moving motorbike, car or lorry. All sounds are made through the vibrations caused when an object moves. This means that sound cannot only be experienced by the sense of touch but sometimes also through sight. One good example of this is when a struck tuning fork comes into contact with a water surface. Ripples spread out from the source of the vibration in a circular pattern and splashes often result due to the vibrations of the moving prongs of the fork.

We know that sound is created by objects vibrating; this means we can also often feel sounds as we can hear the vibrations. This was crucial for the classical composer Ludwig van Beethoven. At the age of 28 he began to lose his ability to hear. To combat this he allegedly sawed the legs off each of his four pianos so the bases were flat on the floor. He would sit on the floor and use the vibrations that were produced when he played which were magnified by travel through the floor before they reached him. This assisted him in his composition. Exploring similar experiences to this can prove to be powerful for young children today. Children can lie down on school floors with large speakers placed on them. They will be able to feel the vibrations and make the links to the sounds. Similarly, observing how rice behaves when on the surface of a drum when beaten demonstrates clearly the movement of the skin and therefore shows the vibrations to young children.

Constant sounds are the result of an object vibrating back and forth. When it moves it pushes the air around it. When the object moves forwards it squashes and compresses the air in front of it. When it moves backwards it creates space for the air to spread out. This movement creates a wave which moves in a column fashion towards the ear.

Figure 10.8 A sound wave

A sound wave moves very differently from the way light moves. Unlike light, sound energy passes through materials from particle to particle. Sound waves are also different to light in that sound waves need to be transported through a medium. Although sound cannot pass through a vacuum because there are no particles for the sound to pass its energy through, sounds can pass through gases, liquids and solids. The image above is a representation of how sound waves move. The rings are pulses of air particles that are pushed forward by the vibrating speaker. Below you can see young children experiencing the vibration and pushing of the air. An airzooka is a great tool to help children feel the way that sound waves work.

Figure 10.9   Children investigating sound waves

Sound travels faster through solids than liquids or gases and sounds can be magnified in water.

Activity

Plan a simple activity to compare the rate at which sounds travel through materials. Don't forget to include solids, liquids and gases.

What conclusion do you come to?

Can you explain your findings?

There are lots of different sounds around us. Sounds can be high. Sounds can be low. Sounds can be loud. Sounds can be quiet. The pitch of a sound, whether it is high or low, depends on the frequency of the sound waves. High-pitched sounds have a high frequency. Low-pitched sounds have a low frequency. Frequency is measured in hertz (Hz) and refers to the number of sound waves per second.

A vernacular misconception often heard when teaching sound is the use of the word volume as the output that is measured. When increasing the loudness of a sound using a remote control, the button is often labelled as volume. Volume, however, is what is measured when seeking to ascertain the capacity of an object. Unfortunately, the capacity of a television does not increase no matter what button is pressed! Amplitude is the correct term to use here. A wave's amplitude can increase and decrease. Amplitude refers to the size of the sound wave and is measured in decibels (dB). Getting children to explore frequency and amplitude through expressive drawing can be very helpful. Playing music which has a variation in terms of frequency or amplitude and asking children to record this provides a non-threatening set of data for children to explore and analyse. Often these drawings can be really useful in highlighting the properties associated with frequency and pitch.

Activity

Take yourself on a sound walk. Stop every five minutes and make a list of observations. You could download sound measuring apps, for example decibel and hertz meter apps, on your smart phone or tablet device.

What do you notice?

What is makes loud sounds?

What makes high-pitched sounds?

What stops you from hearing objects that you can see moving/vibrating?

Turn your observations into questions and seek to use secondary sources to obtain answers.

Case study: The sound garden

Arjinder, a final year part-time undergraduate programme student, was at the same time employed on a part-time basis as a teacher's assistant in a three-form entry infant school. He had a passion for working with children outside the classroom and had read about schools which had used their grounds to teach primary science effectively, such as internationally renowned Coombes C of E Primary School.

Arjinder asked his pupils to bring in from home items that could be reused or recycled. The children worked together to create sound mobiles. The children were tasked to make a mobile that made high sounds and another mobile that made low sounds. The mobiles were hung in the trees in the school grounds. Once hung the children went on a mini-exploration to find the different mobiles. In pairs the children used 'easi-speak' recorders to record the sounds they could hear. The children were also asked to describe what they heard. When the children returned from their exploration to the classroom they were asked to share their observations. The children were able to identify the properties of objects that make high sounds and objects that make low sounds.

Curriculum links

Although sound is explored predominantly in lower and upper Key Stage 2, children are asked to explore the properties of materials in Key Stage 1. One property of a material is the noise it makes when hit or struck. Exploring the sounds that materials make may lead to looking at further properties such as how hard, rough or smooth they are.

In lower Key Stage 2, pupils need to be able to identify how sounds are made, making the link with vibrations. They need to recognise that vibrations from sounds travel through a medium to the ear. They should find patterns between the pitch of a sound and features of the object that produced it and also patterns between the volume of a sound and the strength of the vibrations that produced it. They also should recognise that sounds get fainter as the distance from the sound source increases. With thought, there is a lot of potential for children to work scientifically exploring these patterns through scientific enquiry.

Activity

Look at the National Curriculum requirement for children to find:

- patterns between the pitch of a sound and the features of the sound that produced it;

- patterns between the volume of a sound and the strength of the vibrations that produced it;

- that sounds get fainter as the distance from the sound source increases.

With a colleague, think about how these relationships can be investigated by children in upper Key Stage 2. What sorts of resources might they need to carry out these pattern-finding scientific investigations?

What is electricity?

Electricity can be a tricky topic to teach to young children as it cannot be seen. We are therefore reliant on observing its effects and supporting children's understanding through the use of models. Electricity is a flowing energy that is formed of charged particles. The way in which the particles are charged enables them to either attract or repel each other. Electrical charge is either positive or negative. Particles can be positive or negative or not charged at all. When a particle has no charge we refer to the particle being neutral. Charged particles have an electric field around them. The field around a positive particle repels other positive particles, very like the same poles of a magnet repelling each other, and attracts negatively charged particles.

Have you ever felt the effects of static electricity when rubbing a balloon or heard a crackling when taking off a knitted jumper? Static electricity is a really helpful way to demonstrate the two types of electrical charge. The word static means to stay. Static electricity occurs when two insulating materials such as wool and acrylic rub together. The friction of the rubbing results in some of the negative electrons from one of the materials being removed. This material is now positively charged. The negative electrons join the other material and it becomes negatively charged. Now that they are charged in opposite ways they will attract each other. The build-up of negative and positive charges can only last for a limited period of time. The charges will seek to neutralise each other. Electrons will flow between the materials to once again establish a balance of charges. When this happens we can experience the shock effect.

In electrical currents charged particles flow. Electrical circuits are made up of lots of different components. In order for an electrical current to flow within these components they need to have charged particles within them. A source of energy that can produce an electronic field is required to make a current flow. The power source provides the energy for the electrons that are present within the circuit's components, for example the wire, to move in a desired direction.

Children are often asked to construct simple circuits within the primary phase. For example, a nice way to start a topic on electricity is to ask children to try to light a bulb with a single wire and cell. To support this it is important that resources are well organised and accessible. One way of ensuring easy accessibility is to use small, cheap tool boxes in order that the various components are nicely set out and easy to access, as seen in Figure 10.10.

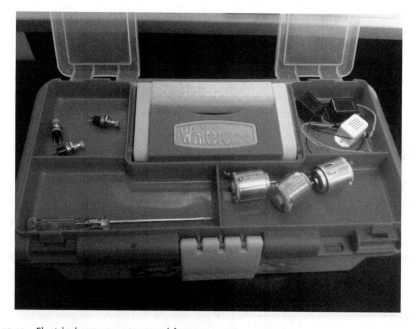

Figure 10.10   Electrical components stored for easy use

Establishing a secure understanding of current is essential. In common circuits where metal wires are used, the current flows from the negative terminal to the positive terminal. Current is the measure of the rate of flow of electricity. Current is measured in amps and is the number of flowing electrons carrying the charge per second. The measure associated with the amount of energy pushing electrons through the wire is known as the voltage. The voltage of a cell, commonly called a battery, for example, refers to the amount of energy it can supply to a circuit.

Electrical components

Components can be added into an electrical circuit. Look at the vocabulary in Table 10.1. Consider what the function of each of these components is within a circuit.

Table 10.1

Wire	Cell/battery	Switch
Bulb	Buzzer	Motor

Each different component has its own symbol. Symbols are especially helpful for creating circuit diagrams. Having knowledge of what each symbol looks like can also assist understanding of the properties of the different components. In particular, children often misuse the term 'battery' when they are in fact referring to a cell. When looking at the symbol for a battery you can clearly see that a battery consists of two or more cells.

Table 10.2

Component	Symbol
Wire	—
Cell	⊣⊢
Battery	⊣⊦⊢
Switch	⌒o o⌒
Lamp	⊗
Bulb	⊖
Buzzer	⊓
Motor	(M)
Resistor	▭

Components each have a specific role to play in a circuit. Each can have an impact on the way the current flows and how the energy is used. For example, bulbs transfer some of the electrical energy into other forms of energy including light and heat. When a component such as a light bulb is added into a circuit the current experiences a level of resistance. We can use models to help teach this concept. The photo in Figure 10.11 shows a group of students holding onto a rope loosely and passing the rope round in an anti-clockwise motion simulating the flow of the current. The tutor placed component hats on students one at a time. The students were instructed that when they had the hat on they needed to hold onto the rope with a tighter grip. By adding several components in the students were able to experience resistance.

Figure 10.11   Students passing a rope round a circuit to experience 'resistance'

Care needs to be taken when using models such as these. Misconceptions can easily be generated when we are trying to represent or recreate a phenomenon using other materials. For example, it may be that after experiencing this model children misconceive that it is the wire and not the current that flows round in a current.

There are two key types of circuits that children might come across or construct. The first is a series circuit (see Figure 10.12). A series circuit consists of a single loop joining different components together. Figure 10.12 also shows the impact of adding several components into a series circuit.

When a component is added the current experiences some resistance. The greater the number of components added the greater the resistance. Additionally, if one of the

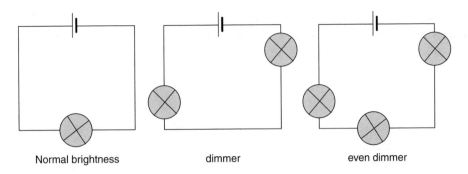

| Normal brightness | dimmer | even dimmer |

Figure 10.12 A series circuit

components in a series circuit breaks, the circuit will be disconnected and all of the components will stop working. This will also happen if components are connected with too high a voltage battery. In this case, one or more of the components is likely to 'blow'. Care needs to be taken not to use high voltage batteries with too low voltage bulbs as this not only can prove to be expensive in terms of replacement bulbs, but is also very frustrating.

The second type of circuit children might make is called a parallel circuit. This has the advantage that the circuit consists of a number of separate branches rather than one continuous circuit. Parallel circuits 'spread out' the total resistance and allow components in one branch to continue working when one in another stops working.

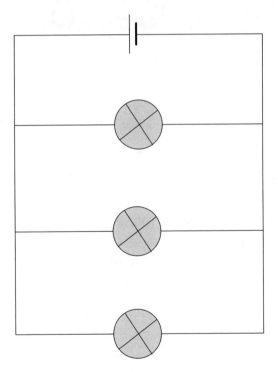

Figure 10.13 A parallel circuit

The parallel circuit creates multiple pathways for the current to travel, reducing the resistance experienced. This is extremely beneficial as it enables the components to work at optimum levels of efficiency.

Activity

To elicit children's understanding of circuits and currents, exploring scenario circuits can be useful. Six different circuits are shown in Figure 10.14. Look at them and try to identify what may be wrong and why they may not work.

Figure 10.14   Photo of electrical circuits

Consider:

What would be the benefits of using similar activities with your children?

How could you record your thinking when engaged in observation activities like this?

Case study: The dolls' house

Kathryn, a full-time PGCE student, was working with children in Year 5. Her topic for exploration was electricity and, in particular, making series and parallel circuits to challenge her more able children. Kathryn was keen to set her teaching within a practical context. She explored the use of circuits within the home. Her children carried out a range of investigations relating to the two different types of circuit.

Wanting to assess the children's understanding of series and parallel circuits, Kathryn worked with the children in focus groups. The children were tasked with making a dolls' house for the Reception class. Kathryn gave the children a list of essential features that ensured that the children would have to construct series and parallel circuits. The children were asked to make paper plans in which they had to use the symbols. They were then allowed to construct the dolls' houses. During each stage of the activity Kathryn recorded what was said and used an observational schedule to help provide a focus to her assessment. Working with the small groups Kathryn was able to hear the children's justifications and choices. She therefore had a clearer insight into what level the children were working at.

Curriculum links

Electricity appears in the 2014 National Curriculum in upper Key Stage 2 when pupils should compare the electrical conductivity of materials in relation to the properties of materials. Following this they should be taught to associate the brightness of a lamp or the volume of a buzzer with the number and voltage of cells used in a circuit. They should compare and give reasons for variations in how components function, including the brightness of the bulbs, the loudness of buzzers and the on/off position of switches. The final requirement is to use recognised symbols for representing a simple circuit in a diagram.

The non-statutory notes suggest that upper Key Stage 2 children should construct simple series circuits to help them to answer questions about what happens when they try different components, for example switches, bulbs, buzzers and motors. They should learn how to represent a simple circuit using recognised symbols. They are not required, at this stage, to learn about parallel circuits.

Research focus

Glauert (2009) undertook a small-scale study with children between the ages of five and six. The children were shown circuits and asked to predict whether the circuits would work and explain their answer. The children were given time to explore and make their own circuits.

Glauert's (2009) findings seem to suggest that:

- concepts such as electricity can be introduced to young children before statutory documentation requires it to be done;

- it is important for Early Years practitioners not to underestimate young children's scientific capabilities;

- when asked, young children can offer views not too unlike those provided by slightly older children or adults;

→

- young children are capable of engaging in a wide range of forms of reasoning;

- teachers need to ensure that they capitalise on young children's capabilities and should not be restricted by narrow frameworks and curricula;

- it is important to use a range of approaches to assessment of young children in science in order that a full and true picture of their knowledge, understanding and skill is established;

- practitioners in Early Years settings need to go beyond mere observation of behaviours and talk and need to get children to explain their thoughts and actions.

Activity

Think about the above case study.

Why may some teachers not wish to introduce topics such as electricity to young children?

Why is there a traditional focus on observation and explanation within Early Years documentation? Is this stance fully justified? Does this lead to a narrow view of young children's capabilities in science at an early age?

Self-assessment questions

1. What is light?
2. How does light travel?
3. How do we see?
4. What is sound?
5. How does sound travel?
6. What is electricity?
7. How do circuits work?
8. What is a battery?

Further reading

Brunton, P. and Thornton, L. (2010) *Science in the Early Years: Building firm foundations from birth to five.* Chapter 10 'Electricity'. London: SAGE.

Brunton, P. and Thornton, L. (2010) *Science in the Early Years: Building firm foundations from birth to five.* Chapter 11 'Sound'. London: SAGE.

Brunton, P. and Thornton, L. (2010) *Science in the Early Years: Building firm foundations from birth to five.* Chapter 12 'Light, colour and shadow'. London: SAGE.

Roden, J., Ward, H. and Ritchie, H. (2007) *Extending knowledge in practice: Primary science.* Chapter 11 'Electricity'. London: Learning Matters SAGE.

Roden, J. Ward, H. and Ritchie H. (2007) *Extending knowledge in practice: Primary science.* Chapter 13 'Light'. London: Learning Matters SAGE.

Roden, J. Ward, H. and Ritchie H. (2007) *Extending knowledge in practice: Primary science.* Chapter 14 'Sound'. London: Learning Matters SAGE.

References

Glauert, E. Bo. (2009) How young children understand electric circuits: Prediction, explanation and exploration. *International Journal of Science Education*, 31(8): 1025–47.

Appendix 1: Model answers to self-assessment questions

Chapter 1 – Working scientifically

1. **What is science?**

A body of knowledge and a way of working.

2. **What are the process skills?**

There is no definitive list. However, this chapter has looked at:

- questioning;
- observation;
- hypothesis and prediction;
- recording, classifying and presenting;
- concluding and evaluating.

3. **What are the different types of investigation that are seen in the primary phase?**

The different types of investigation that this chapter has looked at are:

- classifying and identifying;
- fair testing;
- pattern seeking;
- investigating models;
- exploring;
- making things.

Chapter 2 – Plants

1. **What will your approach be to teaching about plants both in the inside and outside environments? Can you explain why you will adopt this approach?**

Although there are numerous ways to answer this question, a model answer should include the following aspects where children are:

- active learners, being given opportunities for both 'hands-on' and 'minds-on' activities;

- involved in exploration, observation, raising questions, collecting data and involving the use of the other science process skills;

- able to identify plants using keys and other methods? including pictures of trees and other plants;

- given some ownership over their learning.

2. **What are the main points of learning about plants that are important for your age group of children?**

The answer to this question depends upon which age-range you are teaching. Match your answer to the National Programme of Study for your year group, for example EYFS, NC Key Stage 1, NC Lower Key Stage 2 or NC Upper Key Stage 2.

3. **How will this translate into practice in your classroom?**

Look back at the subject knowledge that underpins the teaching of this topic.

1. **Make a quick sketch of the parts of a plant.**

2. **Explain what the roots are for.**

Roots of a plant take in water and mineral salts which pass up the stem to the rest of the plant. Water passes into the root hairs from water around them by osmosis.

3. **Explain why flowering plants have flowers.**

Flowering plants have flowers which are the plant's reproductive system. They carry out sexual reproduction and make sex cells.

4. **Explain the role of the stem.**

Stems transport water from the roots through xylem vessels which is similar to water being sucked through a straw. Stems allow for a continuous flow of water from the roots to the leaves. This is called the transpiration stream.

5. **Explain why a plant has seeds or fruits.**

Seeds and fruits are formed following sexual fertilisation in the flower. Seeds, which are often contained inside a fruit, eventually grow into a new plant.

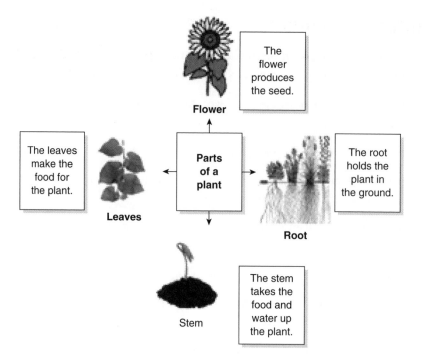

Picture of a plant

6. **Explain how fertilisation occurs in flowering plants.**

Fertilisation in a flowering plant happens when a pollen nucleus joins with an egg nucleus to make a seed.

7. **What do corms, seeds and bulbs all have in common?**

Corms, seeds and bulbs are the storage organs essential for the growth of new plants. They contain stored food that is used by the new plant as it starts to develop until leaves are formed.

8. **Explain the conditions needed for germination.**

Germination will only occur when conditions are right. Germination occurs when the embryo begins to grow. The three conditions for germination are:

- water to allow the seed to swell and burst open;

- oxygen for respiration;

- warmth.

The way that this translates into practice in your classroom should involve a match between your answers to 1 and 2 above.

Chapter 3 – Animals including humans: the parts of the body, the senses, teeth, nutrition and the digestive system

1. **Name the main parts of the body associated with the digestive system. What function does each part perform?**

The main parts of the body associated with the digestive system are the mouth, gullet (oesophagus), stomach, small intestine and large intestine. They perform the following functions.

- Mouth – food is chewed and mixed with saliva in the mouth.

- Gullet – the gullet squeezes the food to push it along through the digestive system.

- Stomach – the stomach contains digestive juices and hydrochloric acid that start to make food ready to be digested. The muscles in the stomach make sure that the mashed food is mixed up with the digestive juices.

- Small intestine – the small intestine slowly squeezes the digested food along towards the large intestine, absorbing digested food through its wall into the blood.

- Large intestine – when food reaches the large intestine there is very little left. Water is absorbed into the blood leaving solid waste products that are stored in the rectum ready for ejection from the body.

2. **Name the different kinds of teeth found in the human body. Explain the difference in shape and the function of each in preparing food for digestion.**

There are three different types of teeth found in the human body:

- incisors – chisel shaped for biting and cutting;

- canines – pointed for piercing and tearing;

- premolars – have uneven 'cusps' for grinding and chewing;

- molars – chew up food.

3. **In this chapter we have begun to explore potential cross-curricular links to support the teaching of humans and other animals. What other possible links can you identify? How might these be developed?**

There are a number of possible cross-curricular links to support the teaching of humans and other animals including hygiene and healthy eating. The important thing here is to remember that it is unwise to make too many cross-curricular links to other subjects because of the potential problem of losing the science focus.

Chapter 4 – Animals including humans: growth reproduction and the circulatory system

1. **What teaching and learning strategies will you employ in the teaching of this topic to avoid the filling in of worksheets or didactic teaching?**

Abstract topics like those in this chapter require a creative approach and the use of models, including role-play, if children are to understand better the aspects of science that are not able to be observed directly.

2. **How would you organise your class into groups for work of this kind to maximise the opportunities for learning of all children in your class?**

Grouping children for science is a very personal thing. Evidence suggests that pairs or groups of three are best for ensuring all children have a role in any practical work. Mixed ability and friendship groups are popular ways of grouping children for science, but ability groups might also be possible. Some teachers find grouping children by their ideas about particular concepts useful to challenge and progress their learning. Evidence suggests that boys and girls approach science in different ways, so all-boy and all-girl groups as well as mixed gender groups might be considered. You might also want to think about grouping your children differently from time to time to ensure that all children take different roles in group work.

3. **What differences are there in the support systems of a) simple animals like the amoeba b) invertebrates and c) vertebrates?**

a) Simple animals like the amoeba consist of one cell. The amoeba moves by changing the shape of its simple cell wall.

b) Invertebrates have an exoskeleton. An exoskeleton is like a suit of armour which protects and supports the body.

c) Vertebrates have an endoskeleton which is located inside the body.

4. **Explain how the bones and muscles work together to move a vertebrate around.**

The bones and muscles work together to move a vertebrate around. Muscles work by contracting and relaxing. They provide the force (pull) to move the bones at the joints.

5. **What are the main functions of the heart and circulation system?**

The main function of the heart is to pump and to continuously circulate blood around the body. Arteries carry blood away from the heart and veins carry blood to the heart. The blood transports essential materials such as oxygen to the parts of the body where it is needed. Blood also collects waste products such as CO_2 for excretion from the body.

Chapter 5 – Variety of life: the characteristics of living things, variation and classification

1. **What are the seven processes of living things?**

The seven processes of living things are:

- feeding – for energy and growth;

- respiration – the process whereby energy is extracted from food;

- movement – both plants and animals move, but in different ways; plants move as they grow towards the light and roots move down into the soil, while animals move their whole bodies;

- growth – all living things grow; plants grow all their lives, while animals stop growing when they become adult;

- excretion – all living things produce waste substances; excretion is the process by which waste products are removed from the body of plants and animals;

- sensitivity – living things react to things around them; plants move towards the light, while animals have sense organs;

- reproduction – all living things need to make new individuals like themselves; otherwise the type of animal or plant would die out.

2. **What misconceptions might you encounter when teaching this topic? How might you challenge these?**

Below are a range of misconceptions cited in other texts.

A. Only 25 per cent of 7 year olds and 60 per cent of 11 year olds consider humans to be animals. As humans do not have four legs, fur or make animal noises they are often not considered animals (Peacock et al., 2009, p24).

B. There are a number of conceptions relating to animal groups that are commonly held by children and many adults. For example, young children will often be confused because although it can fly, a bat is a mammal. Similarly, a penguin can be confusing because although it is a bird, it does not fly, and dolphins are often considered to be fish rather than mammals (Ward et al., 2005).

C. Children believe that humans are a distinct category and not an animal as animals do not have the same senses as humans (Guest, 2003).

D. Children are often confused with regards to the classification of animals. Dolphins are often considered to be fish rather than mammals and the difference between reptiles and amphibians is not always clear (Ward et al., 2008).

Such ideas can be challenged through observation, discussion, classification activities, research and in some instances via practical investigation.

3. What kind of keys can help children in their classification of living things?

Keys come in a number of styles. Some are based on systematic questions or provide a choice of statements to guide identification through observation. Children of all ages can use keys and older children should construct a key to help them to understand the process. Asking older children to construct a simple key for younger children can be particularly effective in progressing their learning about the variety of living things.

4. How would you use the outdoors to further your children's understanding of the characteristics of living things?

There are numerous ways that you could use the outdoors to further your children's understanding of the characteristics of living things. They include such activities as:

- magic spot activities - where children are asked to find a spot and engage one of their five senses;

- string trails – where children follow a coloured string and stop at various points;

- creating living things snap shots of living things (using a strip of card with double-sided sticky tape along its length. As living things are collected, they are stuck acrosss the card as a record);

- undertaking observational drawings of living things;

- placing time lapse cameras facing living things and sharing the recordings with children;

- installing pond and bird box cameras with live feeds to school websites for children to be able to access and observe at any point.

Chapter 6 – Habitats

1. Explain what you understand by the term 'habitat'.

A 'habitat' is a place where living organisms live. Habitats have the conditions that the inhabitants need to survive.

2. Give three examples of different habitats and explain the kinds of animals and plants that might be found in those habitats.

There are many different habitats which have different conditions for survival of the organisms that live there. There are many answers to this question: examples of habitats include dry walls, forests, deserts and polar regions.

3. **Using your answers to question 2 draw:**

- a simple food chain

- a food web

to show the feeding relationships within the organisms in your diagrams.

Your answers in 2 will determine your answers here. It is important to remember the difference between a food chain and a food web.

- Simple food chains show what eats what in a simple habitat. Arrows in the food chain indicate the direction of the energy and the arrow itself shows what is eaten by what.

- A food web is more complex than a food chain indicating that animals eat more than one thing. A food web consists of many food chains.

Chapter 7 – Everyday materials: their uses, properties and changes of materials

1. **What is a material?**

The term 'material' in science refers to any substance – solid, liquid or gas.

2. **What is a mixture?**

A mixture is a number of substances that are mixed together without reacting together in a chemical reaction.

3. **What are the different ways of separating a mixture?**

Mixtures can be separated physically by, for example, sieving, including filtering, and magnetic separation.

4. **Explain the differences between physical and chemical changes.**

Physical changes involve the result of the change of state of the same substance, for example melting ice or boiling water or the mixing of two or more substances that co-exist together, without taking part in a chemical reaction, such as when salt dissolves in water. Physical changes are reversible. Chemical changes are involved when two or more substances are mixed together and they undergo a chemical reaction. Chemical changes are usually not reversible and the substances produced during the reaction are very different from the initial materials in the mixture. The materials have been changed chemically.

5. **Give three examples of physical change.**

Examples of physical change include:

- salt dissolving in water;

- chocolate or ice melting;

- water or perfume evaporating;

- water boiling.

6. Give three examples of chemical change.

Examples of chemical change include:

- fruit ripening or rotting;

- sodium bicarbonate and citric acid in the presence of water;

- vinegar and sodium bicarbonate mixed together;

- an egg being poached or boiled;

- bread becoming toast;

- egg whites becoming meringue;

- placing sherbet on your tongue;

- metal objects rusting;

- the metabolism of food.

Chapter 8 – Forces

1. Explain what you understand by the term 'force'.

A 'force' is simply a push or a pull.

2. What do you understand by the terms:

- air resistance;

- friction;

- upthrust?

Examples of everyday forces:

- Air resistance is a force that involves air and any object moving through it in any direction, for example parachutes dropping to the ground or a ball kicked into the air.

- Friction is a force between two solid objects moving against each other, for example between the tyres of a car or bicycle and the road or between hands when they are rubbed together.

- Upthrust is a force that pushes upwards on an object that is placed in water. It makes an object in water feel lighter.

3. Explain the forces involved in moving a rowing boat through water.

The forces that are involved in moving a rowing boat through water are:

- the pull backwards on the oars by the rower;
- the push against the water by the oars;
- the resulting forward push of the boat through the water;
- the resulting drag of the boat through the water;
- the upward push of the water on the boat (upthrust);
- the weight of the boat acting downwards.

4. Where might you find pulleys in use in everyday life?

Pulleys are in use in everyday life in cranes, pile drivers and in simple lift systems.

5. Why is it important to set the teaching of ideas about scientific and technological applications in a real-life context?

On some occasions it is important to set the teaching of ideas about scientific and technological applications in a real-life context as this may help as a scaffold for new learning to be built upon. Sometimes the best context can be the science itself of an investigation. It does not always have to be an imagined context.

6. Think about your class or a class known to you and about everyday events and routines that regularly involve forces to move things or to keep them still. How could you reinforce some of the scientific ideas met within this chapter in your general teaching?

There are opportunities to reinforce the ideas of forces in everyday events and routines such as:

- opening and closing doors and cupboards;
- making a tricycle, bicycle or skateboard start or stop;
- placing a book on a table.

7. How could you plan to stretch your more able pupils in their learning about forces and their effects?

Planning to extend learning for more able pupils is a constant challenge. One way you could do this is to encourage your children to ask their own questions about forces and their effects and to use their questions as starting points for further work on the topic.

Chapter 9 – Earth, space and rocks

1. **List the eight planets starting with the closest to the Sun?**

The eight planets starting with the closest to the Sun are: Mercury, Venus, Earth, Mars, Jupiter, Saturn, Uranus and Neptune.

2. **Why is it important for children to appreciate the scale of the planets in relation to the Sun?**

It is important for children to appreciate the scale of the planets in relation to the Sun as this will help them to understand how the planets move due to the gravitational fields between the planets and the Sun.

3. **What are the different phases of the Moon and what happens to make them occur?**

The different phases of the Moon are:

- first quarter;

- waxing crescent;

- new moon;

- waning crescent;

- third quarter;

- waning gibbous;

- full moon;

- waxing gibbous.

The phases of the Moon occur because of the Moon's cyclical orbit around the Earth and the Earth and Moon's orbit around the Sun. At the different stages different amounts of light are reflected off the Moon's surface.

4. **How do we get the four different seasons?**

The explanation for the change in the seasons relates to the fact that the Earth tilts on its axis. As the Earth orbits the Sun, its tilted axis always points in the same direction. Over the course of the year different parts of the Earth's surface come into direct contact with the Sun's rays. At times it is the North Pole that tilts to face the Sun and this tilt reaches its height during June and at other times it is the South Pole's turn to tilt toward the Sun, normally reaching its height around December.

5. **What are the different types of rocks and how are they formed?**

There are three distinct groups of rocks: igneous, sedimentary and metamorphic. Igneous rocks are created when molten rock cools and solidifies. Sedimentary rocks are formed from fragments of rock that have been broken away from bigger rocks by the action of rain or wind and are deposited as sediment on the bottom of rivers, lakes and seas. Over time, the sediment becomes a sedimentary rock. Metamorphic rocks are formed when igneous and sedimentary rocks are subjected to great pressure and intense heat and come together to form a new metamorphic (changed) rock.

Chapter 10 – Light, sound and electricity

1. What is light?

Light is a form of energy. The light we can see is called visible light which forms only part of the electromagnetic spectrum.

2. How does light travel?

Light travels in straight lines.

3. How do we see?

Light rays bounce off an object and enter the eye via the pupil. This light gets bent slightly. The bent light rays meet and focus upon the retina. Our eye converts the light into millions upon millions of impulses that are sent to different parts of the brain via the nerves. The brain co-ordinates the messages from the impulses to provide the images that we see.

4. What is sound?

Sounds are made by objects vibrating.

5. How does sound travel?

Sounds travel in waves. Constant sounds are the result of an object vibrating back and forth. When it moves it nudges the air around it. When the object moves forwards it squashes and compacts the air in front of it. When it moves backwards it creates space for the air to spread out. This movement creates a wave which moves in a column fashion towards the ear.

6. What is electricity?

Electricity is a flowing energy that is formed of positively or negatively charged particles.

7. How do circuits work?

There are two key types of circuits: series and parallel. When a current passes through components in a series circuit, it experiences resistance to its flow. The greater the number of components added the greater the resistance experienced. Should one of the components break in a series circuit all of the components will stop working. Parallel circuits create multiple pathways for the current to travel, reducing the resistance experienced.

8. What is a battery?

Batteries consist of two or more cells placed together in a circuit.

References

Guest, G. (2003) *Alternative frameworks and misconceptions in primary science.* Available at: www.ase.org.uk (accessed 19/6/14).

Peacock, G., Sharp, J., Johnsey, R. and Wright, D. (2009) *Achieving QTS in primary science,* 4th edition. Exeter: Learning Matters.

Ward, H., Roden, J., Hewlett, C. and Foreman, J. (2005) *Teaching science in the primary classroom: A practical guide.* London: Paul Chapman Publishing.

Ward, H., Roden, J., Hewlett, C. and Foreman, J. (2008) *Teaching science in the primary classroom: A practical guide.* 2nd edition. London: SAGE.

Science programmes of study: key stages 1 and 2

National curriculum in England

September 2013

Contents

Purpose of study

A high-quality science education provides the foundations for understanding the world through the specific disciplines of biology, chemistry and physics. Science has changed our lives and is vital to the world's future prosperity, and all pupils should be taught essential aspects of the knowledge, methods, processes and uses of science. Through building up a body of key foundational knowledge and concepts, pupils should be encouraged to recognise the power of rational explanation and develop a sense of excitement and curiosity about natural phenomena. They should be encouraged to understand how science can be used to explain what is occurring, predict how things will behave, and analyse causes.

Aims

The national curriculum for science aims to ensure that all pupils:

- develop **scientific knowledge and conceptual understanding** through the specific disciplines of biology, chemistry and physics

- develop understanding of the **nature, processes and methods of science** through different types of science enquiries that help them to answer scientific questions about the world around them

- are equipped with the scientific knowledge required to understand the **uses and implications** of science, today and for the future.

Scientific knowledge and conceptual understanding

The programmes of study describe a sequence of knowledge and concepts. While it is important that pupils make progress, it is also vitally important that they develop secure understanding of each key block of knowledge and concepts in order to progress to the next stage. Insecure, superficial understanding will not allow genuine progression: pupils may struggle at key points of transition (such as between primary and secondary school), build up serious misconceptions, and/or have significant difficulties in understanding higher-order content.

Pupils should be able to describe associated processes and key characteristics in common language, but they should also be familiar with, and use, technical terminology accurately and precisely. They should build up an extended specialist vocabulary. They should also apply their mathematical knowledge to their understanding of science, including collecting, presenting and analysing data. The social and economic implications of science are important but, generally, they are taught most appropriately within the wider school curriculum: teachers will wish to use different contexts to maximise their pupils' engagement with and motivation to study science.

The nature, processes and methods of science

'Working scientifically' specifies the understanding of the nature, processes and methods of science for each year group. It should not be taught as a separate strand. The notes and guidance give examples of how 'working scientifically' might be embedded within the content of biology, chemistry and physics, focusing on the key features of scientific enquiry, so that pupils learn to use a variety of approaches to answer relevant scientific questions. These types of scientific enquiry should include: observing over time; pattern seeking; identifying, classifying and grouping; comparative and fair testing (controlled investigations); and researching using secondary sources. Pupils should seek answers to questions through collecting, analysing and presenting data. 'Working scientifically' will be developed further at key stages 3 and 4, once pupils have built up sufficient understanding of science to engage meaningfully in more sophisticated discussion of experimental design and control.

Spoken language

The national curriculum for science reflects the importance of spoken language in pupils' development across the whole curriculum – cognitively, socially and linguistically. The quality and variety of language that pupils hear and speak are key factors in developing their scientific vocabulary and articulating scientific concepts clearly and precisely. They must be assisted in making their thinking clear, both to themselves and others, and teachers should ensure that pupils build secure foundations by using discussion to probe and remedy their misconceptions.

School curriculum

The programmes of study for science are set out year-by-year for key stages 1 and 2. Schools are, however, only required to teach the relevant programme of study by the end of the key stage. Within each key stage, schools therefore have the flexibility to introduce content earlier or later than set out in the programme of study. In addition, schools can introduce key stage content during an earlier key stage if appropriate. All schools are also required to set out their school curriculum for science on a year-by-year basis and make this information available online.

Attainment targets

By the end of each key stage, pupils are expected to know, apply and understand the matters, skills and processes specified in the relevant programme of study.

Schools are not required by law to teach the content indicated as being 'non-statutory'.

Key stage 1

The principal focus of science teaching in key stage 1 is to enable pupils to experience and observe phenomena, looking more closely at the natural and humanly-constructed world around them. They should be encouraged to be curious and ask questions about what they notice. They should be helped to develop their understanding of scientific ideas by using different types of scientific enquiry to answer their own questions, including observing changes over a period of time, noticing patterns, grouping and classifying things, carrying out simple comparative tests, and finding things out using secondary sources of information. They should begin to use simple scientific language to talk about what they have found out and communicate their ideas to a range of audiences in a variety of ways. Most of the learning about science should be done through the use of first-hand practical experiences, but there should also be some use of appropriate secondary sources, such as books, photographs and videos.

'Working scientifically' is described separately in the programme of study, but must **always** be taught through and clearly related to the teaching of substantive science content in the programme of study. Throughout the notes and guidance, examples show how scientific methods and skills might be linked to specific elements of the content.

Pupils should read and spell scientific vocabulary at a level consistent with their increasing word-reading and spelling knowledge at key stage 1.

Key stage 1 programme of study – years 1 and 2

Working scientifically

Statutory requirements

During years 1 and 2, pupils should be taught to use the following practical scientific methods, processes and skills through the teaching of the programme of study content:

- asking simple questions and recognising that they can be answered in different ways

- observing closely, using simple equipment

- performing simple tests

- identifying and classifying

- using their observations and ideas to suggest answers to questions

- gathering and recording data to help in answering questions

Notes and guidance (non-statutory)

Pupils in years 1 and 2 should explore the world around them and raise their own questions. They should experience different types of scientific enquiries, including practical activities, and begin to recognise ways in which they might answer scientific questions. They should use simple features to compare objects, materials and living things and, with help, decide how to sort and group them, observe changes over time, and, with guidance, they should begin to notice patterns and relationships. They should ask people questions and use simple secondary sources to find answers. They should use simple measurements and equipment (for example, hand lenses, egg timers) to gather data, carry out simple tests, record simple data, and talk about what they have found out and how they found it out. With help, they should record and communicate their findings in a range of ways and begin to use simple scientific language.

These opportunities for working scientifically should be provided across years 1 and 2 so that the expectations in the programme of study can be met by the end of year 2. Pupils are not expected to cover each aspect for every area of study.

Year 1 programme of study

Plants

Statutory requirements

Pupils should be taught to:

- identify and name a variety of common wild and garden plants, including deciduous and evergreen trees
- identify and describe the basic structure of a variety of common flowering plants, including trees

Notes and guidance (non-statutory)

Pupils should use the local environment throughout the year to explore and answer questions about plants growing in their habitat. Where possible, they should observe the growth of flowers and vegetables that they have planted.

They should become familiar with common names of flowers, examples of deciduous and evergreen trees, and plant structures (including leaves, flowers (blossom), petals, fruit, roots, bulb, seed, trunk, branches, stem).

Pupils might work scientifically by: observing closely, perhaps using magnifying glasses, and comparing and contrasting familiar plants; describing how they were able to identify and group them, and drawing diagrams showing the parts of different plants including trees. Pupils might keep records of how plants have changed over time, for example the leaves falling off trees and buds opening; and compare and contrast what they have found out about different plants.

Animals, including humans

Statutory requirements

Pupils should be taught to:

- identify and name a variety of common animals including fish, amphibians, reptiles, birds and mammals
- identify and name a variety of common animals that are carnivores, herbivores and omnivores

Statutory requirements

- describe and compare the structure of a variety of common animals (fish, amphibians, reptiles, birds and mammals, including pets)
- identify, name, draw and label the basic parts of the human body and say which part of the body is associated with each sense

Notes and guidance (non-statutory)

Pupils should use the local environment throughout the year to explore and answer questions about animals in their habitat. They should understand how to take care of animals taken from their local environment and the need to return them safely after study. Pupils should become familiar with the common names of some fish, amphibians, reptiles, birds and mammals, including those that are kept as pets.

Pupils should have plenty of opportunities to learn the names of the main body parts (including head, neck, arms, elbows, legs, knees, face, ears, eyes, hair, mouth, teeth) through games, actions, songs and rhymes.

Pupils might work scientifically by: using their observations to compare and contrast animals at first hand or through videos and photographs, describing how they identify and group them; grouping animals according to what they eat; and using their senses to compare different textures, sounds and smells.

Everyday materials

Statutory requirements

Pupils should be taught to:

- distinguish between an object and the material from which it is made
- identify and name a variety of everyday materials, including wood, plastic, glass, metal, water, and rock
- describe the simple physical properties of a variety of everyday materials
- compare and group together a variety of everyday materials on the basis of their simple physical properties

Notes and guidance (non-statutory)

Pupils should explore, name, discuss and raise and answer questions about everyday materials so that they become familiar with the names of materials and properties such as: hard/soft; stretchy/stiff; shiny/dull; rough/smooth; bendy/not bendy; waterproof/not waterproof; absorbent/not absorbent; opaque/transparent. Pupils should explore and experiment with a wide variety of materials, not only those listed in the programme of study, but including for example: brick, paper, fabrics, elastic, foil.

Pupils might work scientifically by: performing simple tests to explore questions, for example: 'What is the best material for an umbrella? ...for lining a dog basket? ...for curtains? ...for a bookshelf? ...for a gymnast's leotard?'

Seasonal changes

Statutory requirements

Pupils should be taught to:

- observe changes across the four seasons
- observe and describe weather associated with the seasons and how day length varies

Notes and guidance (non-statutory)

Pupils should observe and talk about changes in the weather and the seasons.

Note: Pupils should be warned that it is not safe to look directly at the Sun, even when wearing dark glasses.

Pupils might work scientifically by: making tables and charts about the weather; and making displays of what happens in the world around them, including day length, as the seasons change.

Year 2 programme of study

Living things and their habitats

Statutory requirements

Pupils should be taught to:

- explore and compare the differences between things that are living, dead, and things that have never been alive

- identify that most living things live in habitats to which they are suited and describe how different habitats provide for the basic needs of different kinds of animals and plants, and how they depend on each other

- identify and name a variety of plants and animals in their habitats, including micro-habitats

- describe how animals obtain their food from plants and other animals, using the idea of a simple food chain, and identify and name different sources of food

Notes and guidance (non-statutory)

Pupils should be introduced to the idea that all living things have certain characteristics that are essential for keeping them alive and healthy. They should raise and answer questions that help them to become familiar with the life processes that are common to all living things. Pupils should be introduced to the terms 'habitat' (a natural environment or home of a variety of plants and animals) and 'micro-habitat' (a very small habitat, for example for woodlice under stones, logs or leaf litter). They should raise and answer questions about the local environment that help them to identify and study a variety of plants and animals within their habitat and observe how living things depend on each other, for example, plants serving as a source of food and shelter for animals. Pupils should compare animals in familiar habitats with animals found in less familiar habitats, for example, on the seashore, in woodland, in the ocean, in the rainforest.

Pupils might work scientifically by: sorting and classifying things according to whether they are living, dead or were never alive, and recording their findings using charts. They should describe how they decided where to place things, exploring questions for example: 'Is a flame alive? Is a deciduous tree dead in winter?' and talk about ways of answering their questions. They could construct a simple food chain that includes humans (e.g. grass, cow, human). They could describe the conditions in different habitats and micro-habitats (under log, on stony path, under bushes) and find out how the conditions affect the number and type(s) of plants and animals that live there.

Plants

Statutory requirements

Pupils should be taught to:

- observe and describe how seeds and bulbs grow into mature plants
- find out and describe how plants need water, light and a suitable temperature to grow and stay healthy

Notes and guidance (non-statutory)

Pupils should use the local environment throughout the year to observe how different plants grow. Pupils should be introduced to the requirements of plants for germination, growth and survival, as well as to the processes of reproduction and growth in plants.

Note: Seeds and bulbs need water to grow but most do not need light; seeds and bulbs have a store of food inside them.

Pupils might work scientifically by: observing and recording, with some accuracy, the growth of a variety of plants as they change over time from a seed or bulb, or observing similar plants at different stages of growth; setting up a comparative test to show that plants need light and water to stay healthy.

Animals, including humans

Statutory requirements

Pupils should be taught to:

- notice that animals, including humans, have offspring which grow into adults
- find out about and describe the basic needs of animals, including humans, for survival (water, food and air)
- describe the importance for humans of exercise, eating the right amounts of different types of food, and hygiene

Notes and guidance (non-statutory)

Pupils should be introduced to the basic needs of animals for survival, as well as the importance of exercise and nutrition for humans. They should also be introduced to the processes of reproduction and growth in animals. The focus at this stage should be on questions that help pupils to recognise growth; they should not be expected to understand how reproduction occurs.

Notes and guidance (non-statutory)

The following examples might be used: egg, chick, chicken; egg, caterpillar, pupa, butterfly; spawn, tadpole, frog; lamb, sheep. Growing into adults can include reference to baby, toddler, child, teenager, adult.

Pupils might work scientifically by: observing, through video or first-hand observation and measurement, how different animals, including humans, grow; asking questions about what things animals need for survival and what humans need to stay healthy; and suggesting ways to find answers to their questions.

Uses of everyday materials

Statutory requirements

Pupils should be taught to:

- identify and compare the suitability of a variety of everyday materials, including wood, metal, plastic, glass, brick, rock, paper and cardboard for particular uses

- find out how the shapes of solid objects made from some materials can be changed by squashing, bending, twisting and stretching

Notes and guidance (non-statutory)

Pupils should identify and discuss the uses of different everyday materials so that they become familiar with how some materials are used for more than one thing (metal can be used for coins, cans, cars and table legs; wood can be used for matches, floors, and telegraph poles) or different materials are used for the same thing (spoons can be made from plastic, wood, metal, but not normally from glass). They should think about the properties of materials that make them suitable or unsuitable for particular purposes and they should be encouraged to think about unusual and creative uses for everyday materials. Pupils might find out about people who have developed useful new materials, for example John Dunlop, Charles Macintosh or John McAdam.

Pupils might work scientifically by: comparing the uses of everyday materials in and around the school with materials found in other places (at home, the journey to school, on visits, and in stories, rhymes and songs); observing closely, identifying and classifying the uses of different materials, and recording their observations.

Lower key stage 2 – years 3 and 4

The principal focus of science teaching in lower key stage 2 is to enable pupils to broaden their scientific view of the world around them. They should do this through exploring, talking about, testing and developing ideas about everyday phenomena and the relationships between living things and familiar environments, and by beginning to develop their ideas about functions, relationships and interactions. They should ask their own questions about what they observe and make some decisions about which types of scientific enquiry are likely to be the best ways of answering them, including observing changes over time, noticing patterns, grouping and classifying things, carrying out simple comparative and fair tests and finding things out using secondary sources of information. They should draw simple conclusions and use some scientific language, first, to talk about and, later, to write about what they have found out.

'Working scientifically' is described separately at the beginning of the programme of study, but must **always** be taught through and clearly related to substantive science content in the programme of study. Throughout the notes and guidance, examples show how scientific methods and skills might be linked to specific elements of the content.

Pupils should read and spell scientific vocabulary correctly and with confidence, using their growing word-reading and spelling knowledge.

Lower key stage 2 programme of study

Working scientifically

Statutory requirements

During years 3 and 4, pupils should be taught to use the following practical scientific methods, processes and skills through the teaching of the programme of study content:

- asking relevant questions and using different types of scientific enquiries to answer them

- setting up simple practical enquiries, comparative and fair tests

- making systematic and careful observations and, where appropriate, taking accurate measurements using standard units, using a range of equipment, including thermometers and data loggers

- gathering, recording, classifying and presenting data in a variety of ways to help in answering questions

- recording findings using simple scientific language, drawings, labelled diagrams, keys, bar charts, and tables

- reporting on findings from enquiries, including oral and written explanations, displays or presentations of results and conclusions

- using results to draw simple conclusions, make predictions for new values, suggest improvements and raise further questions

- identifying differences, similarities or changes related to simple scientific ideas and processes

- using straightforward scientific evidence to answer questions or to support their findings

Notes and guidance (non-statutory)

Pupils in years 3 and 4 should be given a range of scientific experiences to enable them to raise their own questions about the world around them. They should start to make their own decisions about the most appropriate type of scientific enquiry they might use to answer questions; recognise when a simple fair test is necessary and help to decide how to set it up; talk about criteria for grouping, sorting and classifying; and use simple keys. They should begin to look for naturally occurring patterns and relationships and decide what data to collect to identify them. They should help to make decisions about what observations to make, how long to make them for and the type of simple equipment that might be used.

Notes and guidance (non-statutory)

They should learn how to use new equipment, such as data loggers, appropriately. They should collect data from their own observations and measurements, using notes, simple tables and standard units, and help to make decisions about how to record and analyse this data. With help, pupils should look for changes, patterns, similarities and differences in their data in order to draw simple conclusions and answer questions. With support, they should identify new questions arising from the data, making predictions for new values within or beyond the data they have collected and finding ways of improving what they have already done. They should also recognise when and how secondary sources might help them to answer questions that cannot be answered through practical investigations. Pupils should use relevant scientific language to discuss their ideas and communicate their findings in ways that are appropriate for different audiences.

These opportunities for working scientifically should be provided across years 3 and 4 so that the expectations in the programme of study can be met by the end of year 4. Pupils are not expected to cover each aspect for every area of study.

Year 3 programme of study

Plants

Statutory requirements

Pupils should be taught to:

- identify and describe the functions of different parts of flowering plants: roots, stem/trunk, leaves and flowers

- explore the requirements of plants for life and growth (air, light, water, nutrients from soil, and room to grow) and how they vary from plant to plant

- investigate the way in which water is transported within plants

- explore the part that flowers play in the life cycle of flowering plants, including pollination, seed formation and seed dispersal

Notes and guidance (non-statutory)

Pupils should be introduced to the relationship between structure and function: the idea that every part has a job to do. They should explore questions that focus on the role of the roots and stem in nutrition and support, leaves for nutrition and flowers for reproduction.

Note: Pupils can be introduced to the idea that plants can make their own food, but at this stage they do not need to understand how this happens.

Pupils might work scientifically by: comparing the effect of different factors on plant growth, for example, the amount of light, the amount of fertiliser; discovering how seeds are formed by observing the different stages of plant life cycles over a period of time; looking for patterns in the structure of fruits that relate to how the seeds are dispersed. They might observe how water is transported in plants, for example, by putting cut, white carnations into coloured water and observing how water travels up the stem to the flowers.

Animals, including humans

Statutory requirements

Pupils should be taught to:

- identify that animals, including humans, need the right types and amount of nutrition, and that they cannot make their own food; they get nutrition from what they eat

- identify that humans and some other animals have skeletons and muscles for support, protection and movement

Notes and guidance (non-statutory)

Pupils should continue to learn about the importance of nutrition and should be introduced to the main body parts associated with the skeleton and muscles, finding out how different parts of the body have special functions.

Pupils might work scientifically by: identifying and grouping animals with and without skeletons and observing and comparing their movement; exploring ideas about what would happen if humans did not have skeletons. They might compare and contrast the diets of different animals (including their pets) and decide ways of grouping them according to what they eat. They might research different food groups and how they keep us healthy and design meals based on what they find out.

Rocks

Statutory requirements

Pupils should be taught to:

- compare and group together different kinds of rocks on the basis of their appearance and simple physical properties

- describe in simple terms how fossils are formed when things that have lived are trapped within rock

- recognise that soils are made from rocks and organic matter

Notes and guidance (non-statutory)

Linked with work in geography, pupils should explore different kinds of rocks and soils, including those in the local environment.

Notes and guidance (non-statutory)

Pupils might work scientifically by: observing rocks, including those used in buildings and gravestones, and exploring how and why they might have changed over time; using a hand lens or microscope to help them to identify and classify rocks according to whether they have grains or crystals, and whether they have fossils in them. Pupils might research and discuss the different kinds of living things whose fossils are found in sedimentary rock and explore how fossils are formed. Pupils could explore different soils and identify similarities and differences between them and investigate what happens when rocks are rubbed together or what changes occur when they are in water. They can raise and answer questions about the way soils are formed.

Light

Statutory requirements

Pupils should be taught to:

- recognise that they need light in order to see things and that dark is the absence of light
- notice that light is reflected from surfaces
- recognise that light from the Sun can be dangerous and that there are ways to protect their eyes
- recognise that shadows are formed when the light from a light source is blocked by a solid object
- find patterns in the way that the size of shadows change

Notes and guidance (non-statutory)

Pupils should explore what happens when light reflects off a mirror or other reflective surfaces, including playing mirror games to help them to answer questions about how light behaves. They should think about why it is important to protect their eyes from bright lights. They should look for, and measure, shadows, and find out how they are formed and what might cause the shadows to change.

Note: Pupils should be warned that it is not safe to look directly at the Sun, even when wearing dark glasses.

Pupils might work scientifically by: looking for patterns in what happens to shadows when the light source moves or the distance between the light source and the object changes.

Forces and magnets

Statutory requirements

Pupils should be taught to:

- compare how things move on different surfaces

- notice that some forces need contact between two objects, but magnetic forces can act at a distance

- observe how magnets attract or repel each other and attract some materials and not others

- compare and group together a variety of everyday materials on the basis of whether they are attracted to a magnet, and identify some magnetic materials

- describe magnets as having two poles

- predict whether two magnets will attract or repel each other, depending on which poles are facing

Notes and guidance (non-statutory)

Pupils should observe that magnetic forces can act without direct contact, unlike most forces, where direct contact is necessary (for example, opening a door, pushing a swing). They should explore the behaviour and everyday uses of different magnets (for example, bar, ring, button and horseshoe).

Pupils might work scientifically by: comparing how different things move and grouping them; raising questions and carrying out tests to find out how far things move on different surfaces and gathering and recording data to find answers their questions; exploring the strengths of different magnets and finding a fair way to compare them; sorting materials into those that are magnetic and those that are not; looking for patterns in the way that magnets behave in relation to each other and what might affect this, for example, the strength of the magnet or which pole faces another; identifying how these properties make magnets useful in everyday items and suggesting creative uses for different magnets.

Year 4 programme of study

Living things and their habitats

Statutory requirements

Pupils should be taught to:

- recognise that living things can be grouped in a variety of ways

- explore and use classification keys to help group, identify and name a variety of living things in their local and wider environment

- recognise that environments can change and that this can sometimes pose dangers to living things

Notes and guidance (non-statutory)

Pupils should use the local environment throughout the year to raise and answer questions that help them to identify and study plants and animals in their habitat. They should identify how the habitat changes throughout the year. Pupils should explore possible ways of grouping a wide selection of living things that include animals and flowering plants and non-flowering plants. Pupils could begin to put vertebrate animals into groups such as fish, amphibians, reptiles, birds, and mammals; and invertebrates into snails and slugs, worms, spiders, and insects.

Note: Plants can be grouped into categories such as flowering plants (including grasses) and non-flowering plants, such as ferns and mosses.

Pupils should explore examples of human impact (both positive and negative) on environments, for example, the positive effects of nature reserves, ecologically planned parks, or garden ponds, and the negative effects of population and development, litter or deforestation.

Pupils might work scientifically by: using and making simple guides or keys to explore and identify local plants and animals; making a guide to local living things; raising and answering questions based on their observations of animals and what they have found out about other animals that they have researched.

Animals, including humans

Statutory requirements

Pupils should be taught to:

- describe the simple functions of the basic parts of the digestive system in humans

- identify the different types of teeth in humans and their simple functions

- construct and interpret a variety of food chains, identifying producers, predators and prey

Notes and guidance (non-statutory)

Pupils should be introduced to the main body parts associated with the digestive system, for example, mouth, tongue, teeth, oesophagus, stomach and small and large intestine and explore questions that help them to understand their special functions.

Pupils might work scientifically by: comparing the teeth of carnivores and herbivores, and suggesting reasons for differences; finding out what damages teeth and how to look after them. They might draw and discuss their ideas about the digestive system and compare them with models or images.

States of matter

Statutory requirements

Pupils should be taught to:

- compare and group materials together, according to whether they are solids, liquids or gases

- observe that some materials change state when they are heated or cooled, and measure or research the temperature at which this happens in degrees Celsius (°C)

- identify the part played by evaporation and condensation in the water cycle and associate the rate of evaporation with temperature

Notes and guidance (non-statutory)

Pupils should explore a variety of everyday materials and develop simple descriptions of the states of matter (solids hold their shape; liquids form a pool not a pile; gases escape from an unsealed container). Pupils should observe water as a solid, a liquid and a gas and should note the changes to water when it is heated or cooled.

Notes and guidance (non-statutory)

Note: Teachers should avoid using materials where heating is associated with chemical change, for example, through baking or burning.

Pupils might work scientifically by: grouping and classifying a variety of different materials; exploring the effect of temperature on substances such as chocolate, butter, cream (for example, to make food such as chocolate crispy cakes and ice-cream for a party). They could research the temperature at which materials change state, for example, when iron melts or when oxygen condenses into a liquid. They might observe and record evaporation over a period of time, for example, a puddle in the playground or washing on a line, and investigate the effect of temperature on washing drying or snowmen melting.

Sound

Statutory requirements

Pupils should be taught to:

- identify how sounds are made, associating some of them with something vibrating

- recognise that vibrations from sounds travel through a medium to the ear

- find patterns between the pitch of a sound and features of the object that produced it

- find patterns between the volume of a sound and the strength of the vibrations that produced it

- recognise that sounds get fainter as the distance from the sound source increases

Notes and guidance (non-statutory)

Pupils should explore and identify the way sound is made through vibration in a range of different musical instruments from around the world; and find out how the pitch and volume of sounds can be changed in a variety of ways.

Pupils might work scientifically by: finding patterns in the sounds that are made by different objects such as saucepan lids of different sizes or elastic bands of different thicknesses. They might make earmuffs from a variety of different materials to investigate which provides the best insulation against sound. They could make and play their own instruments by using what they have found out about pitch and volume.

Electricity

Statutory requirements

Pupils should be taught to:

- identify common appliances that run on electricity

- construct a simple series electrical circuit, identifying and naming its basic parts, including cells, wires, bulbs, switches and buzzers

- identify whether or not a lamp will light in a simple series circuit, based on whether or not the lamp is part of a complete loop with a battery

- recognise that a switch opens and closes a circuit and associate this with whether or not a lamp lights in a simple series circuit

- recognise some common conductors and insulators, and associate metals with being good conductors

Notes and guidance (non-statutory)

Pupils should construct simple series circuits, trying different components, for example, bulbs, buzzers and motors, and including switches, and use their circuits to create simple devices. Pupils should draw the circuit as a pictorial representation, not necessarily using conventional circuit symbols at this stage; these will be introduced in year 6.

Note: Pupils might use the terms current and voltage, but these should not be introduced or defined formally at this stage. Pupils should be taught about precautions for working safely with electricity.

Pupils might work scientifically by: observing patterns, for example, that bulbs get brighter if more cells are added, that metals tend to be conductors of electricity, and that some materials can and some cannot be used to connect across a gap in a circuit.

Upper key stage 2 – years 5 and 6

The principal focus of science teaching in upper key stage 2 is to enable pupils to develop a deeper understanding of a wide range of scientific ideas. They should do this through exploring and talking about their ideas; asking their own questions about scientific phenomena; and analysing functions, relationships and interactions more systematically. At upper key stage 2, they should encounter more abstract ideas and begin to recognise how these ideas help them to understand and predict how the world operates. They should also begin to recognise that scientific ideas change and develop over time. They should select the most appropriate ways to answer science questions using different types of scientific enquiry, including observing changes over different periods of time, noticing patterns, grouping and classifying things, carrying out comparative and fair tests and finding things out using a wide range of secondary sources of information. Pupils should draw conclusions based on their data and observations, use evidence to justify their ideas, and use their scientific knowledge and understanding to explain their findings.

'Working and thinking scientifically' is described separately at the beginning of the programme of study, but must always be taught through and clearly related to substantive science content in the programme of study. Throughout the notes and guidance, examples show how scientific methods and skills might be linked to specific elements of the content.

Pupils should read, spell and pronounce scientific vocabulary correctly.

Upper key stage 2 programme of study

Working scientifically

Statutory requirements

During years 5 and 6, pupils should be taught to use the following practical scientific methods, processes and skills through the teaching of the programme of study content:

- planning different types of scientific enquiries to answer questions, including recognising and controlling variables where necessary

- taking measurements, using a range of scientific equipment, with increasing accuracy and precision, taking repeat readings when appropriate

- recording data and results of increasing complexity using scientific diagrams and labels, classification keys, tables, scatter graphs, bar and line graphs

- using test results to make predictions to set up further comparative and fair tests

- reporting and presenting findings from enquiries, including conclusions, causal relationships and explanations of and degree of trust in results, in oral and written forms such as displays and other presentations

- identifying scientific evidence that has been used to support or refute ideas or arguments

Notes and guidance (non-statutory)

Pupils in years 5 and 6 should use their science experiences to: explore ideas and raise different kinds of questions; select and plan the most appropriate type of scientific enquiry to use to answer scientific questions; recognise when and how to set up comparative and fair tests and explain which variables need to be controlled and why. They should use and develop keys and other information records to identify, classify and describe living things and materials, and identify patterns that might be found in the natural environment. They should make their own decisions about what observations to make, what measurements to use and how long to make them for, and whether to repeat them; choose the most appropriate equipment to make measurements and explain how to use it accurately. They should decide how to record data from a choice of familiar approaches; look for different causal relationships in their data and identify evidence that refutes or supports their ideas. They should use their results to identify when further tests and observations might be needed; recognise which secondary sources will be most useful to research their ideas and begin to separate opinion from fact. They should use relevant scientific language and illustrations to discuss, communicate and justify their scientific ideas and should talk about how scientific ideas have developed over time.

Notes and guidance (non-statutory)

These opportunities for working scientifically should be provided across years 5 and 6 so that the expectations in the programme of study can be met by the end of year 6. Pupils are not expected to cover each aspect for every area of study.

Year 5 programme of study

Living things and their habitats

Statutory requirements

Pupils should be taught to:

- describe the differences in the life cycles of a mammal, an amphibian, an insect and a bird
- describe the life process of reproduction in some plants and animals

Notes and guidance (non-statutory)

Pupils should study and raise questions about their local environment throughout the year. They should observe life-cycle changes in a variety of living things, for example, plants in the vegetable garden or flower border, and animals in the local environment. They should find out about the work of naturalists and animal behaviourists, for example, David Attenborough and Jane Goodall.

Pupils should find out about different types of reproduction, including sexual and asexual reproduction in plants, and sexual reproduction in animals.

Pupils might work scientifically by: observing and comparing the life cycles of plants and animals in their local environment with other plants and animals around the world (in the rainforest, in the oceans, in desert areas and in prehistoric times), asking pertinent questions and suggesting reasons for similarities and differences. They might try to grow new plants from different parts of the parent plant, for example, seeds, stem and root cuttings, tubers, bulbs. They might observe changes in an animal over a period of time (for example, by hatching and rearing chicks), comparing how different animals reproduce and grow.

Animals, including humans

Statutory requirements

Pupils should be taught to:

- describe the changes as humans develop to old age

Notes and guidance (non-statutory)

Pupils should draw a timeline to indicate stages in the growth and development of humans. They should learn about the changes experienced in puberty.

Pupils could work scientifically by researching the gestation periods of other animals and comparing them with humans; by finding out and recording the length and mass of a baby as it grows.

Properties and changes of materials

Statutory requirements

Pupils should be taught to:

- compare and group together everyday materials on the basis of their properties, including their hardness, solubility, transparency, conductivity (electrical and thermal), and response to magnets

- know that some materials will dissolve in liquid to form a solution, and describe how to recover a substance from a solution

- use knowledge of solids, liquids and gases to decide how mixtures might be separated, including through filtering, sieving and evaporating

- give reasons, based on evidence from comparative and fair tests, for the particular uses of everyday materials, including metals, wood and plastic

- demonstrate that dissolving, mixing and changes of state are reversible changes

- explain that some changes result in the formation of new materials, and that this kind of change is not usually reversible, including changes associated with burning and the action of acid on bicarbonate of soda

Notes and guidance (non-statutory)

Pupils should build a more systematic understanding of materials by exploring and comparing the properties of a broad range of materials, including relating these to what they learnt about magnetism in year 3 and about electricity in year 4. They should explore reversible changes, including evaporating, filtering, sieving, melting and dissolving, recognising that melting and dissolving are different processes. Pupils should explore changes that are difficult to reverse, for example, burning, rusting and other reactions, for example, vinegar with bicarbonate of soda. They should find out about how chemists create new materials, for example, Spencer Silver, who invented the glue for sticky notes or Ruth Benerito, who invented wrinkle-free cotton.

Note: Pupils are not required to make quantitative measurements about conductivity and insulation at this stage. It is sufficient for them to observe that some conductors will produce a brighter bulb in a circuit than others and that some materials will feel hotter than others when a heat source is placed against them. Safety guidelines should be followed when burning materials.

Pupils might work scientifically by: carrying out tests to answer questions, for example, 'Which materials would be the most effective for making a warm jacket, for wrapping ice cream to stop it melting, or for making blackout curtains?' They might compare materials in order to make a switch in a circuit. They could observe and compare the changes that take place, for example, when burning different materials or baking bread or cakes. They might research and discuss how chemical changes have an impact on our lives, for example, cooking, and discuss the creative use of new materials such as polymers, super-sticky and super-thin materials.

Earth and space

Statutory requirements

Pupils should be taught to:

- describe the movement of the Earth, and other planets, relative to the Sun in the solar system

- describe the movement of the Moon relative to the Earth

- describe the Sun, Earth and Moon as approximately spherical bodies

- use the idea of the Earth's rotation to explain day and night and the apparent movement of the sun across the sky

Notes and guidance (non-statutory)

Pupils should be introduced to a model of the Sun and Earth that enables them to explain day and night. Pupils should learn that the Sun is a star at the centre of our solar system and that it has eight planets: Mercury, Venus, Earth, Mars, Jupiter, Saturn, Uranus and Neptune (Pluto was reclassified as a 'dwarf planet' in 2006). They should understand that a moon is a celestial body that orbits a planet (Earth has one moon; Jupiter has four large moons and numerous smaller ones).

Note: Pupils should be warned that it is not safe to look directly at the Sun, even when wearing dark glasses.

Notes and guidance (non-statutory)

Pupils should find out about the way that ideas about the solar system have developed, understanding how the geocentric model of the solar system gave way to the heliocentric model by considering the work of scientists such as Ptolemy, Alhazen and Copernicus.

Pupils might work scientifically by: comparing the time of day at different places on the Earth through internet links and direct communication; creating simple models of the solar system; constructing simple shadow clocks and sundials, calibrated to show midday and the start and end of the school day; finding out why some people think that structures such as Stonehenge might have been used as astronomical clocks.

Forces

Statutory requirements

Pupils should be taught to:

- explain that unsupported objects fall towards the Earth because of the force of gravity acting between the Earth and the falling object

- identify the effects of air resistance, water resistance and friction, that act between moving surfaces

- recognise that some mechanisms, including levers, pulleys and gears, allow a smaller force to have a greater effect

Notes and guidance (non-statutory)

Pupils should explore falling objects and raise questions about the effects of air resistance. They should explore the effects of air resistance by observing how different objects such as parachutes and sycamore seeds fall. They should experience forces that make things begin to move, get faster or slow down. Pupils should explore the effects of friction on movement and find out how it slows or stops moving objects, for example, by observing the effects of a brake on a bicycle wheel. Pupils should explore the effects of levers, pulleys and simple machines on movement. Pupils might find out how scientists, for example, Galileo Galilei and Isaac Newton helped to develop the theory of gravitation.

Pupils might work scientifically by: exploring falling paper cones or cup-cake cases, and designing and making a variety of parachutes and carrying out fair tests to determine which designs are the most effective. They might explore resistance in water by making and testing boats of different shapes. They might design and make products that use levers, pulleys, gears and/or springs and explore their effects.

Year 6 programme of study

Living things and their habitats

Statutory requirements

Pupils should be taught to:

- describe how living things are classified into broad groups according to common observable characteristics and based on similarities and differences, including micro-organisms, plants and animals
- give reasons for classifying plants and animals based on specific characteristics

Notes and guidance (non-statutory)

Pupils should build on their learning about grouping living things in year 4 by looking at the classification system in more detail. They should be introduced to the idea that broad groupings, such as micro-organisms, plants and animals can be subdivided. Through direct observations where possible, they should classify animals into commonly found invertebrates (such as insects, spiders, snails, worms) and vertebrates (fish, amphibians, reptiles, birds and mammals). They should discuss reasons why living things are placed in one group and not another.

Pupils might find out about the significance of the work of scientists such as Carl Linnaeus, a pioneer of classification.

Pupils might work scientifically by: using classification systems and keys to identify some animals and plants in the immediate environment. They could research unfamiliar animals and plants from a broad range of other habitats and decide where they belong in the classification system.

Animals including humans

Statutory requirements

Pupils should be taught to:

- identify and name the main parts of the human circulatory system, and describe the functions of the heart, blood vessels and blood
- recognise the impact of diet, exercise, drugs and lifestyle on the way their bodies function
- describe the ways in which nutrients and water are transported within animals, including humans

Notes and guidance (non-statutory)

Pupils should build on their learning from years 3 and 4 about the main body parts and internal organs (skeletal, muscular and digestive system) to explore and answer questions that help them to understand how the circulatory system enables the body to function.

Pupils should learn how to keep their bodies healthy and how their bodies might be damaged – including how some drugs and other substances can be harmful to the human body.

Pupils might work scientifically by: exploring the work of scientists and scientific research about the relationship between diet, exercise, drugs, lifestyle and health

Evolution and inheritance

Statutory requirements

Pupils should be taught to:

- recognise that living things have changed over time and that fossils provide information about living things that inhabited the Earth millions of years ago

- recognise that living things produce offspring of the same kind, but normally offspring vary and are not identical to their parents

- identify how animals and plants are adapted to suit their environment in different ways and that adaptation may lead to evolution.

Notes and guidance (non-statutory)

Building on what they learned about fossils in the topic on rocks in year 3, pupils should find out more about how living things on earth have changed over time. They should be introduced to the idea that characteristics are passed from parents to their offspring, for instance by considering different breeds of dogs, and what happens when, for example, labradors are crossed with poodles. They should also appreciate that variation in offspring over time can make animals more or less able to survive in particular environments, for example, by exploring how giraffes' necks got longer, or the development of insulating fur on the arctic fox. Pupils might find out about the work of palaeontologists such as Mary Anning and about how Charles Darwin and Alfred Wallace developed their ideas on evolution.

Note: At this stage, pupils are not expected to understand how genes and chromosomes work.

Pupils might work scientifically by: observing and raising questions about local animals and how they are adapted to their environment; comparing how some living things are adapted to survive in extreme conditions, for example, cactuses, penguins and camels. They might analyse the advantages and disadvantages of specific adaptations, such as being on two feet rather than four, having a long or a short beak, having gills or lungs, tendrils on climbing plants, brightly coloured and scented flowers.

Light

Statutory requirements

Pupils should be taught to:

- recognise that light appears to travel in straight lines

- use the idea that light travels in straight lines to explain that objects are seen because they give out or reflect light into the eye

- explain that we see things because light travels from light sources to our eyes or from light sources to objects and then to our eyes

- use the idea that light travels in straight lines to explain why shadows have the same shape as the objects that cast them

Notes and guidance (non-statutory)

Pupils should build on the work on light in year 3, exploring the way that light behaves, including light sources, reflection and shadows. They should talk about what happens and make predictions.

Pupils might work scientifically by: deciding where to place rear-view mirrors on cars; designing and making a periscope and using the idea that light appears to travel in straight lines to explain how it works. They might investigate the relationship between light sources, objects and shadows by using shadow puppets. They could extend their experience of light by looking a range of phenomena including rainbows, colours on soap bubbles, objects looking bent in water and coloured filters (they do not need to explain why these phenomena occur).

Electricity

Statutory requirements

Pupils should be taught to:

- associate the brightness of a lamp or the volume of a buzzer with the number and voltage of cells used in the circuit

- compare and give reasons for variations in how components function, including the brightness of bulbs, the loudness of buzzers and the on/off position of switches

- use recognised symbols when representing a simple circuit in a diagram

Notes and guidance (non-statutory)

Building on their work in year 4, pupils should construct simple series circuits, to help them to answer questions about what happens when they try different components, for example, switches, bulbs, buzzers and motors. They should learn how to represent a simple circuit in a diagram using recognised symbols.

Note: Pupils are expected to learn only about series circuits, not parallel circuits. Pupils should be taught to take the necessary precautions for working safely with electricity.

Pupils might work scientifically by: systematically identifying the effect of changing one component at a time in a circuit; designing and making a set of traffic lights, a burglar alarm or some other useful circuit.

Index